I am Special

by the same author

Autistic Thinking
This is the Title
Peter Vermeulen
Foreword by Francesca Happé
ISBN 978 1 85302 995 0
eISBN 978 1 84642 996 5

of related interest

The ASD Workbook
Understanding Your Autism Spectrum Disorder
Penny Kershaw
ISBN 978 1 84905 195 8
eISBN 978 0 85700 427 7

How To Be Yourself in a World That's Different
An Asperger's Syndrome Study Guide for Adolescents
Yuko Yoshida M.D.
Translated by Esther Sanders
ISBN 978 1 84310 504 6
eISBN 978 1 84310 504 6

The Complete Guide to Asperger's Syndrome
Tony Attwood
ISBN 978 1 84310 495 7 (hardback)
ISBN 978 1 84310 669 2 (paperback)
eISBN 978 1 84642 559 2

Asperger's Syndrome
A Guide for Parents and Professionals
Tony Attwood
Foreword by Lorna Wing
ISBN 978 1 85302 577 8
eISBN 978 1 84642 697 1

I am Special

A Workbook to Help Children, Teens and Adults
with Autism Spectrum Disorders to Understand
Their Diagnosis, Gain Confidence and Thrive

Second Edition

Peter Vermeulen

Translated by Beth Junor

Jessica Kingsley *Publishers*
London and Philadelphia

First published in Dutch by EPO Publishers, Lange Pastoorstraat 25-27, 2600
Berchem, Belgium. www.eop.be, in 2005, 7th impression in 2010.
© Vlaamse Dienst Autisme en uitgeverij EPO vzw, 2005, 7th impression, 2010.
This edition published in 2013
by Jessica Kingsley Publishers
116 Pentonville Road
London N1 9JB, UK
and
400 Market Street, Suite 400
Philadelphia, PA 19106, USA

www.jkp.com

Copyright © Peter Vermeulen 2005 and 2013
Translator copyright © Beth Junor 2013

Library of Congress Cataloging in Publication Data
A CIP catalog record for this book is available from the Library of Congress

British Library Cataloguing in Publication Data
A CIP catalogue record for this book is available from the British Library

ISBN 9781849052665

Printed and bound in Great Britain

The translator would like to thank Nathalie Hardy for reading through the translations and providing many helpful suggestions.

Contents

Acknowledgements

It is impossible to thank everyone who has contributed to this new version of *I am Special*. Dozens and dozens of professionals, parents and people with autism from Flanders, the Netherlands and various European countries have contributed directly or indirectly to this new version, through their positive comments and also through their criticisms.

Nevertheless, a number of people deserve to be mentioned and thanked, as their contribution was essential. This includes all those who have made adaptations so new and innovative that they have been included in this version:

- Lisbet Van Gijzeghem, who conceived 'The big book about me', for young children. Sylvie Carette and Marjan Delu have helped Lisbet with corrections and additions to this version.

- Marion Fuijkschot-Timmers and Bart Konings of the *Pleincollege Antoon Schellens* in Eindhoven in the Netherlands, who drafted the worksheets in the section, 'How do I feel with difficulties caused by my autism?'

- Det Dekeukeleire, an educator at *Autisme Centraal*, who developed the version for groups of adults.

- Ann Daelman of *CLB Waasland* in Flanders, who was the first to adapt *I am Special* as a source of information for peers of a child with autism, in a project on inclusion.

- Lies Delameillieure and Annemie Mertens, who took up the challenge of transforming *I am Special* into a complete weekly course.

- Ella Buis of *Vizier* (Netherlands), for her suggestions regarding the registration and evaluation forms in *I am Special* for children, adolescents and their parents or carers as well as for the adapted version of worksheets about character.

- Elke Gilissen, Gudrun Janssen, Sofie Maris, Chris Put, Bert Vanderheyden, Karolien Vermaelen (students at Limburg Catholic University College in Flanders) and Rose-Linde Breels as well as Els Buntinx of *Ter Engelen*, for their creative adaptations and their suggestions for the version for young people with (mild) learning disabilities.

- Howard Childs of Surrey Hants Borders NHS Trust (UK) for his revision of the worksheets on the functioning of the brain.

In addition to these people, I would also like to thank Christel van Bouwel of the Royal Remedial Education Centre in Antwerp, Belgium (*KOCA – Koninklijk Orthopedagogisch Centrum Antwerpen*): with others mentioned above, she contributed enormously to the first version of *I am Special*. Many tutors and assistants used the workbook with their pupils with autism, and Christel organised an evaluation and follow-up day which provided us with most interesting feedback.

I am also very grateful to Beth Junor, who translated *I am Special*. Since the publication of the revised edition in Dutch, many people in the English-speaking world showed great interest in an English translation and quite a few of them promised to help with the translation. Beth was the only one who really kept her promise and she devoted many hours and days of her free time in translating the book and the worksheets. That makes her special!

Finally, many thanks to Jessica Kingsley Publishers, who took up the challenge of publishing this new version. I will always be grateful to Jessica Kingsley, because she was the first one to take the risk of translating my books into English, now more than ten years ago.

Part 1

Theory

Chapter 1

Background

In 1999, when *Autisme Centraal*[1] brought out the very first version of *I am Special* as a book with photocopiable worksheets, we could never have imagined the impact this modest publication would have. Within barely five years, this workbook had become a standard resource used in a variety of ways by a great number of people with autism spectrum disorders.

1 Origins

The story of *I am Special* begins in 1997. Autism in people of average intelligence was becoming more and more recognised. Parents and professionals were clearly no longer the only ones seeking explanations of autism; children, adolescents and adults with autism and good cognitive levels clearly had questions of their own. Although we had been giving information on autism to parents and professionals for years, we were unsure how to inform people with autism themselves. We were facing a challenge. I took up this challenge in 1997, when I wrote *Autism and Emotions: A Closed Book*. I devoted a whole chapter to the subject. At conferences and whenever I gave talks, interest in the subject was obviously very strong. Parents and professionals posed a great deal of questions, particularly about the availability of practical resources. I had of course written the main outline in my book, but the need for a practical manual was considerable. *I am Special* was the first attempt to meet this need.

Over the last few years, the number of children, adolescents and adults with average intelligence who have been diagnosed with autism spectrum disorders has increased dramatically. Although we are still far from perfection in the identification of autism, we have made enormous leaps forward recently. It has also emerged that the number of people with autism spectrum disorders with average intelligence is much more than we had previously imagined. Although previously this group had been designated a 'gifted minority', today, on the basis of recent epidemiological studies, we think that those endowed with a near average intellectual capacity represents at least half of individuals with autism.

At the same time, the need for information, methodology and strategies for informing people about their disability has increased considerably. *I am Special* was clearly an apposite response to the numerous questions of parents and professionals.

2 Extent of use

The success of *I am Special* was not limited to Flanders and the Netherlands. The workbook has been translated into English, French, Danish, Finnish, Norwegian, German, Polish and even Sami and Afrikaans. It is in use all over the world: at the moment, workshops and conferences on *I am Special* are taking place in more than ten countries.

The workbook is used by children, adolescents and adults with autism. It is used in very different ways: for support at home, in mainstream education, special education, psychotherapy, workplace coaching, educational work, in courses and in diagnostic centres. In some special schools, the workbook forms part of the standard curriculum. Some rehabilitation and therapy centres use *I am Special* as part of their social skills training. An employment coaching project adapted the methodology in order to make professional portfolios with individuals with autism. *I am Special* is also used within the framework of inclusive education: peers of a pupil or student with an autism spectrum disorder can gain an holistic understanding of the individual, of disabilities in general and of autism in particular. In Scotland, training offered to Learning Support Assistants and Support for Learning Teachers includes *I am Special* as one of the available ways in which to promote the inclusion of pupils with autism in mainstream education.

In this way *I am Special* came to be a workbook valued in the field of psychoeducation. Psychoeducation informs people about their diagnosis and supports them in finding strategies to cope with their condition or disability. The additions established with a group of students in Eindhoven, the Netherlands, are a telling example. With the first edition of *I am Special*, the students learned they had autism. But then came their question: 'Now I know I have autism – but what can I do about it?' Together with the school in Eindhoven, we developed additional worksheets, called 'The world in fragments' (which are reproduced in full on the CD ROM). Thanks to these additions, children and young people not only learned about their diagnosis, they also learned how to use this knowledge with practical effect.

3 Adaptations and variations

When we published *I am Special* in 1999, we knew that, despite two years' reflection and many trials, the workbook was a first draft and not a finished product. Even though in the old version we had put forward several suggestions for introducing adaptations and variations, these had not been incorporated. This is why, with a view to users working creatively with the workbook, we deliberately launched a plea in the Foreword to professionals, parents and people with autism, that they contribute all kinds of suggestions based on their experience, for the introduction of adaptations, improvements and additions. Many people took this appeal to heart and as a result, there are dozens of versions of *I am Special*. One of the real needs remaining that was mentioned in the feedback was a version adapted to and more appealing for younger children. New, very attractive versions for children have been developed both in Flanders and abroad. Some of these versions now appear as chapters in *I am Special*. Furthermore, the need for a 'digital' version made more and more sense. The teaching profession are employing multimedia techniques more and more and in many families, the computer has become an extensively used, important tool. It is for this reason that we opted for an updated format for the new *I am Special*: the manual being published in hard copy and all the worksheets and illustrations being made available on a CD ROM. This new publication not only facilitates the use of computer-based exercises, but also offers the opportunity to develop new versions with rapidity and ease. It can transform the book into a truly bespoke, personalised tool.

Many professionals and parents have also attended *I am Special* workshops in recent years. These workshops allow us not only to train people in the methodological basis of the workbook, but also to obtain valuable feedback. Many participants at these workshops gave us useful advice and suggestions for the adaptations in the present manual.

The need for specific training on the methodological basis of the workbook, namely the Socratic method, also gave rise to the organisation of special workshops on this methodology. Information about this method and its description were much too brief in the original version of *I am Special*. For this reason, and at the request of many people, the current version includes a detailed description of the Socratic method and its autism-friendly adaptation, called the 'Socra*u*tic method'.

4 Reviews

I am Special has been well received on an international level.[2] Parents and professionals, as well as people with autism, have provided comments –

happily, always constructive – on the original version via e-mail, letters or during personal contact. As far as possible, we have integrated this feedback into the current version. There were a number of criticisms relating to the original version conveying a negative image of autism, despite our explicit intention to present autism in a positive manner. An e-mail from a mother in Mercerville (New Jersey, USA) exemplifies the calls for more positive content: 'Maybe you should not only be interested in the difficulties of autism, but also attach importance to what is nice or positive about autism. It's good to end on a positive note.' According to a review in the *British Journal of Learning Disabilities*:

> …the tone of the book presents autism in a negative way. The writer is clearly aware of the distress that may be triggered by learning more about a disorder that has no cure and will affect people throughout their lives. He stresses the need for ongoing support for individuals in dealing with this realisation. The book assumes a negative reaction to the presentation of the material and describes gaining knowledge about the disorder as 'the bad news'.[3]

However, one can read in different reviews that *I am Special* focuses also on the positive aspects of autism. For instance, the information sheet for Autism West Midlands on explaining the diagnosis mentions that *I am Special* highlights 'their gifts and abilities as well as the areas where they have difficulty'.[4]

A person with autism, as well as another British reviewer,[5] refers to an absence of the social model of disability. This refers to the fact that the degree to which a person is disabled is a result not only of the person's disorder (and its severity) but also of the number of obstacles presented by the environment. A disability is the result of the interaction between personal and environmental characteristics. The extent to which a person with autism experiences difficulties and handicaps in their personal development as well as in the realisation of their dreams is dependent not only on the (degree of) autism but also on the opportunities the environment offers (or does not offer) him or her. Although *I am Special* was intended to be based entirely on the social model of disability, this obviously came across too infrequently in the exercises. This is partly explained by the fact that the terms 'disorder', 'limitation' and 'disability' are undoubtedly abstract and difficult to explain to younger children with autism. Yet a social definition of autism requires a good understanding of these abstract concepts.

Nevertheless, we have tried to meet this challenge, based on our experience of *I am Special* courses for adults. Thus this new edition proposes an explanation of autism as a social disability.

In the autumn of 2002, Peggy Verheijen, a student at the *Fontys Hogescholen* in the Netherlands, evaluated *I am Special* scientifically, thanks to a list of evaluations for preventive pedagogical programmes. According to the findings of this evaluation, the original version of *I am Special*, the aim of which was to serve mainly as a practical tool that would be developed through practical experience, was lacking in conceptual and methodological foundations. This is why, in this revised version, we will describe three main conceptual foundations of *I am Special*. These relate to:

- the evidence base for the self-image of people with autism

- the psychoeducation of people with autism

- the Socratic method as an empowering methodology for people with autism.

Indeed, particularly in this new version, *I am Special* is a psychoeducation programme which aims to teach *self-knowledge* to people with autism, knowledge of (their own) autism and how to manage it, through an empowering method, the *Socratic* method.

The chapter on the self-image of people with autism explains the objectives to be conveyed by the content of *I am Special*, while the texts on psychoeducation and the Socratic method serve as foundations and rationale for the chosen methodology of *I am Special*.

A third criticism concerned the lack of a quality control system for the programme. The fact that *I am Special* was made to be personalised and adapted to each person with autism, in its practical aims, methods, resources used and with content that is not set in stone, makes developing a set of qualitative criteria difficult, if not impossible. However, to respond, in so far as is possible, to this requirement for quality control, we give suggestions for how to evaluate the use of the workbook, in particular through a satisfaction questionnaire sent to the person with autism and those around him/her (parents and teachers). We also include some suggestions for measuring the impact of the workbook on the self-image of the person with autism.

To respond to comments regarding the description of the target groups and aims, we now provide, in the manual, additional information about the target groups, aims and possible methods for measuring impact.

In this way, we hope to have added to a stronger foundation for *I am Special*. We are always on the lookout for more scientific and objective assessments of the possible effects and secondary uses of the workbook, although we know that such a thing is difficult to achieve, given that *I am Special* is not a standardised programme.

When *I am Special* was published in 1999, the book of worksheets was the only one of its kind. With the exception of a booklet by Gunilla Gerland[6] and an article by Carol Gray[7], there was, at the time, no other publication or workbook for children, adolescents or adults with information about their autism. In the meantime, other quite interesting publications pursuing the same aim as *I am Special* have emerged. Anyone wishing to use new ideas and other examples can find inspiration in these publications. A (non-exhaustive) list has been placed at your disposal at the end of the manual.

5 New to this edition

Based on the many adaptations and comments we have received in recent years, the time has come to refresh *I am Special* completely.

For ease of use and to preserve their layout, the colour worksheets have been made available on a CD ROM. The manual and explanatory texts are published here, in book form. The list below gives a brief overview of this updated version.

In the book:

- The manual includes three completely new chapters:
  - a chapter on the 'self-image' of people with autism spectrum disorders

  - a chapter on psychoeducation and autism

  - a chapter on the Socratic method.

- New components have been introduced in Chapter 5, 'Introducing autism', such as the denial of one's diagnosis.

- Chapter 6, 'Working with *I am Special*', has been completely revised.

- The set of worksheets has been revised and supplemented by new worksheets, such as a worksheet on sensory problems.

- The manual includes a concise description of the use of *I am Special* with:
  - peers of a pupil with autism (within the framework of inclusion)

  - siblings

  - adults with autism with average to above average intelligence. This text describes some content from versions adapted for adults, including evening classes and a week-long course.

- Finally, the practical manual (Part 2 chapters) for the new versions of *I am Special* on the CD ROM (see below) are also new.

The CD ROM, in addition to the updates of the original workbook (with new and amended worksheets), also includes adaptations and additions for different target groups:

- *A version for siblings*. Formerly, this was available separately. It is an adaptation of the worksheets on autism, which have been supplemented by the following worksheets: 'What does it mean to have a brother or sister with autism?' and 'How can a child explain their brother or sister's autism to others?'

- *A version for young children*. This version was developed by Lisbet Van Gijzeghem and Sylvie Carette, two colleagues at *Het Anker* in Bruges, Belgium, a residential school for children with autism spectrum disorders. They were already involved in the first trials of *I am Special* and, thanks to their experience with young children, they created this appealing version, which – as well as being in an attractive format – attaches importance to small steps in the stages of reasoning. These stages, as well as more concrete explanations of certain concepts, are generally additions to the original version. In light of many requests this version is included in its entirety.

- *Examples of simplified worksheets on character, the brain and new worksheets on the inside and outside*. Experience has shown us that certain concepts, especially those relating to character and the functioning of the brain, remain abstract for many children and adolescents with autism; they need worksheets which make these concepts more concrete, and which break them down more. Among all the examples we have drawn upon from our practice, we have selected the most captivating and the most attractive. They come from different countries (UK, Denmark, the Netherlands and Belgium).

- *How do I deal with my difficulties caused by my autism?* This set of exercises is a continuation of *I am Special*. With these, adolescents learn how to cope with difficulties arising from their autism. These worksheets cover, among other things, using talents to compensate for limitations, using 'tricks' and tools, as well as learning essential communication skills. In addition, there is a kind of self-help guide to understanding 'autistic blockages'. Such a guide had originally been developed under the name 'De wereld in fragmenten' or 'The world in fragments', by Marion Fuijkschot-Timmers and Bart Konings of the *Pleincollege Anton Schellens* at Eindhoven, in the Netherlands, a special secondary school which particularly caters for young people with autism spectrum disorders.

- *Examples of adaptations and (especially) attractive worksheets for adolescents who, apart from their autism, also have a (mild) learning disability.* As part of a three-year project in the Department of Social Work at the Limburg Catholic University College in Flanders, six students developed, in collaboration with *Ter Engelen*, a school and group home for children and youngsters with learning disabilities, the worksheets for people with learning disabilities called 'That's me?!'. This is a simplified version of *I am Special*, which, in addition to adaptations to page layout (for example, using symbols), includes some appealing activities one can do by oneself. The worksheets on 'My future' are new to this version. Indeed, *I am Special* is an ideal starting point for any form of personal future planning.

- A number of worksheets and supplementary forms, for example for registering with or evaluating *I am Special*, developed by Ella Buis (who works for an outreach autism team at Vizier, in the Netherlands).

- The vignettes and board layout for the *I am Special* board game: a simple game about autistic characteristics. Currently, we are developing a new *I am Special* board game that focuses also on positive aspects of autism, that includes the environment (within a social model of disability) and that involves humour and is more fun to play.

- Some examples of worksheets for people with autism spectrum disorders and average or above average intelligence.

- Suggestions for all sorts of activities one can do by oneself, based on a weekly course of *I am Special* organised by *Autisme Centraal*, for adults with autism. These activities that can be carried out by oneself are also suitable for children or adolescents.

This new version of *I am Special*, therefore, is much more than a new cover. The target groups, content and layout of the worksheets have all been thoroughly revised, as is shown by the comparison between the old and new versions in Table 1.1.

Table 1.1 Comparison between old and new versions of *I am Special*

	I am Special, 2000 edition	*I am Special,* 2013 edition
Target group with autism	Children and young people from 10 to 16 years, with below average to average level of intelligence[8]	Children from 9 to 12 years with (near) average intelligence ('The big book about me' version of the worksheets) Young people from 12 to 17 years with below average to average intelligence (revisions to worksheets in the original version) Adolescents from 12 to 18 years with a mild learning disability ('That's me?!' version) (Young) adults of average intelligence (different ideas to develop worksheets and activities around the diagnosis for adults)
Other target groups	Not covered	Siblings Peers of a child with autism
Content	What is autism?	What is autism? What can I do about my autism? ('The world in fragments' version) My future ('That's me?!' version)
Layout	Manual and worksheets in the same book	Theory and practical manual in book form Worksheets and resources on CD ROM

6 Is *I am Special* evidence based?

To start with, *I am Special* is definitely research based. The content of the workbook and worksheets is based on what scientific studies revealed about the self-knowledge of people with autism spectrum disorders and the difficulties they experience when trying to understand their diagnosis. The chapter on self-image (Chapter 2) summarises this body of research. But the backup by research is not confined to the content of the workbook.

The strategies and methods used in the workbook are based on what scientists have taught us about the cognitive style of people with autism. Informing someone about his or her diagnosis involves giving information, obviously. Research has shown that autism involves specific information processing difficulties, such as: difficulties with understanding abstract concepts (and 'autism' is a very abstract concept!), difficulties getting the gist of a message, weak central coherence, difficulties in understanding mental states, difficulties putting information in context, sensory issues such as easily being distracted by certain stimuli or being overwhelmed by them. The autistic style of processing information fortunately also has its assets, such as good visual processing, a logical, often almost mathematical, straight-forward style of thinking, good memory for facts, and a good eye for details. The way concepts are introduced and explained in *I am Special* and even the layout of the worksheets takes into account this specific autistic cognitive style, as we currently understand it based on numerous studies.

On top of the research based character of *I am Special*, the workbook is also evidence based in terms of clinical expertise. The workbook is the result of the work of a group of experts in the field, who have done try-outs with the materials with more than 100 youngsters and adults with an autism spectrum disorder in different settings (education, clinical treatment, counselling, social skills groups). Each try-out resulted in worksheets and strategies being adapted.

I am Special is currently being used in countries all over the world and has received many positive evaluations. It has been recommended by several authorities in the field (e.g. Tony Attwood) and organisations (such as Geneva Centre for Autism, Toronto, Canada). *I am Special* has been included in the Autism Toolbox: An Autism Resource for Scottish Schools.[9] Patricia Howlin, Professor of Clinical Psychology at St. George's, University of London, mentions *I am Special* in her article on self-help books about autism.[10]

Of course, these recommendations and references are far from synonymous for 'evidence based'. Because psychoeducation is a relatively young method in psychological support, especially in the field of autism spectrum disorders, evidence for its positive effects are almost nonexistent. However, several experts in the field underline the usefulness of psychoeducation in the treatment of autism for example, 'Psycho-education plays a pivotal role in the treatment of autism spectrum disorders. It is considered to be essential in the support of people with autism'.[11] The Dutch guidelines for diagnosis and treatment of autism spectrum disorders in children and youngsters by the Dutch Psychiatric Society[12] state that although there is a paucity in the research of psychoeducation in autism spectrum disorders, it should be considered as essential in the treatment, because it can have positive effects, as has been shown for other disorders.

Indeed, for other disorders, such as schizophrenia and bipolar disorder, there is already some scientific evidence for the beneficial effects of psychoeducation,[13] including a positive effect on quality of life. For the time being, we cannot generalise these findings to the area of autism, but they do support the use of psychoeducation.

Even after more than ten years since the first publication and despite being used all over the world, *I am Special* has not caught the attention of researchers. However, there are some small studies (regrettably no RCT studies)[14] that have shown positive effects:

- In the UK, Sally Rickhuss did a so-called N = 1 study (a case study with a single subject) in 2006 with *I am Special* and reported positive effects.[15]

- In her research of methods for informing youngsters about their autism diagnosis, Abigail Cann mentions *I am Special*.[16]

- At the Canadian universities, Université du Quebec en Outaouais (UQO) and University of Montréal, Jocelyne Sylvestre studied the effects of a psychoeducation programme that involved a combination of *I am Special* and the anxiety programme developed by Tony Attwood. The study was developed in the framework of suicide prevention in adolescents with Asperger's Syndrome. The results of her study were promising. Jocelyne also developed a specific questionnaire to evaluate *I am Special*: 'Le test Connaissance de soi et du diagnostic TED' (The Test for Self-Knowledge and Knowledge of the ASD Diagnosis).[17] Côté, I. (2009). *Programme visant l'appropriation du diagnostic et la gestion de l'anxiété chez les adolescents atteint du syndrome d'Asperger afin de réduire leurs risques suicidaires.* Université de Montréal, Ecole de psychoéducation.

- The University Hospital in Oslo did a study of the effects of (the Norwegian version of) *I am Special.* Parents, professionals and adolescents with autism reported positive experiences with the workbook.[18]

- Finally, Dutch clinicians reported positive effects of *I am Special* in a group of 45 teens who were in treatment in a project that combined special education and psychiatric treatment.[19]

7 The future of *I am Special*

I am Special will never be 'finished'. A specific feature of the workbook is that neither its form nor content will ever be final. *I am Special* is more of a process than a finished product. A new version can be seen every day, thanks to the interaction between the facilitator and the person with autism.

This new version proves that many professionals (and parents) have been working creatively with *I am Special*. I hope there will be no limit to this creativity. The autism spectrum clearly has a much wider range of colours than previously thought: diversity in autism is huge and people with autism perhaps differ from each other more than they resemble each other. Users must encourage this diversity in *I am Special*, and continue to work as creative people, in order to procure personalised information on autism.

We are always interested to hear suggestions that will enable us to introduce amendments and additions.

Chapter 2
Self-image

Self-knowledge is the source of wisdom, as taught by the Greek philosopher Socrates in the fifth century BCE. The maxim γνωθι (*Gnothi seauton*: know thyself) is, as it were, the starting point for *I am Special*. We work from the assumption that anyone who has a good understanding of himself or herself can thrive and make choices in life more easily.

1 Self-knowledge and self-determination

Therefore, in essence, *I am Special* should serve as an instrument for furthering self-determination. Self-determination represents the knowledge, understanding and skills which, in conjunction with one another, enable one to gain 'power' over one's own life. We wish to give people with autism the best possible opportunities to define and defend their rights and to flourish (self-advocacy). To achieve this empowerment, three steps are necessary:

1. Self-knowledge, that is, being aware of one's needs, potential and limitations.

2. Taking action to realise one's dreams, whilst taking into account one's own limitations and potential, as well as those of the environment.

3. Weighing up the effects of one's actions.

The first step, 'self-knowledge', is not insignificant. Exercising control over one's life requires an understanding and knowledge of oneself. Zimmerman,[20] one of the founders of the current self-determination movement, sees the amelioration of critical consciousness as one of three key junctures in self-determination, after the gaining of control and fostering of social involvement.

I am Special has been designed so that people with autism can learn more about themselves from a perspective of self-determination. More specifically, this means:

- getting to know one's autism, understanding it and being able to describe it oneself

- being able to describe the effects of autism on one's functioning and on one's life

- being able to specify, in concrete terms, difficult situations linked to one's autism

- being able to identify strategies that can be used for managing difficult situations (as well as new strategies and skills that need only to be taught)

- being able to give autism a place in one's self-image, in such a way that self-esteem will be positive, or remains so.

Accordingly, these practical principles are the five primary objectives of *I am Special*.

2 Self-knowledge and autism

On reading these objectives, those who already have some experience in the field of autism will immediately ask: is this possible? Understanding yourself and taking into account your limitations and potential, is this really achievable for people with autism? In this regard, Alec Webster,[21] professor of psychology at Bristol University, called *I am Special* a 'paradox': according to him, *I am Special* requires the very skills affected by the impairments in autism, such as self-reflection.

Do people with autism spectrum disorders have a realistic image of themselves? It is well known that people with autism spectrum disorders have a unique style of perceiving and understanding the world, quite different from so called neurotypicals, people without autism. So, given their 'autistic perception and thinking', what sense do they make of themselves? How do they see their autism? What consequences arise from these factors, for assimilating their disability? These are crucial issues when it comes to informing someone about their autism.

We know from experience that from a certain age, many people with autism become aware that they are different – and this process is sometimes painful. This realisation is largely dependent on intelligence and therefore appears primarily among individuals with an average level of intelligence, but also often among those who are less gifted. We even know of some adolescents and adults with moderate learning disabilities who have reached a certain level of awareness. However, their understanding of this difference is often very concrete and based on minute details, without any real understanding of the more fundamental differences.

In fact, we know only very little about the way in which people with autism see and understand themselves. Most of our knowledge of this subject remains anecdotal and is based on unsystematic experiences and examples. Autobiographies of people with autism can shed light on this world and some authors with autism may even provide insightful and completely accurate self-descriptions. We must not forget that these are a very small minority of talented people, who have already advanced far in the process of coming to terms with their disability. We must not think that all people with autism are or will become like Temple Grandin, Gunilla Gerland, Ros Blackburn, Luke Jackson or any other person with autism who shares their self-knowledge through first-hand accounts.

2.1 Neurotypical projections

In addition to autobiographies, there are of course the experiences of all those who work in the field of autism every day, from parents to professionals. Usually, they have their ideas, too, about the self-image of people with autism. An important disadvantage is that, often, those around the person who do not have autism start from their own way of thinking, when interpreting the way in which a person with autism sees himself or herself. We assign neurotypical personalities to people with autism. Starting from this recognition, we need to describe how 'neurotypical' projections come about. Neurotypical projections result from our impertinence in considering our non-autistic mental lives as being a given, or as the norm. We believe everyone is thinking and feeling like us. We are perhaps too ready to presume that people with autism see things as we see them. Are we not then making the same mistake they do, when they are unable to place themselves in someone else's world?

Due to these neurotypical projections, we sometimes see problems that do not exist or we consider them to be more serious than they actually are. Not all adolescents with autism fall into a depression or have difficulty in accepting their disability. With many of the attendees at our *I am Special* workshops, I notice a certain anxiety before using the workbook, a fear of being faced with possible negative reactions from the person with autism when they are informed of their diagnosis: aggression, anger, sadness. However, not all children and young people with autism react in this way. Just as one of the criticisms levelled against *I am Special* quite rightly shows,[22] assuming that each individual with autism will consider being informed of their diagnosis as bad news is an erroneous generalisation.

The opposite also happens: sometimes, there are certain problems which we do not see or we underestimate the emotional state of the person with autism. This is how some people with autism who, according to those around them, had no worries, have all of a sudden – to their relatives' greatest shock – taken their own lives or attempted to do so.

However, most of the time, it is not a case of erroneous assessment of the 'problematic level' of someone's self-image but an incorrect *qualitative* estimation. For example, Marie tells her mother that in the playground, she is always in the corner. We promptly interpret narratives such as Marie's as a feeling of loneliness or an unfulfilled desire for social contact. But is this the case? Instead, we ought to check how Marie sized up the situation: she doesn't find it serious. On the contrary, she has the best view of the crowded playground and others speak to her less.

We should not assess the remarks of people with autism from our own point of view; instead, we need to start from theirs. In other words, we should not take our own experience into account, but rather take the perspective of the person with autism. We need to put ourselves in their way of thinking and living. This is what we call empathy or perspective taking. This concept is very close to a very prevalent term in the literature on autism: 'theory of mind', the ability to understand, predict and anticipate the mental states (such as thoughts, feelings, wishes) of others and one's own. Generally, the theory of mind of the person with autism and ours, professionals and parents, do not coincide. Misunderstandings are legion, and far from being the exception.

Scientific research is one solution in the fight against these projections, interpretations and anecdotally based knowledge. Unfortunately, research in the field of self-image and self-knowledge in people with autism is very rare.

2.2 Theory of mind and self-image

Thanks to research, we do know that theory of mind constitutes a problem for people with autism. The world of mental states poses a real challenge for people with an autism spectrum disorder.

Curiously, in nearly all of the studies on theory of mind in autism, only half of the picture is taken into account. The bulk of the research studied whether or not people with autism face problems with recognising, describing and understanding the 'mind' of others. However, theory of mind applies to one's own 'mind', too, as shown in the definition of Premack and Woodruff[23] in their innovative article on the theory of mind of chimpanzees: 'An individual has a theory of mind if he imputes mental states to himself and others.' Theory of mind is therefore about one's own 'mind' as well as the 'mind' of others.

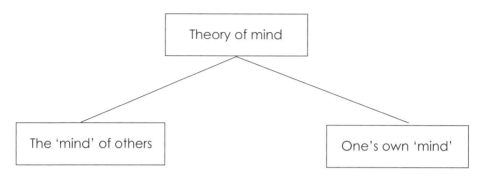

Figure 2.1: Theory of mind and self-image

Numerous studies have shown a deficit or, at the very least, a delay in the development of theory of mind in people with autism. Logically, we can deduce that their theory of mind regarding their own minds may also suffer a delay or present with deficits. We assume therefore that people with autism will encounter problems and difficulties when they learn about themselves, a hypothesis that has been corroborated by scientific research. An experimental study of three people with Asperger's Syndrome has shown that performance on theory of mind tasks was strongly related to their capacity for introspection.[24]

If people with autism present with theory of mind deficits in relation to others, then what about their 'theory' of their own 'mind'? Can people who find it difficult to reach a good judgement of others assess themselves accurately? If you wear glasses that give a distorted view of others, these glasses will also distort your view of yourself in a mirror. According to David Williams from City University (London), autism indeed also involves a particular deficit in 'theory of *own* mind'.[25]

In contrast to the abundance of literature and scientific research on the difficulties encountered by people with autism with regard to their empathic faculty, studies on the way in which they view themselves are extremely rare. They are, nevertheless, very informative.

3 Self-image and autism

In the mid-1990s, Lisa Capps and colleagues[26] were among the first to study the perceptions children with autism have of themselves. They did not however study the totality of that perception but a small part, specifically, the way in which the children perceive and assess their social competence. Capps and her colleagues found a negative correlation between the children's assessment of their social competence and their IQ and emotional understanding. The more intelligent children, who, as reported by their parents, were better able to access their own emotional experiences and had greater understanding of others' emotions, perceived themselves as being less socially competent.[27] This finding is very plausible: due to their higher level of social intelligence, these children see the differences which set them apart from others and are therefore more conscious of their deficits. This awareness often arises during puberty or adolescence (although, depending on intelligence level, it can also appear earlier). In many adolescents with autism, we have observed a more negative self-esteem, from this time in their lives. We can therefore assume that children with autism with a good level of intelligence are more susceptible to developing a negative self-esteem.[28] This is therefore a priority target group for *I am Special*.

Knowing whether someone has a positive or negative self-image and knowing *what* they think of themselves are two very important aspects. It is just as important to know *how* a person sees him/herself. The form one's self-image takes (good or bad, positive or negative) is pertinent for obtaining an indication as to how to begin psychological support or psychoeducation, but the *quality* of self-image is important for assessing the way in which we need to go about providing this support. The question is: is the self-image of people with autism, in itself, different from ours?

Anthony Lee and Peter Hobson's study[29] offers us an answer. They analysed the statements able adolescents with autism made about themselves, and compared these with statements of young people without autism. They compared four categories of self-concept:

- physical: speaking about one's appearance or physical characteristics, for example, 'I have beautiful grey hair'
- activities: speaking about one's activities and aptitudes, for example, 'I often read articles on autism'
- psychological: speaking about one's inner life, such as one's thoughts, emotions, hopes, values or other mental states, for example, 'I like jazz'
- social: speaking about oneself as a social being, for example, 'I have nice colleagues and I like to talk with my close friends'.

The results for adolescents with autism did not differ greatly from results obtained from young people without autism as far as the first three categories are concerned. They spoke as much, even a little more (but this was not significant) about their appearance and their activities. Surprisingly and contrary to the predictions of the researchers, the adolescents with autism spoke as much about their psychological self as the control group, for example by evoking their hopes or emotions. The most notable difference lies in the descriptions of their social self. On average the young people with autism spoke four times less about their relationships with others than the control group. Not one of the young people with autism spontaneously made a statement that referred to friends or to being a member of a particular social group.

The results are not related to IQ or developmental age. In total, adolescents with autism gave as many self-descriptions as the control group. They do *not have an impoverished self-image*. It seems, instead, that the image people with autism have of themselves is much less socially anchored than that of ordinary individuals. Whereas, according to their statements, the self-image of so-called normal young people consists mainly of social elements (who am I in relation to others?), the foundations of an autistic self-image lie mainly in factual information regarding their appearance and activities.

Qualitative results from this study were just as informative as the quantitative results, showing a different quality to autistic self-image. If one refers to theories about autism, the fact that young people with autism have provided as many psychological self-descriptions as so-called normal adolescents is rather surprising. Indeed, according to some psychological theories, people with autism are less gifted in matters of psychology ('folk psychology') than in more concrete and physical matters ('folk physics'), such as your appearance and your activities.[30] When the researchers qualitatively analysed the psychological statements of the participants, striking differences immediately emerged between the two groups. The adolescents with autism mainly spoke about their material or physical preferences, especially the things they would like to do or possess and much less about their social and psychological preferences or aversions. They spoke as much as the control group about their emotions but the content was much less varied. What is also striking, is that they spoke about their past, but only three people with autism spoke about their future. When the researchers explicitly asked them (how do you see yourself in the future?), a certain number of answers provided very good illustrations of the autistic style of thinking (literal and concrete):

- I'll stay the same.
- My voice will change.

The best answer of all:

- I won't change because my name will remain the same.

Lee and Hobson's study[31] gives us information on how young people with autism see themselves, but not on the way in which they understand their disability from this insight. Regarding this aspect of self-image, we can find some answers in another study, by Jonathan Green and his colleagues.[32] Through comparing psychosocial functioning in adolescents with Asperger's Syndrome with that of adolescents with conduct disorder, this British team also studied self-awareness in 20 adolescents with Asperger's Syndrome. To do this, the researchers utilised three sources of information: parental reports, those of the adolescents themselves and the interviewer's rating.

According to the parents, approximately half had some awareness of their autism. However, only one adolescent in four could give an adequate description of it. According to the parents, the adolescents had particular difficulties understanding their own contribution to their interpersonal problems. They also found it hard to understand why others found them different. Green and his colleagues also asked the young people direct questions about their differences. It emerged that although one adolescent in three was able to describe their autism, even so, the same number of young people (approximately 30%) were completely unable to say how they were different from young people of the same age.

According to the researchers, only 10 per cent of those with Asperger's Syndrome had an accurate perception of how others think of them and around half had no idea at all of how others view them. Thus, the researchers concluded that only a minority (around 15%) had a realistic view of their disability. Knowing and being aware of the consequences of autism for everyday, practical situations are clearly two complex tasks. These difficulties are in line with the limitations adolescents experience in the social sphere. Able adolescents and young adults often have a good abstract understanding of relationships and social behaviour but do not possess practical social skills. This also applies to their understanding of autism. Their theoretical knowledge of autism is sometimes impressive and striking, but knowing what autism means for them practically and in their daily lives is much more difficult.

We can conclude that, when informing someone about their autism, it is not enough to have them go through all the literature on autism or have them check out some websites. This would extend their theoretical and abstract knowledge of the subject but not necessarily their understanding and self-awareness. It is for this reason that one works with *I am Special* in an interactive way, particularly through exercises that will make the general information on autism practical and personalised.

One valid, general definition of self-image, or a synonym for self-concept does not exist, which is strange because self-image is one of the most studied themes in psychology and even in philosophy. Famous figures such as Descartes, Freud and Rogers have examined this theme. It is generally agreed that the concept of self refers to a complex, organised and dynamic system of ideas that each person holds about themselves.[33]

Self-concept or self-image is composed of two parts: a descriptive element (self-concept) and an evaluative and positive element: self-esteem. According to Rita Jordan and Stuart Powell[34] the descriptive aspect of the self is less affected in autism than the evaluative aspect. According to them, it is possible for people with autism to construct an image of themselves from autobiographical facts, facts they can gather together from their experiences and from what others tell them about their past. People with autism are often even gifted at remembering autobiographical facts. Knowing their age, sex, where they live, what they like to do, etc. does not usually pose a problem for them. The autobiographical knowledge of people with autism, especially those with a higher level of intelligence, is often astonishingly detailed and accurate. In the Lee and Hobson study a substantial proportion of the participants with autism, but no comparison participants, spontaneously provided vivid and descriptive recollections of their own birth. What is much more difficult for them is reflecting on these self-concepts and evaluating them. As Jordan and Powell express succinctly but quite correctly, 'they lack a sense of themselves'. They are therefore capable of describing who they are, but what it means to be this person that they describe is much more difficult.

Damon and Hart[35] make the distinction between self-as-object, numerous 'me's (cf. Lee and Hobson's study: the physical me, the social me, etc.), and the self-as-subject, 'I', at the heart of the concept of self. It is the 'I' that permits an individual to take into consideration past events, to analyse present impressions and to give form to future experiences. What Jordan and Powell call the 'sense of self' may be compared to the 'I' in Damon and Hart's model. Autism will therefore have an impact particularly on the subjective concept of the self and less on the objective aspects. This is in line with the hypothesis of David Williams[36] about an autism specific deficit in 'Theory of *own* Mind': according to Williams, there is in autism a diminished awareness of the psychological, but the awareness of their physical selves remains remarkably unimpaired.

Further evidence for a more objective, factual and less subjective, psychological self-awareness comes from studies of the memory of people with autism. One study for instance,[37] showed that children with autism recalled events performed by themselves less well than the events they saw peers perform. These difficulties can be linked to a deficit in what is called (personal) 'episodic memory'. Episodic memory is the memory for personal experiences, and can be distinguished from 'semantic memory', the memory for knowledge about facts. Several studies have given evidence for an autistic deficit in this episodic memory. Laura Crane and Lorna Goddard,[38] for instance, found a distinctive pattern of remembering in adolescents and young adults with ASD: in the light of an unimpaired personal semantic memory (recalling facts about yourself) these young adults showed a deficit in their personal episodic memory. Remembering their personal involvement in all kinds of life events is a difficult process. Occasionally, they feel more like spectators than actors in their own life; or as Wendy Lawson (who has autism herself) says, it is like 'life behind glass'.[39]

As if that is not enough, there are additional obstacles relating to problems with theory of mind. For example, self-esteem is not based solely on success and failures, but also on the mirror that others hold up to us. The difficulties people with autism experience in evaluating how others react to them are in turn reflected, entirely logically, in how they evaluate themselves.

In a study we carried out on the diagnostic history of adults with autism and high levels of intelligence,[40] we asked participants to describe themselves. Due to the fact that open questions are difficult, we used a sentence completion test.[41] One of the sentences simply begins with: 'I…'.

As with Lee and Hobson's[42] findings, many answers were clearly related to concrete activities and physical characteristics, as shown in the examples below:

I…

…really like wearing shorts and a t-shirt.

…have green eyes.

…have a dog.

These responses were especially typical for adults who had received an early diagnosis, who had a markedly autistic style of thinking and a slightly lower level of intelligence (but they all had an average level: the participants' average IQ was 115).

Individuals with a higher level of intelligence and more subtle manifestations of autism gave quite different answers, the most telling examples of which are the following:

I…

…am a Taurus: faithful, slow, compassionate.

…am someone who is unique but not more or less so than my friends.

… = a limited and complex concept for many people.

These responses suggest a style where difficulties with self-description are compensated for by using known scenarios, such as astrology or theoretical definitions from psychology. The last example quoted above was not written by chance, but by someone who had studied psychology and pedagogical sciences.

There is still a third category of responses. Those who are familiar with autistic thinking will not need any further explanation on reading the example below:

> I...am me!

The differences between the three categories seem profound. Nevertheless, these differences are only superficial. Each of the three categories has at source an identical way of thinking: an autistic mode of thinking characterised by difficulties with describing oneself in a personal, vivid, coherent way (see also Jordan and Powell's 'sense of self'). An individual picture of the person is missing across the three categories. The answers are either hyperselective and concrete, or hyperabstract or very literal, but they reveal very little about the individual. People with autism therefore do not seem able to escape the influence of their autistic way of observing and thinking, with regard to self-concept.

We currently describe the typical autistic cognitive style as context blindness:[43] people with autism find it difficult to use context when giving meaning to stimuli. Here is an example of context blindness. When the doorbell rang, the mother of a seven-year-old boy with autism asked him to open the door. He opened the back door instead of the front. His reaction was logical, but his choice of door was out of context. To put it more simply: the autistic brain thinks in an absolute way, rather than a relative, contextually defined way. The door = the back door. Or, in the case of Raymond in the movie *Rainman*: 'Don't walk' means only one thing: 'Don't walk', so he stops in the middle of the intersection when the sign changes to 'Don't walk'. Raymond does not understand that 'Don't walk' means many different things, depending on the situation or context. When you're halfway through the crossing, it means 'Hurry up' instead!

We often see that people with autism think about themselves in rather absolute terms, in black and white. A child with autism that failed one difficult test at school can think he's 'stupid', not taking into account the context of the difficulty of the test. Or the adolescent who thought he was ready for independent living because he could take care of himself: 'I can cook!' Well, he was able to bake himself an egg for breakfast... The self-concept of people with autism is often a-contextual: they find it difficult to contextualise their self-concept and to build up a self-concept related to numerous personal experiences.

Some of the other sentences in the Sentence Completion Test that I used in my research with the able adults also provided information about their self-esteem and self-concept. Many of them appeared to reveal a negative self-image, as in the following examples:

I sometimes think of myself that…

…I'm not as good as other people.

…I can do better.

…I only cause trouble for others.

…there's not much I can do.

On reading such statements, we should not leap to the conclusion that it is a question of negative self-image. Although people with autism and an average level of intelligence are more susceptible to developing a negative image of themselves (as shown by Capps and colleagues), a number of negatively charged statements do not necessarily mean a negative self-image is being subjectively experienced by a person. In people with autism, negative self-descriptions more often express dissatisfaction with the way in which they are treated by those around them, or, quite frankly, they are a sophisticated form of echolalia. In an interview during the same study, one of the participants stated that his answer that he 'only caused trouble for others' was based on what he had often heard. He himself did not think this response corresponded with his own and he thought he also had positive relationships with his colleagues and members of his family. Despite the negative self-description, this person did not therefore hold a negative image of himself.

As is the case for ordinary individuals, the self-descriptions of people with autism find their origin mainly in what others say of them. Self-image is based in part on the mirror held up to us by others. In the case of autism, the reflection is not always rosy and positive. This is particularly apparent in the responses given by participants to the following phrase:

Others think…

…I'm an idiot.

…I could be faster and more active.

…I'm shy.

Fortunately, not all suffer from negative feedback.

Difficulties with 'theory of mind' can also sometimes be positive as they protect the person with autism from too much negative feedback. Sometimes it feels much better not knowing what others think of us. And during testing, this was the case with one participant in five. One of the literal answers given to the question above was: 'I don't know, obviously!'

However, in one way or another, most of the able people felt that others sometimes regard them as being less than 'normal', odd or less skilled. They deduce this notably from the criticisms they hear, sometimes even from their peers, parents, professionals, colleagues, employers. For many children, young people and even adults with autism, the distinction between criticism of their behaviour and that of their personality is blurred. Because of their difficulties putting remarks 'in context', this distinction is even harder to make for someone with autism than for a so-called normal person. And that has repercussions for self-image.

On the other hand, parents and professionals also regularly tell us that people with autism overestimate themselves. It would then also be a question of a self-image that is too positive.

During our study, when we were looking for information on adaptive functioning, we used the Interview on Social Functioning (Huskens).[44] This interview, which we converted into a list of written questions, focuses on functioning in a number of social domains, such as the home, shopping, outings, free time and scheduled time. We used two versions: one for parents' reports and one for adults with autism. We were very curious to find out whether people with autism spectrum disorders evaluated their adaptive skills differently from their parents. In general, the account of a person with autism did not differ in significant ways from that of the parents. But strangely, there was a difference between people diagnosed at an early age (before age 15) and those diagnosed later (after 15 years). The former evaluated their functioning less well than their parents, while the latter arrived at better evaluations than their parents. We do not yet have a conclusive explanation for this surprising observation. Several factors may come into play, such as awareness of one's disability, the importance of support from those around one and support behind the scenes (which is therefore unseen by the person with autism). This was especially so with people diagnosed later: often, they did not see how many of their activities, like outings, were largely supported by their parents. In all cases, our findings indicated a link between the time of diagnosis and the self-image of the person with autism. Those who have worked with *I am Special* for some time regularly tell us that providing information on autism goes a bit better with children and adolescents who were diagnosed very early compared to those who were diagnosed later. In the latter group, there is sometimes a strong resistance to information about their own limitations.

Incidentally, this resistance is not limited to autism. In order for our self-concept to remain quite stable (imagine having a different image of yourself every day!), a certain tendency to resist change emerges. Every experience that is contrary to one's self-image may be perceived as a threat. As these experiences become more numerous (and receiving a diagnosis may be considered such an experience), the more a certain rigidity may appear in one's self-image, simply for protection and self-preservation.[45] We can draw an important lesson for *I am Special* from this. With young people and adults who have a positive image of themselves and thus a certain tendency to overestimate themselves, it is advisable to provide our 'corrective' information in doses and to take time to give new information sparingly.

In summary, we can draw the following conclusions about the self-image of people with autism. The image people with autism have of themselves is not necessarily more limited or any poorer than the image ordinary individuals have of themselves. The number of self-descriptions and, hence, the extent of the self-image is linked mainly to intellectual level:[46] more able people with autism know more things about themselves than less able people with autism.

By contrast, the self-image of people with autism differs or diverges *qualitatively* from that of people without autism. The principal difference lies in the level of coherence. The self-image of people with autism seems to be less socially anchored and also less anchored in a subjective self, a 'self as actor'. Such individuals encounter problems with *coherent thinking*[47] and *contextual sensitivity*[48]; they find it hard to connect the knowledge of themselves to the context, especially in the social and personal realms, where feelings and thoughts are found. They can be aware of what's happening, but not always aware of what's happening to them (nor of the part they played in an event). They are spectators of their own life, where they do not sufficiently recognise themselves as actors.

The difference between an autistic and non-autistic self-image therefore lies not in its extent, but in its depth. Self-knowledge in terms of remembering experiences and facts is unimpaired. The problem lies instead in the level of awareness of one's own present experience.[49]

As with any human being, the image which people with autism have of themselves results from their own thoughts. Thus, this image also reflects their style of thinking. The self-image of people with autism is generally very objective, absolute and linked to concrete details. The difficulties individuals with autism experience with placing things in different and shifting perspectives often results in a black and white way of thinking, which they apply also to themselves. Combined with a large dose of failure and negative feedback from those around them, this leads above all to a very negative self-image. However, the opposite can also be produced: a very positive self-image or an overestimation of oneself.

4 Working on self-image

One question still remains: do people with autism have a realistic image of themselves? The answer to this question is short and concise: no! But let us immediately add that no one has a realistic self-image. Each one of us nurtures our own illusions about ourselves and our image of ourself is never the same as that held by others.

It is not the aim of *I am Special* to arrive at a realistic self-image. Its impact on daily functioning and psychological well-being are much more important. And according to studies, self-concept yields further information about how a person deals with life's stresses (Bandura).[50] The question is whether one's self-image enables one to go through life in harmony with one's surroundings and oneself. Or, when self-image leads to depression, to a refusal of necessary support, to fear of failure, to permanent conflicts with those around one, everything indicates that we must work on this image. It is not therefore a matter of knowing whether the person with autism has a realistic self-image. The image that people with autism have of themselves is, by definition, autistic. Someone who thinks and observes in an autistic way also views himself in an autistic way (which also affects how they regard their autism, as we will see later in 'Reactions to the diagnosis'). People with autism have a right to an autistic image of themselves. The question to ask is whether, and to what extent, someone with autism suffers from their self-image in their everyday struggle for survival and in their self-satisfaction.

Given the importance of self-image for survival, for how one deals with stress and for a person's well-being, it is necessary to dwell on how we can positively influence the self-image of people with autism.

One of the five fundamental aims of *I am Special*, previously cited, is to promote positive self-esteem. Despite this aim, the weight given to supporting the self in the totality of actions and interventions in the psychoeducational sessions is minimal.

One crucial variable for promoting positive self-image resides in our attitude towards autism. A positive attitude of acceptance and self-determination in relation to people with autism is one of the explicit conditions we set for all those who wish to work with *I am Special*.

Questions about how people with autism see themselves and how they regard their autism are worth asking. But how do we see them, and their disability? Such reflection is essential, in light of the influence our views and attitudes have on the self-image of people with autism. Psychologists think that self-image is, in large part, acquired.[51] No one is born with their self-image: it develops, through our experiences. It is mainly experiences ranging from success to failure and those involving the significant people directly around us that exercise a major influence on the development of our self-image. Through their respect, criticisms and comments they make on our behaviour, others hold up a mirror to us. What feedback do we give to people with autism in our daily relations with them? How do we talk about autism?

I have begun some workshops with the following task: what is autism? With few exceptions, the definitions of most participants are an enumeration of all sorts of limitations, shortcomings, differences, disorders and problems. Of course, there is no denying autism leads in general to several deficits, but when we think of autism, we think firstly and exclusively of deficits and not of talents. This view influences our interactions with people with autism and the mirror we hold up to them. How can we hope that people with autism will have a realistic and positive self-image, if we show them predominantly one facet of autism, namely the negative side, the shortcomings and problems?

Our view of autism influences not only what we tell people with autism about themselves, but also, and especially, what we do with them. It is not enough to tell them they are 'OK'. Imagine someone telling you how nice and pleasant they find you, how talented they find you, but at the same time they recommend you take a course on social skills and receive some therapy, as well. What would be the effect on your own self-image?

Social skills courses, special education, psychotherapy and all that we offer to support people with autism leave traces on their self-image, even though all this help may be appropriate and necessary. Can someone who needs this kind of support be OK? Is psychotherapy a cause of depression or the treatment for depression?

This is not a plea for romanticising autism, which has recently become very popular in all kinds of publications and texts, especially on the internet. Clearly, people with autism have gifts. But a simplistic association that combines autism with eccentric genius and ridiculous lists of 'positive models' (lists of famous people who have or probably had autism, such as Einstein, Yeats, Bill Gates, etc.) can sometimes exercise a negative influence on self-image. Not only are most of these 'legends' far from having unanimous backing, but these romantic views of the concept of autism also place the bar very high for anyone who has autism. So try to equal Bill Gates or Einstein!

Success is the keyword for increasing self-confidence and self-esteem. William James[52] already knew this when, in his book *The Principles of Psychology*, he invented a formula for self-esteem, namely: self-esteem = success/expectations. This formula tells us that self-esteem will be positive when success exceeds expectations. Whoever does not achieve their set aims will not generally have a high opinion of themselves.

This formula also teaches us that there are two ways of increasing someone's self-esteem:

- Let the person experience more success.

- Adapt your expectations to his or her potential and to his or her limitations.

Ensuring that people with autism experience more success in their lives is perhaps more important than any psychoeducation or any counselling. Programmes such as *I am Special* are only a drop in the ocean when someone with autism continually endures failure. 'They tell me I'm OK, but nothing goes right in my life and it's a real mess', etc. If their world does not adapt itself in order for success to supplant failure, *I am Special* can do little to help children and adolescents who have a poor self-image.

In order for people with autism to keep their heads above water, we need to adapt their environment to situations and tasks that encourage them to thrive. To survive having autism is a noble aim, but it is not enough. Succeeding in life, despite autism, means much more in terms of quality of life. It is no coincidence that the words 'happiness' and 'success' go together.

We can increase the feeling of self-esteem in people with autism by adjusting the environment and our expectations to their difficulties, as well as by giving them space for expressing their talents.

I am Special can be useful for adapting their own aims and expectations. Here, we return to the starting point of the chapter: self-knowledge as the source of wisdom.

We would like children and young people with autism to learn all kinds of self-assessment. Generally, people with autism are assessed by others: their parents, teachers and helpers. Even if these evaluations are communicated, they remain somewhat external because the person with autism is less involved. As a result, external assessments do not always lead to a person adjusting their expectations: 'We've already told him he can't drive, but even so he still wants to get his licence,' etc.

Self-assessment is not obvious to people with autism. Indeed, self-assessment requires difficult skills, calling upon imagination and coherent thinking. Studies[53] show that even able adults with autism experience difficulties in reporting on themselves and self-awareness. This does not mean they are unable to think about themselves or that they are unable to say something about themselves. Their autobiographies are the most conclusive evidence of this. In practice, we see[54] that what is particularly difficult for them is mainly related to the cohesion between self-description and actual functioning in everyday contexts.

So self-assessment in general and abstract terms such as 'I'm slow at getting down to work' or 'I need structure' have little effect, in our opinion. Such general self descriptions may be accurate, but someone with autism will still have trouble getting down to work in practical terms. These observations remain too vague and are therefore quite useless for the concrete thinker that a person with autism is. We sometimes see children and adolescents talking about themselves in an impressive way and in theoretical and abstract terms, yet if one continues to question them about the consequences for very practical situations, they are silent and have no answers. It is a form of echolalia of the highest level. Above all, transfer and flexible application in daily life remain problematic for people with autism.

Therefore we prefer more practical and concrete forms of self-assessment. Just as in many other areas, here also, we are in favour of very concrete communication. We are not looking for an understanding of oneself, but for a better knowledge of all kinds of concrete situations. It is not an approach for reaching greater understanding but for more knowledge, since, for people with autism, knowing practical things is a much more achievable aim than understanding vague things such as 'the self'. For them, knowledge of specific situations is more easily attainable than knowledge of the abstract self, since making situations concrete is more feasible than materialising the 'self'. You can see situations and thus can make them concretely observable (for example by showing a photo or video), you can analyse them with diagrams and information (for example through 'Social Stories™') and you can make static visual representations (such as a cartoon strip). In short, concrete situations are much more useful when working on self-knowledge than abstract self-descriptions, and with concrete situations, there is less need for complicated applications or transfer of what you teach them.

In practical terms, this means, for example, that we are not going to teach someone to evaluate himself in terms of social skills ('how would you rate your skills on a scale from 0 to 10?'); but with this person, we can draw up lists of social situations that may be problematic or difficult for him.[55] This can consist of a database of, for example, 'situations to avoid'. It is easier to work with this kind of list than with the brief description 'I'm very naive in social situations.'

Using self-assessment in terms of increasing the person's knowledge of situations (rather than knowledge about one's personality, skills and deficits) also involves a lot less confrontation, stigmatisation and is less threatening. Indeed, it relies upon a social model of disability: our starting point is that the situation or environment also plays a role in the presence of problems and difficulties. It is sometimes easier to make environmental adaptations than to modify personal characteristics such as 'naivety', 'uncertainty' or 'rigidity'.

Finally, an overview of easy and difficult situations can allow one to devote more attention to easier situations and thus increase the chances of success. This opens the door to discussions about possible strategies for dealing with problems, and to concrete plans of action for difficult situations. And it is in line with what is called the 'solution focused approach' in therapy (contrary to 'problem focused approach').

This is the vision which forms the basis of the practical objectives of *I am Special* concerning self-knowledge, namely the last three objectives on the list of five objectives (see p.25).

The aim of *I am Special* is not merely to give the person with autism information about their disability. Increasing self-knowledge and above all promoting a feeling of self-esteem are equally important aims for all who want to work with the workbook. In this regard, the manual mentions a number of practical tips as well as suggestions for identifying or assessing the self-image of someone with autism.

Chapter 3

Psychoeducation

I am Special is a psychoeducation programme. We are not the only ones to have described it as such. Others, too (notably Van Doorn and Verheij),[56] situate the workbook within the field of psychoeducation. But what is psychoeducation?

1 Origins

Psychoeducation is a fairly recent methodology which falls within the scope of help given to individuals with a disorder, illness or disability. The exact origin of psychoeducation is somewhat unclear.

As far as we have been able to discover, the term was mentioned for the first time in Canada, in Montréal to be precise. In 1953, a certain Jeannine Guidon founded the *Centre de Psychoéducation du Québec*. In this centre, specialised teachers were trained to re-educate young 'delinquents'. The situation is not clear, but it seems that in the Canadian context of the time, the term 'psychoeducation' was more related to what we now call special education rather than to what is generally meant by psychoeducation at present, that is to say, 'informing patients'. With Guidon, the term is both a reference to specific special education methodology as well as to a training programme for teachers[57] specialising in the treatment and education of children and young people with challenging behaviours. Moreover, these teachers are called 'psychoeducators'. As a result, the meaning of the term 'psychoeducation' in the School of Psychoeducation at the University of Montréal is exceptional. In the rest of the world, psychoeducation has a completely different meaning.

Ivey[58] was one of the forerunners of current conceptions of psycho-education. We believe he was the first to give a definition for the term 'psychoeducation': 'The aim of the psychoeducation model is to equip people with the skills necessary to take charge of their lives in their own way.' In its strictest sense, psychoeducation refers to the programmes and methods employed to inform psychiatric patients and their families about the illness that affects them. We found this origin in the treatment of schizophrenic patients (among others, Anderson[59]). Originally, psychoeducation was limited to family members of someone with schizophrenia, but gradually and to a degree, this was extended to the patients themselves.

Psychoeducation allowed a number of advances to be achieved in this period. First and most importantly, the popularity of cognitive-behavioural therapy grew and paid particular attention to the cognition of the person. Psychoeducation is entirely in keeping with the modern image of the patient as a consumer. In certain texts, consumer-education is even synonymous with psychoeducation.[60] For a long time, patients with purely physical illnesses, such as diabetes, had come together and fought for accurate and comprehensible information about their illnesses, as well as about their treatment. Information sessions for patients with various conditions such as diabetes or cancer thus already existed, but this was not yet the case for people with a mental illness or disorder. Within the current model of welfare work, where the patient is transformed into a discerning and autonomous consumer, the provision of information to patients about their illness, its progression and its treatment has become a fundamental right.

Finally, psychoeducation was also used during the 1970s when a number of criticisms were made of the current medical model in psychiatry and psychotherapy. The emphasis was more and more on the acquisition of skills through a model described as educational and didactic psychosocial support.[61] At this time, all sorts of skills training, such as social skills and relaxation, were popular.

Little by little, it became evident that psychoeducation, particularly as a complement to more traditional treatments including medication and psychotherapy, had a positive effect on a patient's well-being as well as on the severity of the symptoms.[62] The popularity of psychoeducation continued to grow and, by the late 1980s, the first tentative attempts to define and systematise[63] the method (for example, Goldman[64]) had begun. For a long time, psychoeducation had no longer been limited to people with schizophrenia. Since the 1990s, this method has commonly been applied to all areas of psychiatry and is used in cases of anorexia, mood disorders and eating disorders, among others. Strangely, psychoeducation has rarely been applied in the area of developmental disorders. Moreover, in general there are very few programmes for children and adolescents. *I am Special* was the very first comprehensive programme in the field of psychoeducation for people with autism.

2 What is psychoeducation?

Despite the number of articles on psychoeducation, especially in the literature related to schizophrenia, there is no unanimous definition at an international level. Furthermore, a lot of confusion surrounds its definition. Some see it as a form of cognitive-behavioural therapy while on the other hand, some argue for abandoning the prefix 'psycho' to speak only of education. Sometimes, the term encompasses a very narrow definition: communicating a diagnosis to a patient can be synonymous with psychoeducation, as can handing out a brochure on medication. Others opt for a much broader interpretation and describe all kinds of psychotherapeutic interventions under the name of psychoeducation. In some defined programmes, psychoeducation refers to informative meetings for family members and/or other involved persons or even a course for parents. In some fields, psychoeducation is limited to patients and in others, it focuses on both the patient and those around him. Sometimes it is individual programmes, sometimes group meetings. Furthermore, the aims can also differ: to provide information, counselling, support, self-advocacy, self-help, etc.

For almost 20 years, we have used a broad definition of psychoeducation. This term refers to all kinds of educational and pedagogical interventions whose aim is to 'provide people with the tools (skills, knowledge and self-confidence) necessary to take (back) control of their own lives'.[65]

This definition makes it clear we are not limiting psychoeducation to people who have an illness, a developmental disorder or a psychiatric disorder. Everyone can lose their grip at some time in life, and then it is useful to receive the knowledge and skills necessary to recover.

Nevertheless, psychoeducation takes on its full meaning for those who have to face a chronic illness, pathology or disorder. The chronic and therefore permanent character of an illness must involve, alongside the treatment of the illness, help so that the patient may manage the limitations and disabilities arising from the illness. To be able to manage the situation and to encounter as few obstacles as possible, it is essential that the person knows about their illness, their disorder or their syndrome, knows the limitations that result from it and knows how to deal with these. Psychoeducation aims to help patients so that they will encounter the fewest possible restrictions in the face of certain illnesses or disorders.

3 Psychoeducation: more than information

3.1 Knowledge

The provision of information is therefore one of the key aims of psychoeducation. By providing information, this method enables a person to increase their knowledge of their illness, disability or disorder. Some of the more limited applications of psychoeducation bring together information on causes, symptoms, progression of the disorder or illness and treatment (including information on medication, which, most of the time, is about the required dosage). In a much wider sense, such as that which we propose, information is not limited to the illness or disorder but also includes the psychological and social consequences of the problem as well as ways in which the person can deal with these.

In practical terms, we include the following themes in psychoeducation, themes on which information may be provided:

- the characteristics of the disorder, illness or disability

- causes of the disorder, illness or disability

- the progression of the disorder, illness or disability and its prognosis (outcome)

- treatment (different forms of treatment, including medication)

- consequences of the disability for those around the person (for example lack of understanding or stigmatisation)

- ways of coping with the disability (strategies for managing the situation)

- support options (in both formal and informal networks)

- self-advocacy: defending one's own rights and needs.

Psychoeducation thus encompasses the biological, psychological and social aspects of disability at the same time.

3.2 Acceptance and positive self-image

However, knowledge alone of the implications of a disability does not suffice. Many young people and adults with autism possess an in-depth theoretical knowledge (see the chapter on self-image) but even so, face huge problems related to their disorder.

Information and a simple transfer of knowledge therefore is not enough. In addition to providing information, Van Doorn and Verheij[66] saw still two more characteristics specific to psychoeducation, namely:

- encompassing the psychological context (hence the term *psycho*education)

- interpreting the disorder according to the patient's personal context.

The aim of psychoeducation is not only to acknowledge, know about and understand a disability but also to accept it. We are not talking about a total and absolute acceptance. No one is capable of this – there will always remain an element of anger, dissatisfaction, pain. Sometimes, these feelings are useful: some dissatisfaction can motivate a person to (continue to) work on their disability. Instead, we are referring to a degree of acceptance that contributes to peace of mind and particularly to a positive self-image. In psychoeducation, we pay particular attention to the self-image and mindset of the person with autism. Our aim is to increase self-confidence. Thus, when we provide information on the causes of autism, we place emphasis on a 'no-blame' attitude; a person must not feel guilty about their autism.

The aim of psychoeducation is not pure knowledge, but real-life, 'lived' knowledge.[67]

Here, psychoeducation moves nearer to *counselling* (psychosocial help) and to psychotherapy. Although psychoeducation clearly differs from psychotherapy, particularly on the methodological level, generally, it too includes patient assistance and support. Depending on the style and training of the psychoeducator, psychoeducation sometimes also corresponds perfectly with psychotherapy. However, psychoeducation's main emphasis is on learning, and therefore more on cognition than on emotions. As soon as someone becomes blocked in the process of assimilation, it is psychotherapy, rather than psychoeducation, which will take over.

Nevertheless, psychoeducation can have recourse to psychotherapeutic techniques, as well, although these differ from those used in psychotherapy. Here, we are talking primarily about techniques from cognitive-behavioural therapy. Indeed, the degree of acceptance of disability in a person is related to certain conceptions they have, for example about their disability and about themselves. With regard to people with autism in particular, some of their ideas can be quite irrational and therefore lead to low feelings, such as anxiety, depression and stress. For example, someone who associates their disability with disaster, lack of happiness, having no future and being a big failure will have difficulty assimilating their disability and will find it very difficult to find, or may never find, a form of acceptance.

This is why those who work with *I am Special* pay particular attention to any irrational thoughts of the child, young person or adult regarding themselves, an illness, their disability, their autism or their expectations.

3.3 Action

A 'lived' knowledge of disability is not an end in itself. The aim of psychoeducation is that a person acts upon this knowledge and transforms it into actions. The ultimate aim is that the person has total control over their life. In this sense, psychoeducation is aimed towards self-determination (Henselmans[68]): by knowing one's limitations but also one's potential, by knowing how to manage one's disability or illness and by knowing about different kinds of help, everyone can exercise more control over their life. Psychoeducation offers people the information they need to make informed decisions. Self-knowledge is not only the source of wisdom, it is also the source of control over one's own life. Knowledge is indeed real power.

Two essential elements follow from the self-determination perspective, namely individualisation and the transfer of knowledge to everyday behaviour.

3.4 Individualisation

In contrast to psychotherapy, psychoeducation generally proceeds in a more structured way. Most of the time, work is done on the basis of well-defined programmes consisting of a series of sessions and modules. Didactic material is used often, such as workbooks, information brochures, literature or even videos. Therefore, there is less pressure not only for the eventual user (it is easier to sign up for a course than to undergo psychotherapy) but also for those who wish to recommend psychoeducation for their patients. Ready-made products, such as workbooks or programmes, are popular with professionals and patients, particularly in the field of well-being. Today, everything has to happen in a faster, shorter and more efficient way, which increases the pressure to reduce psychoeducation to a 'quick fix': 'a couple of information sessions, a video, one meeting and a brochure will be fine for me'.

However, studies have shown that these 'products' in themselves have very little or no effect, and certainly not in the long term. The effect of a brochure,[69] for example, or even of one information session with a video[70] is very superficial and minimal. One reason may be that standard products rarely lead to *lived* knowledge, since the relationship to the participant's personal situation is missing or is far from being obvious.

Psychoeducation as education does use programmes and didactic material, but this must in no way prevent the 'psychoeducator' from tailoring these programmes and material to the user or patient, so that they truly will derive benefits. Individualisation is essential: information about an illness or a disorder is given for an individual's own, personal situation. In the first place, not everyone who undergoes psychoeducation wishes to have more knowledge about their disorder or illness in general, but, of course, about their own disorder or their own illness: 'my problem'. This personalisation of information is particularly necessary for people with autism. Given their difficulty with seeing context,[71] they do not always spontaneously make the connection between information on autism in general and themselves. *I am Special* pays particular attention to this, among other things, through all kinds of exercises where the person is invited to translate information into their personal context.

Furthermore, not everyone needs the same information at the same time. *I am Special* has taken this, too, into account: the worksheets do not have any page numbers, so that exercises may be left out or added in. A solid psychoeducation programme is a flexible programme, one that can be offered on request and is tailor-made.

3.5 Transforming knowledge into practice

During the sessions, conveying information in ways that take into account someone's personal circumstances is one thing. The transfer to daily life is another, particularly for people with autism. For them, knowledge does not always transform itself into actions. Knowledge of their own potential and limitations does not always lead to making wise choices, simply because making choices is difficult for them. Similarly, knowing about all kinds of support does not always result in calling upon this support, due to a lack of the necessary communication and social skills, for example. The impact of psychoeducation on self-determination can therefore be deferred, if we do not help them put information into practice, in concrete situations in everyday life.

3.6 Skills training

This involves *acquiring skills*, namely social and communication skills (for example asking for help) and skills for solving problems (being able to cope). Social and communication skills are essential for accessing the help that will enable one, for example, to defend one's rights and articulate one's needs. Meeting these challenges in relation to a disability requires problem solving skills. These latter constitute the vital link between knowledge and action, and represent an essential part of psychoeducation.

From this point of view, the first version of *I am Special* does not measure up. The programme was limited to providing information on autism; actions for working on the autism remained general and vague. We had to remedy this shortcoming. This is why the current version includes, for example, a detailed section on the way in which adolescents can translate their knowledge into scenarios for managing their autism, particularly with regard to the blockages related to their autism. In terms of social and communication skills, autism's essential features, we make references to all kinds of existing programmes, since apart from *I am Special*, others are available for developing these skills.

3.7 Collaboration with the environment

The difficulty with transferring skills to everyday life necessitates collaborative working with the environment. We are convinced that the effects of psychoeducation are increased tenfold when both the person and those around him are kept informed. An isolated programme of psychoeducation results in isolated effects, not in integration into everyday life. Without collaboration with the environment (parents, teachers, tutors, etc.), *I am Special* is nothing but a drop in the ocean.

Working with the network around the person provides a broader base from which to gain a perspective on the person's future prospects: if everyone is looking in the same direction, more people can support the individual in his plans for the future.

In addition, the network also plays an important role in providing emotional support for the person. The emotional impact of information about disability is often felt after the psychoeducation sessions, in particular with people with autism who need more time to process information (especially that which is emotionally charged). Those around the person are crucial for good follow-up to the psychoeducation.

In the case of autism, the environment is often key for the application of knowledge and skills learned during psychoeducation. Thus, a child or young person with autism may come up with a scenario in a psychoeducation session for coping with difficult social situations, but actually using this when necessary will depend greatly on the way in which the environment activates this scenario, especially in the beginning. The environment often has to 'push the start button'.

Finally, there is another reason why working in collaboration with the environment is indispensable. The person with the disability is not the only one who has to adapt to the limitations arising from the disorder or illness. The environment also must learn to live with the disability. The degree of acceptance in the environment exerts a great influence on the weight of the burden a person carries due to his illness or disorder. One of the principal aims of psychoeducation is to increase self-confidence and improve self-image. The image a person with autism has of herself will not become more positive if that person continually suffers setbacks because her environment is not open to autism. As we have described in Chapter 2 on self-image, adapting situations so that the person with autism may experience more success in life is the best guarantee for the development of a positive self-image.

One can hardly expect a person with autism to accept their disability through psychoeducation, if their environment does not accept it. For this reason, in the workbook we emphasise the importance of close collaboration with the network of people around the person with autism.

4 Psychoeducation in practice

As we have already mentioned, support of an educational nature takes many forms. It can be implemented individually or in a group. An essentially educational approach is characteristic of *I am Special*. Psychoeducation is closer to education than to 'psych', it is more a course than therapy, and, for our purposes, the prefix could even disappear. Psychoeducation is training in life skills. More precisely, it teaches skills that help a person to give their disability a place in their life.

4.1 Didactic

The educational dimension is reflected in the methods and techniques used, as well as in the attitude of those offering psychoeducation.

In psychoeducation, the trainer presents him or herself primarily as an 'educator' or 'teacher', someone who wants to enable others. The fact that psychoeducation consists of acquiring knowledge, attitudes and skills, demands *pedagogy*. Pedagogy is the science that deals with the study of and development of theories about the processes of teaching and training. Pedagogy consists of a reflective and reasoned set of methods for the transfer of knowledge and skills. Various ideas and precepts derived from pedagogy are required in psychoeducation.

For example, attention is given to what in pedagogy is called the search for an accurate assessment of the initial situation. This latter consists of the set of personal and environmental characteristics that can exert an influence on one's aims and that will be used to achieve these aims. The important variables in the initial situation are, for example, the motivation of the person and their level of understanding of autism. In accordance with this data, one will choose a specific style for conveying information as well as a set structure for the programme. Thus, before commencing work with *I am Special*, it is very important to know whether the child or young person has any knowledge of their autism. If this is the case, it will be necessary also to establish what their knowledge is and what attitude the child or young person has adopted towards it (for example, a denial of the diagnosis). For a young person with a very negative attitude towards their autism, it is preferable not to begin with the worksheets 'what are the positive sides to my autism?'

In the analysis of the initial situation, the issue of conditions is also important: what conditions must be met in order to start a particular programme and how can we influence these conditions, if necessary? Here, we believe the agreement of parents to work with *I am Special* is particularly crucial.

Learning style is another important point in pedagogy. A good teacher adapts resources and methods to the pupil. In the context of *I am Special*, it is essential to know about the particular learning style of people with autism, as well as their specific needs: information provided in stages, a preference for concrete and visual information, etc. This knowledge is a prerequisite for anyone wishing to use *I am Special*.

In addition to the importance attached to the initial situation and learning style, pedagogy also pays particular attention to underlying values and norms, to aims, to the choice of the form and method of work (the programme plan), to transfer and to assessment. In 1985,[72] we developed a pedagogical model for practising social skills and other 'life skills'. This model has served as a guide and has led to the development of a model for psychoeducation, the EDUCATOR model, comprised of eight components or phases:

- **E**xploration of norms and values (for example, what are your views on self-determination, your views on disability?).

- **D**etailed evaluation of the initial situation (what does the person know about autism?).

- **U**sefulness: defining a set of objectives that are useful for the client and that are in accordance with the initial situation and values (what goal do you want to achieve, mainly knowledge about autism or a better self-image?).

- **C**urriculum design: development of a concrete curriculum or programme (which sessions do you want, how many hours, what resources, sessions organised in groups or individually?).

- **A**ction: carrying out the programme (who will lead the sessions, where and when?).

- **T**ransfer: applying the knowledge and skills acquired (what do you want the person who acquires this knowledge to do – where, when and how?).

- **O**utcome: evaluation of the results and effects (how will you assess whether the person has a more positive self-image?).

- **R**ecycling: based on the evaluation, you can review or repeat some parts (e.g. use the section on 'being unique' once again, with different resources and in a different way).

When setting out to work with *I am Special*, ensure enough time has been allowed to consider each of these steps, and if necessary, consult others, such as the parents of the child or young person. Preparation is at least half of the work!

Finally, with psychoeducation, we also opt for a markedly pedagogical attitude, more precisely, the Socratic attitude (see next chapter). Here, we focus on the self-discovery of knowledge.

4.2 Resources and tools

All kinds of resources for acquiring knowledge and skills can be used in psychoeducation. Resources may differ with regard to:

- the number of participants (individual learning sessions or group meetings)
- the main tool (online learning, computer courses, courses on television or by video, written courses, discussion groups, etc.)
- the degree of active participation by the participants (low for a supporting video or for reading a brochure, higher for a group discussion)
- the information source (paid professional, friend, book).

A number of psychoeducation programmes combine different resources, for example an information brochure, a certain number of group discussion sessions, a talk given by a specialist and one by a friend.

Specific resources may also vary greatly.

Examples of concrete resources in psychoeducation:

- information brochures
- interactive workbooks with 'exercises' (such as *I am Special*)
- videos
- writing
- authoritative lectures or courses
- group discussions
- role play
- homework
- video feedback
- interviews
- board games

- group games, especially designed for psychoeducation
- quizzes
- collages
- cartoon strips.

The choice of materials and practical tools depends on different factors, such as the learning style of the participant, the time available to the person, the aim of an investigation. To avoid boredom, it is advisable to vary the resources and tools. Finally, there are particular resources and tools which, unless you adapt them, are less suitable for people with autism, such as conventional group discussions.

Psychoeducation is a relatively new method in the range of forms of support given to people with developmental disorders. Psychoeducation specific to autism is just at the embryonic stage. We are keeping an eye on further progress and with this book, we hope we have drawn out a preliminary sketch.

Chapter 4

The Socratic Method

1 Context

One of the methodological bases of *I am Special* is the Socratic method. I mentioned this method for the first time in my book on Asperger's Syndrome, *Brein bedriegt* (*The Deceiving Brain*), as a method for clarifying the world to people with an autism spectrum disorder.[73]

As a result of their *context blindness* and their particular style of perceiving and thinking, people with autism sometimes fail to understand things the way other people do. Being unable to involve important contextual elements, having too concrete an understanding or understanding in a way that is too detailed are barriers in their everyday functioning and complicate 'right' decision-making. By asking questions – the hallmark of the Socratic method – we nudge them towards a sound understanding, from which basis they may take independent and autonomous decisions. Like Socrates, we do not provide any answers, but through questioning, help them to discover the best meaning and the right context for themselves. In addition to its empowering effect, the Socratic method also has a positive impact on self-image, as individuals with autism feel they have reached a good understanding and found good solutions by themselves.

The Socratic method and the inductive way of working which ensues from it have already been mentioned in the first version of *I am Special*. The workbook as a whole as well as each section taken separately may be presented in a deductive or inductive way. An inductive or Socratic work method may be used when the person with autism already holds his own views about autism, ideas that we would wish to correct or question in a critical way.

In our workshops, we offer parents and carers an opportunity to practise this way of working. After a brief presentation on Socrates and a description of the method that bears his name, we show adaptations of this method particularly related to autism: what we call the Socrautic method. It may seem obvious that Socratic questioning should motivate the listener to reflect on their own ideas and opinions. Thanks to the experience gained in a workshop, however, one realises that the practical application of these principles and establishing a Socratic dialogue are far from easy. As well as a Socratic attitude, some training is necessary to be able to use this method.

2 Socrates

A Greek philosopher who unsettled others with his questions. He died after drinking hemlock, the poison which was the traditional death penalty in Athens.[74] That is the common answer to the question, 'Who was Socrates?' Socrates was the child of a sculptor and a midwife. He lived in Greece from

Photo 4.1: Socrates

470 to 399 BCE. The sculpture bust capturing his image depicts a realistic reproduction of his appearance and proves that he was not particularly an Adonis.

Like many other philosophers of the era, Socrates was 'teaching'. By comparison with his colleagues, Socrates was a maverick: for example, he did not ask his students for payment for his lessons. He was not bound to a specific school nor to particular students. He spoke in public places, such as markets, squares, at festivals or simply in the place where he found himself. Furthermore, he refused to participate actively in political life, unlike many other philosophers of the time. On the contrary, he continually delivered sarcastic remarks about the political regime, was frequently critical, and regularly turned politicians into objects of ridicule: 'Athens is like a sluggish horse and I am the gadfly that will try to sting you into life.' It is this attitude which ultimately cost him his life. He was accused – wrongly – of corrupting the young. On three occasions he was forced by the authorities to account for his actions; the third time proved fatal.

Socrates seems to have been a very ironic figure. The proof of this is in the famous answer he gave to the young man who asked him whether he should marry or not: 'Do what you want…either way, you will regret it!' His response to the death sentence was also characterised by this same irony. He refused to ask for a stay of execution.

Unlike his colleagues, he did not leave behind any writing. What we know about him comes from Plato, one of his students. Plato was Socrates' interlocutor in the many dialogues written by Plato. It is through these dialogues we have come to know Socrates and to understand how he differed from most other teachers and philosophers of the era. It is also through these that we have discovered the main reason why he became famous, namely, the way in which he taught.

3 Socrates' method of work

According to Socrates, all wisdom comes from within. Unlike his colleagues, he did not teach in the classical way. He completely reversed the traditional teacher–student relationship. In a conventional relationship, the student, being ignorant, asks questions to the teacher who, as the one who knows, answers. Socrates did exactly the opposite: he did not give any answers but asked questions in such a way that the student discovers the answer for himself and comes to an understanding of the situation. Socrates compared his work to that of his mother, a midwife. Just as a midwife helps other women bring their child into the world, Socrates helped his students to give birth to new insights. Referring to the Greek obstetrics term ('maieutikè' or Μαιευτική), the Socratic method is also referred to as the maieutic method or maieutics.

Socrates did not represent truth as something to be given but helped his students to find the truth hidden within themselves. In his characteristically ironic style, he also claimed he knew nothing. At best, he knew only one thing, namely that he knows nothing. Naturally, this was not the case. However, Socrates began each dialogue by playing the role of the ignorant one.

He confronted students with questions which cast doubt on their own choices, ideas and assumptions. The questions he posed seemed very innocent, from his point of view as someone who is ignorant and naive, but this was in appearance only. It was rigorous and critical questioning which repeated the arguments of the interlocutor, the ultimate goal of which was that the latter would make revisions or corrections. This method of working is known in Greek by the term 'elenchus' (ἔλεγχος), and can be compared, at best, to a cross-examination. Socrates interrogates the student until he becomes confused and has the feeling of no longer knowing anything. In Greek, this state is called 'aporia' (ἀπορεία). According to Socrates, it is at this point that the student's knowledge acquired from the outside, learned from others, ends. Indeed, according to this philosophy, many people possess knowledge in a particular area without having any real understanding of the subject. They also adopt the false ideas of others all too easily. According to Socrates' vision, to know nothing is better than to have false knowledge. And ignorance arouses curiosity, a search and a quest for knowledge and truth. Thus critical questioning breaks away from that, to begin with a clean slate, a blank page, to construct a new and better understanding from the inside. Through induction, Socrates was trying to bring about new ideas and thoughts in his students, thus students were invited to draw conclusions for themselves. The ultimate goal for Socrates was not to arrive at THE truth – Socrates was too critical a thinker for such a thing – but to reach a consensus between the interlocutors.

4 The Socratic method
4.1 History and present application
Our current knowledge of Socrates and his merits is limited to knowledge of his method. Apart from philosophers, very few people know what philosophical ideas and opinions Socrates held. As a result, the contribution of Socrates is more pedagogical than philosophical. Socrates is praised for his method, not only in philosophy but also in other disciplines such as psychology, where he is quoted by Sigmund Freud.[75]

The current interpretation and contribution of the Socratic method does not directly reflect Socrates' original way of working, but is based primarily on that of the German philosopher and educator Leonard Nelson (1882–1927).[76] Nelson attracted new attention to the Socratic method, inspired by the German philosopher Immanuel Kant (1724–1804) whose 'critical' philosophy and 'critical' method were in fact new forms of the Socratic method.[77]

Today, the Socratic method is popular in various areas, such as philosophy for children, work psychology, management and psychotherapy. Many universities, particularly law schools, as well as American secondary schools offer courses in the Socratic method. Given the heterogeneity of areas in which the Socratic method is employed, interpretations and additions also vary greatly. The term has become commonplace, yet its practical application sometimes seems very far from the original working method and objectives. Furthermore, it is sometimes very much like a caricature. Some professors at these law schools give absolutely no lectures or theory for a whole semester but drive their students to despair and abandonment with their continual critical questioning.[78]

4.2 General structure of a Socratic dialogue

Most of the time, the Socratic method is applied in group discussions on ethics, philosophy, psychology and other abstract and fundamental subjects, such as freedom, truth, authenticity and equal rights for all. Then, the group seeks consensus on the principles of the subject of the conversation. The structure of such a Socratic conversation closely resembles that of an hourglass: starting from an initial general question (for example, what is creativity?), the leader of the conversation reduces the discussion to one or more concrete experiences of the participants. Questioning these experiences further tightens the net around the subject of the conversation to arrive at a central position (for example, creativity is creating something new which is appreciated by others). Then, the group examines the hidden assumptions and arguments behind this position (for example, that creativity must be something new, or that something which is not appreciated by others cannot be creative). This phase opens up a new discussion, to reach a consensus on the theme's general principles (for example, innovation; a social component).

4.3 Induction

The Socratic method we propose for use with people with autism is somewhat different. To begin with, it is often a dialogue and not a group conversation, although the latter is not ruled out for people with autism (but they are not easy!). In general, the themes also are much more concrete than those for which the Socratic method is used most of the time. The basic principle of a Socratic dialogue nevertheless remains the same: *induction*, inferring from individual cases that there is a general rule.

Instead of starting from general principles to reach specific conclusions, we start with concrete experiences, sometimes even small details and examples, to draw more general conclusions. This does not mean that the dialogue always begins with examples or specific experiences. A Socratic dialogue always begins with what the other person says, whether this is a general or specific remark. Taking circumstances into account, we make 'inductions' from the specific to a more general rule, or, more precisely, we will question these experiences and specific examples so that starting from the concrete, we can critically discuss a general rule and thus deduce another general principle.

4.4 Directive, not authoritarian

As a result of a reversal of the teacher–student relationship and use of an inductive work method, a Socratic dialogue is non-directive. Nothing is being postulated and the 'instructor' in a Socratic dialogue is following the 'student' in his thoughts. Nothing could be further from the truth. Remaining completely faithful to the character of Socrates, this is precisely the irony of the Socratic method: the ignorance which Socrates employed as a main tool is not truly ignorance on the part of the 'teacher'. This is the ironic paradox of the Socratic method: if the 'teacher' really was ignorant, he could not ask the questions by which the 'student' could attain knowledge. The word 'irony' is derived from the Greek 'eirōneia'([Eironeia:] ειρωμαι), which means feigned ignorance. The remarkable thing is that 'eirōneia' has more or less the same root as 'eirōmai'([Eiromai:] ειρωμαι), the Greek word for…'to ask' or asking questions. Coincidence, or not?

At heart, a Socratic dialogue is well and truly directive. Although modern interpretations of the Socratic method focus on openness, a Socratic dialogue is not a true dialogue between peers. A Socratic dialogue was and remains a dialogue in which one learns, where the leader of the conversation assumes the role of guide and director. The questions he or she poses are not neutral, but on the contrary are suggestive, or 'leading questions', questions that lead the student to a point – more precisely, to a questioning critique of their own ideas and conceptions. The role of the ignorant person could become so caricaturist that the dialogue can take an ironic turn, where the 'student' has a feeling of being made fun of.

In this sense, it is very important to make the distinction between authoritarian and directive. Many people consider the two terms synonymous, but they are not at all. Being directive means to guide, whereas being authoritarian is related to the use of power.[79] Someone who is authoritarian imposes themselves on others. The notion of authoritarianism is linked to superiority in a relationship, powerful versus powerless, while 'directive' is associated with the idea of being guided or not guided, towards clarity or ambiguity.

Figure 4.1 clarifies the situation. We have placed different communicative functions along two axes (authoritarian or not and directive or not).

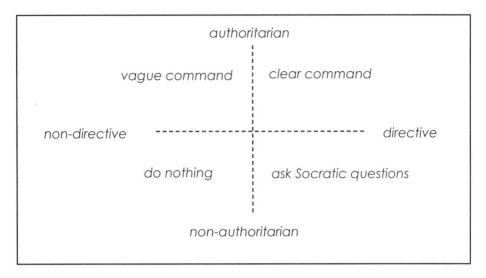

Figure 4.1: Authoritarian vs directive forms of communication

Anyone who acts in an authoritarian way is using power and operating in a decisive manner with respect to the other. Orders are given in this context too. Clear orders (such as 'go to school!') direct the person and as a result are unambiguous (in the example given, you know exactly where you have to go). Someone who is authoritarian but does not guide or direct also gives orders but in too vague a manner (such as 'stop that!', an order that does not actually say what you need to do). Someone who acts in a non-authoritarian way but is also non-directive does absolutely nothing. This is what is called a '*laissez-faire*' attitude, which leaves someone completely free.

A Socratic attitude is non-authoritarian. Indeed, the starting point is that any belief comes from the inside, and that which is imposed by others is not a true conviction. This is why, in a Socratic dialogue, one does not determine what the other person should think or do. Socratic questions guide a person towards a critical questioning of their own opinions or towards a definite conclusion. Socrates was the last person who would want to force anyone to accept unreflected conclusions.

However, a Socratic dialogue could also be used as an authoritarian instrument. Given that at first sight a Socratic dialogue features few directive characteristics (giving no orders, opinions or suggested truths), it lends itself perfectly to a fake democratic dialogue. It is no coincidence that the Socratic method has been very successful in management, despite the 'democratic' tendency of many managers. A Socratic dialogue is nothing more than a method or tool, and every method or tool can be used for democratic purposes or not.

The Socratic method that we propose is directive but non-authoritarian. Indeed, self-determination, or empowerment, is the premier attitude adopted in *I am Special*. The image that best suits this attitude is that of a guide. A guide points out the direction to follow but does not exercise power. It is the person with autism who makes the crucial choices and takes the final decisions.

The combination of directive and non-authoritarian methods has advantages, particularly with regard to autism. On the one hand, many people with autism, particularly adolescents and adults with average intelligence, wish to make their own decisions and require a non-authoritarian attitude from others. On the other hand, they have a considerable need for clarity. Someone who works in a directive manner provides more clarity than someone who uses a non-directive method. The combination of directive and non-authoritarian methods is the best way to ensure a positive collaboration with the person with autism, as shown in Figure 4.2. This shows how people usually react to the forms of communication depicted in Figure 4.1. Orders often provoke opposition. A lack of clarity leads to confusion.

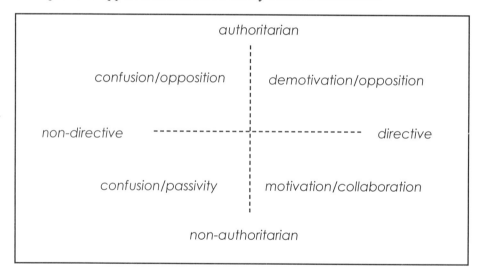

Figure 4.2: Authoritarian vs directive forms of communication: consequences

Given that choices and decision-making constitute real challenges for people with autism, they may regularly ask us to resolve a problem and to choose or decide for them. The Socratic method provides advantages in these instances, too. By asking targeted questions, we can guide them towards a choice or decision, without necessarily taking these for them.

4.5 Developing a Socratic dialogue in practice

The ideas and experiences of the 'student' have their place in a Socratic dialogue. This attribute renders a Socratic dialogue unpredictable. Nevertheless, it does develop in a very structured way. A Socratic dialogue develops as follows:

1. Determine your goal and define what you want in concrete terms. The objectives of a Socratic dialogue can be very different (convincing someone to adopt another point of view, helping a person to make a decision, etc.). A Socratic dialogue is not the same as idle chit-chat in a cafe. As the one leading the discussion, you need to determine in advance what the objectives of the dialogue are.

2. Think about the 'steps' necessary for reaching the final objective.

3. Think of a pertinent initial question, a question that will arouse the curiosity of the 'student' and provide motivation to reflect further. A good initial question takes into account the individual's interests and desires.

4. Ask the initial question.

5. Listen to the person's answer and ask a new question. The cycle of questions and answers is repeated until a certain 'step' in the plan has been passed.

6. If this step has been accomplished (partial conclusion or a specific opinion), summarise the whole, or let the person summarise.

7. Lastly, let the person draw a final conclusion.

Example

A boy's teaching assistant (TA) is convinced that symbols are a good means of communication for this young man. But as the teacher of this boy, you know from your experience that the boy finds it hard to understand symbols and that he prefers to use more concrete forms of communication, such as objects. The boy never uses symbols to say he is thirsty, for example, but will simply go to the fridge himself to find something to drink. The TA thinks this is not a good attitude and regards this conduct as a behaviour problem.

Your objective: to ensure that the TA asks critical questions regarding his idea that it is preferable for this boy to use symbols as a means of communication.

The different 'steps' are, notably:

- Does the TA see a link between the challenging behaviour and the young boy's communication problem?

- Does the TA know the different levels of means of communication (objects, two-dimensional aids such as photos, line drawings and symbols, spoken language)?

- Does the TA consider objects as a possible form of communication?

- What options are there for identifying the young man's level of comprehension?

Given that the TA considers 'taking a drink from the fridge' to be a problem, we should take this as a starting point for the dialogue. We explain to him that during this dialogue, we would like to talk about the boy's communication, more particularly about the fact that he does not ask for a drink but simply helps himself from the fridge. An initial question could be the following: 'In your opinion, why does he not ask for a drink?'

Another example

The mother of a child with autism asks you, a professional, whether her child should go into special education rather than to a mainstream school. From the point of view of self-determination, you are not going to take this decision for the mother. The objective of the dialogue is that the mother makes the decision herself. The different 'steps' are, among others:

- consider the opportunities as well as the limitations of special education and mainstream education

- consider the educational needs of the child

- consider the preferences of the person who must make the decision (according to the mother, what is it that is important for the child?).

By asking questions on all these aspects, you are giving the mother some criteria by which she may make her decision.

These examples demonstrate that the Socratic method can be applied to a wide variety of situations.

4.6 Socratic questions

Questions are the key to the success of a Socratic dialogue. Depending on circumstances and the stage of the dialogue, in your capacity as leader of the dialogue, you will use up your prepared questions. In fact, not every question will help to advance the dialogue in the desired direction. There are different kinds of questions, each with their own function. Before analysing these, we will examine some general criteria that apply to questions in a Socratic dialogue. These criteria are obvious – even so, we have drawn up a list.

All questions should be:

- Interesting and provocative, such that the interlocutor is, so to speak, guided towards reflection.

- Constructed in a logical way, that is, linked to previous thinking. Sudden and unexpected turns can derail the interlocutor and impede the dialogue. It is necessary to choose another angle sometimes, for example when one has the impression of stalling on a particular discussion point. Taking a new direction is possible, but it must be done carefully.

- Direct. Ultimately, a Socratic dialogue is the sort of conversation in which we learn. To promote concentration and increase its effectiveness, we should not blight the dialogue with unnecessary elements.

> *Socratic questions are provocative, logical, direct and neutral.*

- Neutral. A Socratic dialogue already carries a degree of risk from irony, which can give the impression that the interlocutor is stupid or has erroneous ideas or opinions. Although the two participants in the conversation are not equal, since they have different roles ('teacher' and 'student'), they are counterparts, all the same. It is preferable to avoid certain forms of questioning, both verbally and non-verbally, which may give the impression to the other person that they are being stupid or getting it all wrong. Here are some examples of questions that convey a judgement: 'Honestly, how can you…', 'Do you really think…', 'Think about it seriously now. What is…'. Suggestive questions like 'Do you also find that…' also contain a value judgement, as they suggest your vision is the right one.

Overall, questions can be divided into two categories: *exploratory questions* and *leading questions*. Within the two categories, we can make further subdivisions. Table 4.1 gives an overview of the types of questions, illustrated by some examples.

Table 4.1 Categories of questions in a Socratic dialogue

Exploratory questions	Leading questions
Questions for obtaining clarification What do you mean by…? Can you give me an example? How can I picture it? Can you explain it differently? **Questions for clarifying assumptions** What is your basis for saying that…? Could you give an example of…? Why should that be the case? How could it be possible that…? How did you come to this conclusion? You seem to think that… Is it possible?	**Questions for verifying certain ideas** How do we apply that in this case? How can we tell whether this is the case, and when is it the case? Where could we check this? It is true, you think, that…but could it be different? What would be another solution? **Questions for checking implications and consequences** If that is true, what will it result in? If that is true, what does it mean for…? If that happens, what else will happen then? What is the consequence of…?

The aim of exploratory questions is to learn about the ideas or opinions of the other person. As a Socratic interlocutor, you are trying to obtain information through asking these questions. In the exploratory questions category, we distinguish between questions for obtaining clarification and those for clarifying assumptions.

Through questioning to obtain clarification, we are checking to see whether we have understood the other person properly. In order to sound out the underlying ideas of a person, the opinions on which a certain position or conception was based, we can use the questions for clarifying assumptions.

With leading questions, the aim is not to obtain information but to give information, albeit in an inductive way. For example, we can invite the interlocutor to monitor and verify their own ideas and opinions by asking questions about the application of a particular principle. By asking questions about the consequences of an event, we can guide the interlocutor towards one or more conclusions.

Example

A man with autism calls and asks me if it would be right for him to attend a course for people with autism. Through exploratory questions, such as 'Which course are you referring to?', I try to discover what his real question is. His response clearly indicates it is specifically a course on autism and relationships, a course mentioned in the brochure of programmes we have sent him. I ask why he would (or wouldn't) attend this course (I'm testing the unspoken assumptions). He replies that he needs to be in a relationship to attend this course and at the moment he's not in one. He therefore thinks that he will not be allowed to attend the course on relationships. I ask him whether he is sure he needs to be in a relationship in order to attend the course. He says he is not really sure but he assumes this. I ask him how he can be certain that having a relationship is a requirement for attending the course (a verification question). He says he doesn't know. I ask him whether there are any other requirements. He responds: 'An official diagnosis of autism.' I ask how he knows this. He responds that this is mentioned in the brochure. I ask whether other requirements are also mentioned. He enumerates the other requirements. I ask him: 'If being in a relationship were a requirement for attending the course, what would this result in?' (a question on implications). He deduced that any requirements would be mentioned in the brochure and ends with the following remark: 'So, even I can take this course!'

Although Table 4.1 above clearly offers a distinction between different kinds of questions, in reality many questions generally serve several objectives, sometimes simultaneously.

For example, a question about the consequences of a certain position can be used both to bring the person to a particular conclusion and to confront them with their own views. However, this question can also tell us more about what the person thinks (exploratory question). The response to the question can also give information about the person's underlying assumptions.

Questions asking for *examples* are very useful. Generally, examples are indeed more concrete, and the more concrete a Socratic dialogue is, the more effective. The examples will shed light on the assumptions of the person and give us a picture of the type of experiences on which to base some advice or share thoughts. They also allow us to test whether we understand each other properly; abstract terms like the word 'good' have innumerable meanings. Ultimately, examples also allow us to verify assumptions and thus to monitor the person's ideas in relation to reality.

> *Questions asking for examples and hypothetical situations enhance the dialogue's effectiveness and provide rich information.*

Hypothetical situations are very handy when we wish to invite the interlocutor to verify or test the validity of their own assumptions and ideas. Through this hypothetical situation, we are testing the concrete consequences of the person's ideas. Hypothetical situations enable an experiment in thinking to be carried out, where one can modify or verify an assumption or hypothesis that has evolved. Most of the time, the experiment in thinking begins as follows: 'OK, let us presume/suppose/that…' Then, we can see what concrete consequences arise from this. We can verify these consequences through more thorough questioning.

We could use the example of the man who was worried about the course, for a hypothetical situation. The experiment in thinking would be the following: OK, supposing having a relationship did indeed constitute a requirement, what would be the consequence for the brochure? The consequence would be that the brochure would mention it, just as it does the other requirements. The man can take the brochure in hand and verify this. This requirement is not mentioned and the man modifies his own assumption.

A question often posed during workshops on the Socratic method is the following: 'Which questions are best, open or closed questions?'

Closed questions are questions with very limited options for answers: 'yes' or 'no'. For example: 'Do you find this book boring?' Most of the time, closed questions begin with a verb. Open questions begin with words such as *who*, *what*, *where*, *why*, *when* and expand the range of choice of possible answers. For example, 'What do you think of this book?'

In a Socratic dialogue, we use both open and closed questions. They both have their purpose and usefulness, and their use therefore depends on the information you need and the objective of your search. Closed questions direct one's attention to a precise point and help to obtain clear confirmation or refutation of a matter. Generally, open questions result in a broader answer and are thus more informative. They can be used particularly in the initial phase of the dialogue, when we are still in the process of exploring the ideas and views of our interlocutor. However, open questions can also bring out too much information. They also carry the risk of receiving much too detailed an answer from the other person. The dialogue can be derailed as a result and you could lose the thread of it. This risk is particularly present with people with autism who are talkative. Unlike closed questions, open questions encourage critical thinking in the interlocutor, particularly when you ask them to verify their own ideas. Closed questions, on the other hand, allow you much better control of the dialogue.

In short, you need to adapt a question to the needs and objectives of the dialogue.

4.7 Additional essential elements

Naturally, a Socratic dialogue is composed mainly of questions. However, it is neither an enhanced quiz nor a cross-examination. Questions are the *leitmotif* of the Socratic method, but throughout the dialogue, the leader of the conversation also grants time and space to other things.

Let's start right away with the first piece of advice: take your time and give the other person some space. A Socratic dialogue demands a great intellectual effort. Particularly when facing directive questions and those implying confrontation, it is necessary to give enough time and space for your interlocutor to think.

> Advice:
> ✓ Take and give time for reflection.
> ✓ Mention context and give any necessary explanations of your question.
> ✓ Summarise regularly.
> ✓ Concretise!

Pauses in the dialogue are a particular tool. When the other person does not respond right away to your question, we often tend to reformulate it – or even worse – to ask an additional (sub-) question. This can severely disrupt the interlocutor. You are interrupting his thinking processes and you will probably get an answer to your additional question and not to your first question, which was perhaps much more important. Give yourself time to think, too. Indeed, the questions that you ask are crucial and it is necessary to give yourself some time to think.

When you want to give another direction to the dialogue, or you notice that your interlocutor is frowning, it is advisable to explain the context of your question or to explain where you are going with it. You and your interlocutor will thus avoid getting lost in your surprising question. An *explanation* helps towards receiving a direct answer, especially when you are asking an open question, because it includes the objective as well. By giving an explanation or a justification of your question, you can also motivate the other person. If your interlocutor understands the purpose of the question, he or she will put more effort into thinking of an informative answer.

It is very helpful to *summarise* the main points regularly during the dialogue. A summary helps maintain the line of discussion and allows you to check whether it is still working, but above all it provides a foothold for your interlocutor. Thanks to your summary, the other person can also see whether you have understood them properly and if necessary, can correct you or supplement their answer.

Finally, a recommendation of utmost importance is: *concretise the dialogue!* The advantage of examples and hypothetical situations is in fact that they make the dialogue concrete. Experience has shown us that the success of a Socratic dialogue depends on the extent of concretisation. This is particularly of benefit for those who wish to use the Socratic method with people with autism, who are models of concrete thinking. Which leads us to how we can make a Socratic dialogue *autism friendly*, the so called Socra*u*tic method.

5 The Socrautic method

By definition, a Socratic dialogue is communication. People with autism communicate differently and often encounter problems with 'ordinary', non-autistic communication. We will now show why it is necessary to adapt a 'normal' Socratic dialogue or traditional style of communication for people with autism. We call this adapted version the Socra*u*tic method. Before presenting this version of the Socratic method adapted for autism, it is useful to situate this method within all the kinds of help available for people with autism.

5.1 The Socratic method's place within interventions offered

The term 'method' in Socratic method evokes many expectations as well as a number of misunderstandings. We have noticed that many professionals and parents think that the Socratic method is an nth 'treatment' for autism, such as Sunrise, TEACCH, Applied Behavioral Analysis, etc. Nothing could be further from the truth. The Socratic method absolutely does not belong on this list and its aim is not at all to have an immediate impact on autism or on a person's development. A Socratic dialogue is nothing more than a technique for learning from a specific dialogue and therefore belongs within the category of group discussions, role play, songs, stories – which are all pedagogical work methods. The Socratic dialogue is a practical means that can serve different aims and can be applied in a variety of contexts, as can a group discussion or role play. We can also use it within many programmes and methods: in psychotherapy, in teaching, in social skills training, psychosocial assistance, in the counselling field and in courses of all kinds.

Naturally, the Socratic method, as we have presented it, also refers to a particular attitude and vision, namely, that true understanding comes from within. Better still, it is even possible to work in a Socratic way without having a literal dialogue with someone, for

> The Socratic method is not a treatment method for autism!

example when you help someone to make a decision using a guide or manual written in a Socratic way.

In all cases, to serve as a treatment is not the purpose of the method. This feature makes it secondary to general work methods and approaches to people with autism. First of all, people with autism require clarity, predictability and explanations, not a Socratic dialogue. When someone with autism encounters difficulties, holding a Socratic dialogue is not the immediate solution. The first need is to carefully analyse their difficulties. Confusion, lack of clarity and structure, unpredictability, too high expectations, excessive demands of the environment, sensory overload, etc. appear very quickly in your focus then. You will have to act upon the sources of distress, rather than starting a Socratic dialogue with the person.

Example

During a workshop, a participant, the father of an adolescent with autism, chose as an application of the Socratic dialogue to get his son to understand that he has to do his homework. In fact, the problem was that his son often doesn't do his homework, and that, as a result, he is reprimanded and punished. When we examined together as a group what the real problem with the homework was (N.B. this was through a Socratic dialogue we had established as a group and in which we asked questions of the father), it turned out that the homework tasks were vague and too imprecise for the adolescent. For example, the teacher did not give enough detail about what was needed, about the deadline for the homework, time needed to spend on it, etc. Furthermore, the young person couldn't tell when was the best time for starting his homework at home, he didn't know what to do if he didn't understand or what he could do to remember to bring home any equipment he needs for his homework. In short, the communication around homework was not concrete enough. The young man was willing enough to do his homework, but could not manage without structure or additional support. In this case, a Socratic dialogue was not necessarily needed, what was needed was clarification, details about the homework and good communication around it.

In order to convey this clarification to the boy with autism, it is possible to use a Socratic dialogue. In the previous example, a support for not forgetting anything at school at the end of the day is one of the adaptations that may be introduced in a homework scenario. Different means and adaptations were offered to the young person (a classmate telling him everything he needs to take home, making up a list himself of what he needs, asking a classmate) and through a Socratic dialogue, his parents helped him choose which one he prefers.

5.2 Conditions

A Socratic dialogue is not always possible. It requires a number of intellectual skills on the part of the person with autism. During a Socratic dialogue, we are asking someone to reflect and this reflection necessitates a certain level of cognitive functioning. This does not mean that it is only possible to conduct a Socratic dialogue with individuals of average intelligence. With a very concrete theme and well-adapted communication, it is also possible to use a Socratic dialogue with people with autism and a learning disability.

Other than a required minimum level of intelligence, a person with autism must also be able to carry on a two-way conversation in a Socratic dialogue. We do not mean that they must be able to carry on a 'normal' dialogue (one that is very verbal, rapid and abstract). In fact, in a Socrautic dialogue, we use a style of communication adapted to autism (that is to say, very visual, slow and concrete). However, a certain level of understanding of dialogues is necessary and a question must be understood as such, even if the form of communication is adapted to autism.

Time is a significant limitation in a Socratic dialogue. It takes time, a lot of time. This statement is especially true when one wishes to use the method with people with autism who – much more than so-called neurotypical people – need time for reflection. To illustrate with a rather dramatic example: if, all of a sudden, a child wants to cross the road without looking right and left, you are not going to embark on a Socratic dialogue about safety in traffic. In many urgent problem situations, action and intervention will take precedence over conversation. In situations where the person with autism panics or becomes confused, a Socratic dialogue is not the best way to address the problem, especially not when there are fits of crying or anger. Of course, we can discuss the incident later, when the person with autism is calm enough to concentrate, and then the Socratic method can be used.

A Socratic dialogue takes time not only during the conversation, but also in preparation. As a conversation in which we learn, a Socratic dialogue always has a specific aim. It is recommended that you think about that aim beforehand and prepare the Socratic dialogue: what is the objective? What is the logical sequence of steps to be achieved? What supports will I use?

5.3 Developing a Socrautic dialogue in practice

Fundamentally, a Socratic dialogue with people with autism unfolds in the same way as with ordinary individuals. However, since predictability and clarity are maximised, more structure is required with people with autism.

First of all, this means that, usually, from the beginning of the conversation, we will mention its purpose. Often, people with autism do not perceive others' intentions or don't understand these spontaneously, and find it particularly difficult to guess others' aims. If, from the beginning, we articulate the aim, as well as, as much as is possible, the steps to go through, we are sparing them a huge amount of reflection and uncertainty. That benefits their motivation and concentration.

It is also advisable to summarise regularly, more often for people with autism. Since people with autism experience great difficulty with predicting things and can easily get lost in details, writing down each partial conclusion on a piece of paper is not a bad idea – especially for more complex themes. In this way, the person with autism can literally see how the dialogue is unfolding; he or she has a clear overview and, if necessary, can refer easily to conclusions that have already been drawn.

Time allotted to the phase in which you are exploring the person's assumptions is also different from the progression of a 'normal' Socratic dialogue. When we set out to discover the underlying ideas and views of a person who does not have autism, we can hang on to our own thoughts. This statement does not apply to dialogues with people with autism. Indeed, the latter have a particular way of thinking and understand things in a totally different way. It is therefore preferable not to draw too hasty conclusions about what they think. In order to avoid the danger of 'neurotypical projections', it is advisable to take enough time and to ask enough questions to assess what the person with autism thinks. Behind the questions and discourse of those with autism, one does not always find the same reasoning as that which would lead so-called neurotypical people to using the same words.

Example

Take the man who phoned us to find out whether it would be right for him to take a course organised by *Autisme Centraal* for people with autism. We immediately thought that this man wanted to know what such a course might give him. Indeed, when someone asks if something is a positive thing, it is because they want to know the potential benefits. However, this was not this man's question. He was not asking whether it would be right for him, but for us. After having asked some exploratory questions, we understood he wished to attend a course on relationships and that he assumed he did not meet the requirements. His question was in fact: 'Can I participate in this course even if I'm not in a relationship at the moment?' He thought, wrongly, that a relationship was a necessary requirement for the course.

Lastly, the ending of a Socra*u*tic dialogue also differs from that of a 'normal' Socratic dialogue, which usually ends with one final conclusion. Our experiences have shown us that conversations with people with autism sometimes have little effect on their everyday lives. Even the conclusions written on paper often go unheeded. This is a consequence that stems from problems with 'transfer' that are characteristic of autism. People with autism can learn and understand a great deal during conversations, but they experience significant difficulties with applying everything they have understood and learned to everyday life. These difficulties

> In a Socrautic dialogue, we pay more attention to:
> ✓ predictability (specify the aim of the dialogue)
> ✓ having an overall view (keep a written log)
> ✓ transfer (what will we do with these conclusions?).

with application and transfer notably explain why training programmes in 'theory of mind' unfortunately have very little effect on the everyday social functioning of children and young people with autism, even if their results in 'theory of mind' exercises have improved dramatically. To help them apply what they have learned and understood in a Socratic dialogue, one must not only draw one or more conclusions at the end of the conversation. It is also necessary to talk very concretely about what they need to do with these conclusions: who, what, where, when and how. In the phone conversation with the man who has autism, the dialogue ended with the question of whether he would enrol in the course, how he should enrol (by e-mail or post) and when we could expect his enrolment.

A Socratic dialogue is not an end in itself, but always serves to attain a purpose that is outside of the conversation. Taking into account the difficulties people with autism have with applying what they have learned, it is recommended to remain at length with the results at the end of a dialogue and – if needed – establish concrete and necessary agreements.

5.4 The Socrautic dialogue: adapted communication

A Socratic dialogue is communication. If we wish to establish a Socratic dialogue with a person who has autism, of course we need to adapt our style of communication. People with autism prefer *concrete communication*, communication that is clear, precise and explicit. Always be precise about what you mean and concretise your words. Avoid any embellishments in your communication, whether friendly or disconcerting introductions (like, 'Dear Pierre, we are both comfortably settled. Let's engage in a very interesting conversation on…') or needless digressions.

Generally, people with autism also like a visual style of communication. Seeing makes understanding much easier. And they retain that which is visual longer than fleeting words. It is preferable to use pencil and paper – write down the main themes of the dialogue. A simple log also works miracles sometimes if you wish to clarify certain things or give an overview.

Diagrams and lists help people with autism in their communication with others. Making choices is not always easy for them, and lists of the different options available can help. For outlining their own autism's characteristics, you can ask an open question: 'Give me some examples of the difficulties you experience with communication.' In *I am Special*, we use a worksheet on which a certain number of communication difficulties are already provided and the young person

> Adapt your communication. Make it:
> ✓ concrete
> ✓ visual
> ✓ mathematical and logical
> ✓ use diagrams and lists.

can tick whether they apply in their case or not. The participant thus has much less need to rely on their imagination. Recognising given examples is somewhat easier than thinking of some oneself.

When people with autism need to select what is relevant in an exchange of information, writing out their responses is very useful, since this is an area of difficulty and they generally give too little or too much information.

You will find more examples of visual communication and lists of questions in the possible applications outlined below.

In a Socra*u*tic dialogue, as a conversation in which we learn, a low-key, logical style of communication is used. Avoid emotional arguments which rarely work with people with autism. Rather, try to convince them with logical arguments. These are better suited to their sometimes hyperlogical way of thinking. *Mathematising* things is also very helpful and is in keeping with their systemising mindset.[80] Traditional arguments had no impact on a young person who had a fear of being killed in a road traffic accident on his way to school (nothing's going to happen to you, you're very careful, it's not a very busy road, your dad's a sensible driver, etc.). A statistical calculation of the chances of being killed in an accident on the road to school (0.000056 in 1,000 chance, a calculation based on statistics for accidents in the area) was a relief and gave him something to hold on to.

5.5 Possible applications

When do we use a Socratic dialogue? In fact, there is no limit. However, it is advisable to use with moderation and with a specific objective in mind.

We will review a number of possible applications and provide one or more examples for each.

PROMOTING INDEPENDENCE AND SELF-CONTROL

Parents and professionals often complain about the lack of independence in people with autism: they are too dependent on support, they are capable of so many things but cannot spontaneously put them into practice, they take too few initiatives, you always have to help them to remember certain things, etc.

Children and adolescents with autism are capable of acquiring a lot of knowledge and learning many skills, taking account of course of their intellectual capacity. Often the main problem is with transfer, the spontaneous putting into practice of what they have learned. They remain dependent on instructions and on the person who pushes the 'start' button at the right time. The Socratic method can be a useful tool when the individual wishes to be more independent in applying what he or she has learned. Instead of giving instructions, we can ask questions whereby the person with autism can employ a skill or newly acquired knowledge themselves. Thus in an exercise analysing a specific activity, such as tidying up, making coffee or packing a bag, we are going to replace instructions with questions.

Example

A pupil with autism always forgets to put the things she needs for her homework in her school bag. Her teacher constantly has to remind her to take her work diary, her English book, homework and other school equipment. And this never changes. Instead of telling her what she has to do every time, the teacher could approach the problem in a Socratic way:

Teacher: 'So, Anne, what are you going to do when you get home?'

Anne: 'First I'll have a piece of fruit, then feed my cat, then do my homework.'

Teacher: 'Good. And what do you have for homework?'

Anne: 'I have to colour in a map of Europe and write in the capitals.'

Teacher: 'And how are you going to do that? What do you need?'

Anne: 'My homework page of the map of Europe, my colouring pencils and a ballpoint pen.'

Teacher: 'And do you have all this equipment in your school bag?'

Anne: 'Yes, look. No, I haven't put my colouring pencils in yet. I'll put them in right now.'

Teacher: 'Very good. And do you already know the capitals of Europe?'

Anne: 'Lots, but not all! The Eastern European ones are really hard to remember.'

Teacher: 'That's true. And how will you find out these capitals?'

Anne: 'Oh, yes, right, in my atlas. I haven't put that in my bag yet, either.'

Teacher: 'Good thinking, Anne!'

By asking Socratic questions, we can teach a person to think for herself about what she needs to do. It is also more rewarding, because, like the teacher in the example, we can give them a compliment because they have figured something out for themselves.

By repeating this method frequently, we are teaching people with autism to ask themselves good questions, so that they become less dependent on others when performing certain tasks. To encourage transfer in Anne's case, we can for example put the questions in writing and stick the page in her work diary. This page goes over the questions to ask in order to know what she should put in her school bag, such as, 'Do I have homework today? If yes, what book do I need to take? Do I need anything else?'

In teaching someone with autism to ask the right questions, we are encouraging not only independence but flexibility, too. Asking questions is an essential skill for monitoring and self-control, and it makes a person more sensitive to context. It is a known phenomenon that people with autism do certain things in a too rigid or too routine way. 'I always need to put my atlas in my school bag, even if I don't need it.' As a result, people with autism often repeat needless steps or miss out essential ones, depending on which ones, given the context, are unnecessary or necessary.

Children who are a bit older and young people with autism, in particular, will no longer put up with being controlled or corrected in a routine way. The Socratic method teaches them to control themselves, which is positive both for their self-image and for the relationship between themselves and those who support them.

Example

The way you dress and what you take with you when you go out depends on the context: what is the weather like? Where are you going? What are you going to do? In the courses organised by *Autisme Centraal*, we sometimes go on an outing with the participants, for example to a fair, a sports hall, for a walk or to a theatrical performance. We need to 'check' with some of the participants whether they have brought everything they need. What they need to bring naturally depends on where we're going. Instead of exercising complete control, we ask questions whereby they can decide for themselves what they need: what's the weather like today? Do you need to pay an entrance fee? What's the Underground fare? We do not always ask the questions orally. For many outings, these questions are already written down in a leaflet participants received about the course. Sometimes they are explicit and sometimes more general, such as 'What should I take for this activity?'

MAKING CHOICES AND EVALUATIONS

Making choices is a fundamental right. Generally, for people with autism, it is also a complex task. What is especially difficult for them in decision making is weighing up the different choices, one against the other, and knowing what criteria to apply, on which to base this weighting. The same applies to evaluation: on what basis can one decide whether a thing is good or not? What are the degrees of difference?

We can help them to resolve these problems by asking the 'right' questions.

Example of decision making

For people with autism, leisure time is not always as relaxing and enjoyable as it is for others. Knowing what to do in their leisure time and, taking contextual circumstances into account (such as how much free time there is, where you are), how to use this time in the most judicious and agreeable way there is, is sometimes very difficult for children, adolescents and also for adults with autism.

To help with this, on a course organised by *Autisme Centraal*, we conducted a Socratic dialogue on leisure. First of all, we gave the participants, all adults, an outline of the week, which they had to fill in with the times when they would be free, when they would be working, sleeping, etc. Then, we asked them about their interests, what they like doing. They had to write down on a sheet of paper their preferred leisure activities. Through Socratic questioning, we brought them to the subsequent discovery that deciding on an activity depends on many factors: the time available, availability of any necessary equipment, the difference between an indoor and outdoor activity, between an individual and group activity. Based on these criteria, we asked them to sort their favourite activities, for example, short or long activities, individual or group activities. In this way, the participants developed their own guide to leisure activities. For their leisure time, they can ask a number of Socratic questions (or these are asked by the facilitator), such as: how much time do I have available? Is there any equipment? Based on the answers to these questions, they can make a decision completely independently – thanks to their guide to leisure.

In this example, we mainly used a ballpoint pen and paper. We also let the young adults with autism do the writing. This is of course a very difficult level of visual communication. However, Socratic questioning can also take other forms of communication. Thus, we can let a person with autism set out a list of their favourite activities or meals by sorting photos and drawings of activities or meals into two trays, one tray with a happy face and one with a sad face.

For yet another person, we have even used a computer. The Socratic questions were recorded in an interactive programme where a person can answer by choosing from options given or by typing in any other answer. Some questions also took the form of drawings and photos.

Example of evaluation

One organisation particularly values the views of their clients, adult residents with autism. At their long-established meetings, residents had been invited, on several occasions, to share their views and had ample opportunity to put across their comments. Despite all this, the information they sought remained elusive. Some residents gave the same answer every time, some said nothing and others' evaluations were lacking in subtlety (it's brilliant, or it's horrible). Through Socratic questioning, it was possible to learn about what some clients appreciated and what they were less keen on. Here, we also used an overview of the week. We asked those with autism to complete a weekly schedule. Then, we asked them to colour code each activity according to a very precise code: green = I thought it was great, or good; orange = I thought it was average; red = I thought it was awful. For each activity coloured in red, we asked them afterwards what changes they would like to make: a different support worker? Have it last for a shorter time? Have it at another time of day? Is it the activity itself or only one aspect of it? (For one of the residents, the problem lay not with the activity but with where it took place.) Lastly, we asked them to place the changes they wanted in ascending order, i.e. which changes do they wish to implement first?

Giving people with autism the option of carrying out an evaluation themselves and of evaluating their environment promotes self-determination. The Socratic method offers them this chance, as shown in the example above. Here is the structure of a Socratic dialogue in which we allow adults with autism to act by themselves, to find out about their partner's expectations. The Socratic questions are as follows:

- What do I expect from my partner?

- What does he or she expect from me?

- Amongst my expectations, which have not been satisfied? (The partner can also answer this question, with respect to what concerns him/her.)

- How can I get these expectations across? How can I make them clearer for my partner?

The attention given to transfer, as an additional step for people with autism, consists mainly of the forward planning and preparation of a dialogue about the partner's expectations.

TEACHING COMPREHENSION AND KNOWLEDGE

The Socratic method, as a conversation in which we learn, or as a pedagogical instrument, lends itself naturally to the input of certain knowledge or to a new understanding of things. We have already come across this objective in Socrates.

In this sense, the Socratic method is perfect for conversations in which the aim is for people with autism to learn more about themselves or to have a better understanding of their functioning. We are thinking particularly of psychological support, psychosocial support and conversations with a mentor, but also of workplace coaching. By using the Socratic method, a workplace coach may increase the awareness of a person with autism of their potential, limitations and interests in relation to employment.

The section, 'How do I deal with difficulties caused by my autism?', an addition to *I am Special*, was constructed in an entirely Socratic way, in particular the part about the management of difficult moments and blockages. Here is a brief resumé of the questions in their order of appearance:

- What is a blockage of thoughts or action?

- When do blockages occur? When do you get stuck?

- What is your reaction during a blockage?

- Amongst these reactions, which are appropriate and which ones are not?

- From those which are appropriate, what behaviours can you adopt in the future, during a blockage?

Example

As a workplace coach, you want to help someone with autism to understand the potentially negative consequences of sending untimely e-mails to colleagues, about a variety of trivial subjects. You have two aims related to consciousness of the situation:

- for the person with autism to realise she is sending too many e-mails to her colleagues

- for her to know also that others don't appreciate these kinds of e-mails.

You do not say these things point blank to the person with autism, but you want her to make the discoveries in a Socratic manner. You ask her to count how many e-mails she sends in a week. If, based on this calculation, she does not reach the conclusion on her own that this number is too many, you can invite her to ask her colleagues how many e-mails they send on average per day. If you wish, you can even present the flow of e-mails sent by her colleagues on a graph. Regarding the effects of 'spam', you can invite the person with autism to ask her colleagues (a short enquiry via e-mail) about this. She could also search, for example on the internet, for information about spam and how people react when they receive too many trivial e-mails.

CONVINCING AND PERSUADING

The aim in the example above is not only to increase self-knowledge but also to convince the person with autism that it is important to modify her behaviour. In addition to informing through knowledge and consensus, at least in the fields of education and management, the Socratic method, more often, seeks to bring about a change in someone's views, ideas or behaviour. This is linked to the fact that, from the outset, the objective of the method is to bring someone to reflect upon their own ideas and assumptions.

We can also work in this way with people with autism. Because their style of observation and thinking is different, they often have 'distorted', 'bizarre', 'insensitive', 'mistaken', in short, 'autistic' ideas. These adjectives were deliberately placed in quotation marks. From the point of view of the person with autism, their own ideas, of course, are never bizarre, insensitive or mistaken. Indeed, THE truth does not exist. Each has their own truth. The negative connotations attributed to autistic ideas are only negative from the point of view of a non-autistic brain. Thus, one could conclude that to bring about a change in someone's views, to correct their ideas and conceptions, is not sympathetic to autism and is unnecessary. One hears more and more frequently that there are two world views, one autistic and one non-autistic, and that both groups have a right to their own truth. Moreover, we read here and there that people with autism are not hampered by their emotions in decision-making and that, consequently, they have a more objective view of reality.

Although this is undoubtedly the case in many situations, we nevertheless believe it is justifiable, in particular circumstances, to bring about a change of mind in a person with autism. This is exactly the case in situations where the person with autism himself, or those around him, are handicapped or held back by the ideas and views of the person in question. It is also the case when the ideas of the person with autism are manifestly unrealistic or potentially harmful for the person himself or those around him. Most of the time, these situations go hand in hand and it is precisely these unrealistic views that cause problems for the person and for those around him. Truth does not exist. In contrast, reality certainly does exist. You can have your own truth about the place on the road where you yourself feel most at ease when driving, but if the law says you need to drive on the left, you will quickly collide with reality, embodied by another car on the road. In situations where the person with autism or those around him are hindered by certain views, in situations where certain ideas hold back or threaten someone's functioning, or when a person's views are contrary to reality, one must be allowed to make corrections and take action. Naturally, assessing the negative consequences of an idea or view comes within the realm of the subjective. Consulting others or the person with autism (does he or she also find this idea limiting?) can increase motivation or vindicate a corrective intervention.

Example

A young person with autism, who lives in a home for young adults with the same disorder, has been very tired lately. In fact, two other young people have been staying in his room until the middle of the night, listening to music and chatting about their favourite subjects: girls, music, outings, etc. During a conversation, the young person in question disclaims any responsibility and blames the other two for being the cause of the problem: 'I ask them to go back to their own

room and tell them I'm tired but even then, they stay in my room.'
When these two people are called upon for further explanation, they
declare that the young person has never made such a request. In
the end, it appears they are right. The mentor of the young person
organises a role play: they act out the situation in the room and, in
fact, the young person says nothing. When the mentor remarks upon
this to the young person, he replies, 'But you can even see by my
eyes that I'm tired and I want you to leave!' To convince him that the
others can't see such things, the mentor decides to set up a new role
play. Together with the adolescents, he writes five states of mind (for
example, boredom) and five requests (such as 'open the window')
on bits of paper. Several times, the mentor takes a piece of paper at
random, without the young person seeing, and sits down beside him
without saying anything. The young person has to say what his state
of mind is and what he wants him to do. To his greatest surprise, the
young person finds he isn't able to tell. Through Socratic questioning,
which establishes the link with the nocturnal visits, he drew the 'right'
conclusion: 'So I have to actually "say" that I'm tired?'

This example clearly shows that Socratic questioning can also take the form
of role play. This method does not always have to find expression literally in
a 'question'.

Almost all of the applications cited can be found in *I am Special*. In the
workbook, we use the Socratic method so that the child or young person:

- acquires knowledge (for example, that everyone is different and
  unique or that autism is invisible)
- gets to know themselves (e.g. to know their own interests)
- can self-assess (e.g. the different kinds of intelligence)
- can make choices (e.g. 'Who can I tell that I have autism?')
- can be convinced of certain facts (e.g. that there's no point in
  comparing my own autism to that of others).

Lastly, there is one final remark on potential applications of the Socratic
method. We have already mentioned that, in practice, the results of applying
the method are not always rapid, especially at the outset. The method demands
training and above all, an enormous amount of practice. Workshops have
shown that many people want to use it primarily to make someone with autism
have 'better' ideas, to correct certain autistic conceptions and replace these
with the views of others. This was Socrates' way of working, too. Originally,
the Socratic method did involve a character confrontation. The most difficult

Socratic dialogues are those in which we try to confront and convince the participant. The order in which we have described the potential applications is based on the degree of difficulty of each application. Anyone who wishes to use the Socratic method should start not with the most difficult applications but with the easiest, that is, those in which we are supporting the person with autism to make certain choices or to perform certain tasks and activities by asking questions.

5.6 Advantages and disadvantages of the Socratic method

We will conclude this chapter with a short evaluation of the Socratic method in general and the Socra*u*tic method in particular.

The greatest disadvantage of the Socra*u*tic method is that it takes a tremendous amount of time, especially with people with autism. It demands a lot of patience. Giving an order, sharing a view or an opinion is much quicker. Telling someone he should put on a warm jumper, take his waterproofs or his wallet for going on an outing is much quicker than making him understand through Socratic questioning that it is preferable if he does all these things.

With the Socra*u*tic method, we are bringing the participant, step by step, to a certain understanding or idea. It is not our preparation that is the guiding principle, but the other person's thinking. That is why one often makes long detours in order to reach the final aim, especially with people with autism.

A Socratic dialogue does not necessarily need to last a long time. Everything depends on the pertinence of the questions. It is precisely the questions which bring a person to a rapid understanding of a certain concept.

This is where the second disadvantage of the Socra*u*tic method lies: it requires a great deal of knowledge and experience to have 'Socrates on call'. The Socra*u*tic method is not easy to master and a multitude of questions can confuse the person with autism, rather than bring him to a different understanding or to a different evaluation.

Finding the right questions requires a lot of training,[81] but in the case of autism, another element is also necessary: a more in-depth knowledge of autistic thinking. It is this knowledge that you are going to rely upon for being able to predict, to some extent, the reasoning of the person with autism, for harmonising your questions accordingly, and also for selecting those which are going to be concrete enough and therefore comprehensible.

Another disadvantage is the danger in irony. This danger is intrinsically linked to the Socratic method. The interlocutor can be irritated by the so-called ignorance of the other person and may therefore become wound up during the conversation. However, they can also get the impression that this person is completely stupid. Both types of reaction can occur in people with autism, especially with young people and adults with average intelligence.

The ironic character of a Socratic dialogue is linked above all to the attitude of the person who is leading the conversation but also – again – to the type of questions posed. If the 'right' questions are asked, and if they are neutral, irritation and frustration on the part of the interlocutor can, for the most part, be avoided.

Nevertheless, these disadvantages do not outweigh the advantages of the method.

In the Socratic method, we employ an analytical and intellectualist style. The questioning is structured, unfolds in stages and functions by means of logical arguments. This style is in perfect concord with the mode of thinking of persons with autism, a mode oriented towards logic, intelligence and order.

Moreover, the second advantage, but not the least, is that it is precisely thanks to the Socratic method that we can have an overall view of the thinking of a person with autism as well as the specific and sometimes idiosyncratic meanings which follow from this way of thinking. It was only thanks to the mentor's Socratic work method that it became clear that the young man who had problems getting a good night's sleep was assuming that others could read his wishes and feelings directly on his face. Anyone who devotes time to the exploratory phase of the Socrautic method, in particular, learns a great deal about the autistic style of thinking.

In the same way, the Socratic method allows one to test the comprehension of someone with autism. If you only ever give an order to take money for an outing, you do not know whether the person with autism has established the link between the Underground and the money in their wallet ('Ah, I need to pay for the Underground, too?').

Another advantage of the Socrautic method is that it allows people with autism to draw their own conclusions, in their own terms and in their own style. This prevents an echolalia-based knowledge, which would have been absorbed from the outside and which – without true comprehension – would simply be repeated. You could simply have told the young man who thinks others can read his wishes on his face that this is not the case. And if you're lucky, he will repeat it and tell the others. But it is impossible to tell whether he truly understood what that meant. By making him experience the situation, you increase the chances of real comprehension and reduce the risk of echolalia. You forget less quickly what you learn by yourself than that which is taught by others. The effect of a conclusion induced in a Socratic way subsists much longer than an instruction, statement or remark which comes from the outside.

Finally, the Socrautic method also has a positive impact on self-image. Since the other person understands the problem by himself, you can reward him: 'What a great idea you've had!' Having the feeling of being able to choose by oneself, even if that means with the help of someone else who asks questions, is more beneficial for the image you have of yourself than if others choose for you. Being able to ask yourself questions in order to find out what you need to put in your school bag is much more constructive for the 'self' than if you depend on someone else who tells you exactly what you need to take home. The Socrautic method is an empowering tool *par excellence*.

Chapter 5

Introducing Autism

1 Explaining autism to someone who has autism

Explaining autism to someone who has autism is not easy. Autism is a particularly complex subject. Even professionals who have worked in the field for many years do not always know precisely what characterises autism. If specialists in autism are confused themselves, how can we explain autism to people with autism who are already easily confused? We cannot pass our confusion on to them.

People with autism do not make sense of an event in the same way as us. Traditional neurotypical communication, which involves a lot of *talking*, can be very confusing for them. *Talking* about autism with someone who has autism is a bit like explaining what blindness is to a blind person through drawings and photos.

People with autism have particular difficulty understanding abstract concepts. It is especially the concretisation of the abstract concepts that is difficult for them.[82] Autism is a highly abstract concept, as it summarises many symptoms, which are unique in each person and which are the consequence of something invisible, a different cognitive style. Making autism concrete is very difficult. However, concrete information is precisely what people with autism need.

Absolute thinking, thinking in terms of 'either/or' or 'black and white', is also typical for autism. Even the most carefully phrased qualification with the most obvious nuances can be interpreted as an absolute general statement. For example: 'You have autism, but that does not mean you don't have any talents' can be understood as, 'I'm autistic, therefore I'll never amount to anything' or on the contrary, as 'I can do anything.'

Just like other people with a disability, people with autism conceal or compensate for their disability. This means we have to be extra careful when trying to estimate their real comprehension. It is easy to overestimate this and, as a result, to speak with them about things that in fact they do not understand.

Finally, just like anyone else, people with autism who are told that they are different and that they have certain deficits or challenges, have to assimilate this information. This is why explaining their autism to them requires more than a simple conversation. It is a real process.

2 Why?

There are several different reasons for starting the process of explaining autism to someone with autism.

- The person with autism obviously has had unrealistic expectations about his or her future, for a considerable time. For example: later on, I'm going to get married, have children, build a beautiful house and drive a convertible. For many people with autism, such future prospects are not achievable. Only a few rare individuals are going to manage it. It is better to prepare people in time that they are not likely to have such a future, than to wait until they become more and more frustrated and depressed.

- The person with autism is or shortly will be facing unprotected and therefore potentially 'dangerous' situations. For instance, when a young person is going to have to start using public transport to get to his work placement or when he is going to start going to the cinema or to the pub with his friends. In these situations, the person with autism will react differently from the others, and sooner or later, problems can arise. If the person with autism is aware of his difference and his vulnerability, he can learn how to avoid certain situations or how to escape from them. Above all, he can put the reactions of those around him in perspective, instead of being surprised at being laughed at or being turned down again and again. An awareness of one's autism therefore plays a preventative and protective role. It can help the person with autism to put into perspective their own behaviour, which might be disturbing or annoying for others. Indeed, if someone knows their own disability, they may be (better) able to express their needs so that other people can adapt themselves. Self-knowledge is a condition *sine qua non* for defending oneself.

- The person with autism is confronted with all kinds of difficult situations. For example, being bullied, having relationship problems, not being able to find work. It is easier to find solutions to these problems if the person knows what is causing them. Then, it will be easier to motivate someone to find a job in a sheltered workshop rather than a regular job and this won't come as such a surprise to them.

- The person with autism is asking: 'What's wrong with me?'; 'Why does that lady come to the house and talk with you about me?'; 'How come my friends don't come over to play?'; 'Why do people tease me so much?'. There is a risk of over-interpreting these questions. Because of their different way of making sense of an event, it is very possible that people with autism mean something completely different from what appears at first sight. Before answering, you must always try to detect the question that lies behind their question.

3 At what age?

There is no fixed age. Everything depends on the person's intelligence, what they are going through and how they react to their environment. Furthermore, it is best to let sleeping dogs lie. It is best not to give more information to the person with autism than he or she can absorb. Both starting too early and starting too late can have negative consequences. Telling them too soon can confuse them. If they are told too late, this can leave them too long in uncertainty unnecessarily, thus causing frustrations. Or they create their own idiosyncratic explanations, which are sometimes hard to correct.

With children with an (almost) average level of intelligence, it is advisable to start pre-emptively, when they start primary school, by explaining about our 'inside' and 'outside' and about being different. This requires a minimum developmental age of four years. Explaining to a child that they are different from others demands a certain amount of skill and insight that children at too young a developmental age do not have, such as being able to understand abstract words, being able to look back on past events and on their own behaviour, being able to reflect on oneself, understanding the causes and consequences of an event and above all, displaying evidence of perspective-taking. In order to understand oneself better, one must be able to look at oneself through the eyes of others.

Assessing whether someone is ready to receive information about their disability is particularly difficult, especially as there is no precise age. *I am Special* takes this difficulty into account. The workbook does not begin expressly with 'explaining autism to someone who has autism'. It is also strongly inadvisable to start right away with this step, particularly with younger children. The worksheets in the chapters 'I am unique', 'My body' and 'Being different' which precede the section on autism are more concrete and, above all, they have an assessment function. They serve not only to inform but also to make one reflect on what the participants already know about themselves, namely to determine what style of communication it is preferable to use, etc. In fact the first three parts of *I am Special* serve as an assessment: a way to find out whether we can begin the chapter on autism and if so, how to do it.

4 Who?

Explaining autism to a person with autism cannot be done in a single conversation. It is a long-term process, requiring long-term support. Anyone who starts this process should therefore be able to guarantee sufficient continuity. Moreover, they must be available to answer, frequently and in a timely way, the numerous and sometimes urgent questions of the person with autism.

Parents can often guarantee both continuity and availability. However, it is not recommended that they be the primary ones in charge of the process.

Parents are parents in the first instance and not therapists for their children. If they also have to take on the task of communicating a diagnosis to their child, there is a risk of role confusion. The child should always be able to turn to his or her parents for support and comfort when he or she becomes emotionally upset by the bad news. It is not easy to seek comfort from the same person who broke the bad news to you. There is a genuine risk that the person with autism will start to evade his or her parents, when they try to make him or her aware of his or her disability. Alongside the risk of role confusion, there can also be a loss of confidence in their parents. Even though the parents themselves may be able to assume both roles, people with autism find this extremely difficult. Irrespective of the resultant negative consequences for the parents, it is, in any case, very confusing for the individual with autism.

This does not mean that parents have no role to play in the process of their child becoming aware of their disability. On the contrary, they play an essential role in the support they provide while their child assimilates their diagnosis. They can help their child to understand their autism better and to accept that there are positive sides, too. By showing that they, too, have given autism a place in their lives, parents can help to lessen any feelings of guilt, anger or sadness their child may feel as a result of these mysterious differences.

The same applies to support workers and/or educators who work with the child on a daily basis. It is better for the children if they do not learn about their autism from them, but from an unfamiliar person, instead, such as a speech and language therapist, specialist teacher, educational psychologist or a support worker from another team or another establishment. Sound knowledge and sufficient experience in the field of autism as well as experience of communicating with individuals with autism are more important than a diploma! Ideally, the person with autism will be able to call upon a professional as someone they can trust. Of course, there needs to be close collaboration between this professional and the child's parents. Parents can help to set the priorities and they should receive timely, adequate information about the process, including regular feedback on what is happening with their child and how he is understanding and assimilating the information he receives.

5 The different stages

Explaining autism to someone who has autism is a process that should unfold by stages. It is no use trying to start right away with explaining autism. We must first provide the knowledge and concepts required for an optimum understanding of the diagnosis when it is given. This stage consists of:

- knowledge of the human body (your own body), the outside as well as the inside
- basic knowledge of the features of the brain and of how the brain works (autism is, after all, a brain disorder)
- understanding the difference between people's 'outside' and 'inside' and knowing that other people are different on the inside and outside
- understanding the concepts of illness, disorder and disability.

It is only when these concepts have been grasped that we can combine them into a sort of conclusion: 'You are good at certain things and not so good at others. For the things you find more difficult, that you do less well, there is a name: autism. Autism is a disability and not an illness. It is the result of a brain disorder. The brain of someone with autism works differently from the brain of someone without autism. Because autism has to do with the brain, autism cannot be seen from the outside. But autism is not entirely invisible. People with autism sometimes behave and react differently. You are also different from other people with autism you know. But you have some things in common with other people with autism, too.'

6 Paying attention to self-esteem

Talking about autism with someone consists of much more than simply explaining it factually or providing information. Just as for other people, such information stirs up thoughts, desires and emotions. In other words, you cannot just tell them. It is a process which requires commitment and taking responsibility for giving the person with autism support for any emotional repercussions of the news. We must always keep an eye on the effect of the information on the person's self-esteem.

People with autism are very sensitive to criticism and negative comments. Not because they do not want to hear, but because they are unable to put these in perspective and are unable to protect themselves emotionally, as we are able to. For them, criticism always comes like a bolt from the blue. Criticisms come as a shock to them, as they appear suddenly and too unexpectedly. They are unable to anticipate them. To talk about their problems and make comments on things they are not very good at could cause a negative reaction or even denial. The person who breaks the bad news needs to be prepared for that.

However, there is no sense in hiding the truth. There is no point in telling them they are capable of accomplishing a specific task when this is not the case. It is difficult enough already for people with autism to get a good sense of themselves. We must not make things even more complicated by giving them a rose-tinted image of themselves or their abilities. Honesty comes first. Because of own very absolute style of thinking, people with autism will really appreciate that.

At the same time, we need to take care not to undermine their self-esteem. Talking with people with autism should never lead to frustrations. They have enough stress and frustration as it is. The whole process of informing them about their disability must take place, and above all finish, in a positive atmosphere, but at the same time, without awakening any false hopes.

The following tips may help a person with autism to cope with the news:

- Intersperse the sessions with enough breaks for the person with autism to let off steam, preferably physically.

- Measure out the information in doses – don't give it all in one go.

- Ensure a healthy balance between confrontation and affirmation.

- Ask about their favourite topics of conversation or favourite activities.

- Adapt your communication style so that all their attention is focused on the content of the message.

- Underline the fact that there are ways of addressing autism's limitations.

- Highlight the fact that a person is much more than their limitations or their disorder.

- Devote enough time to questions and reflection.

- Above all, use your sense of humour! Anyone who imparts information on autism as if they are an employee of a funeral parlour can hardly expect a positive reaction…

7 Adapted communication

It is very well known that people with autism experience difficulties in the area of communication, particularly verbal communication. Therefore we must adapt our communication when we are with people with autism and take account of the fact that they understand language differently.

As we have already said, people with autism understand the world differently from us. They often assign different meanings to certain words and concepts. For example, when a person with autism talks about her friends, it is possible that they are talking about people who are friendly, who simply say hello. When we speak with a person who has autism, we need to be cautious in our interpretations. We should not be too quick to think we understand what they mean. We need to remain vigilant regarding our own communication style.

Due to the risk of misinterpretation (and because people with autism can become desperately lost in these too), when informing someone about their autism, we have chosen to start not from their point of view, but from a highly structured whole which we present to them: a workbook.

Remember that the terms we use when talking about problems linked to their autism are not easy for them to understand. How do they understand terms such as 'stereotypical behaviour', 'ritual', or 'social interaction'? Even apparently more simple terms can sometimes take on a strange meaning for people without autism. To avoid these misunderstandings, we pay particular attention in *I am Special* to definitions and to explaining concepts such as 'disorder', 'disability' and 'communication'.

When we are speaking with someone with autism we should constantly check what is being understood from the conversation. The best way to do that is by regularly asking the person with autism to repeat what has been said in their own words.

Talking with someone with autism also means keeping a constant eye on the long-term effects. For them, an apparently minor detail can have a snowball effect. The message is: always think autistically and look beyond the present moment. This is why it is best to use *I am Special* only after having discussed with those around the person (parents, in the first instance) how it will be followed up in the future. People with autism assimilate information much more slowly than other people, especially when it comes to emotional information. They are also less likely to talk about their emotions spontaneously and this is why certain questions and comments may only come to the surface weeks or months after the *I am Special* sessions. When they do, though, the safety net must be there.

Just as in any communication with people with autism, one has to adapt one's use of language when explaining their disability, too. Concrete descriptions, and referring to things that they can see are very important. Speaking hurriedly is ruled out. Talking about feelings can also be delicate. Nevertheless, their feelings do need to be discussed. People with autism do have feelings, but for them it is not a very concrete or tangible matter. Moreover, experience has shown us that talking about feelings excessively and for too long can only get out of hand. They become entangled in abstract terms and overwhelmed because they find it difficult to make the distinction between talking about feelings and actually experiencing them. Sometimes, they become lost in this sea of words. This is why *I am Special* is very factual and very concrete.

In conversations about autism, it is important to talk in the first instance about concrete actions and only then about feelings. If people with autism have something to do, then they have something concrete in hand with which they can continue to work. The best insights and solutions are usually reached through tasks, such as 'write down an example of an aid you use'. Talking about autism comes back to *doing* something together, rather than simply talking about the topic. This is exactly why *I am Special* is not a *book about autism*, but a *work*book.

Just as for communicating with people with autism in general, the golden rule in talking about autism is the *visualisation* rule: convey your message using as many concrete means as possible. A simple drawing can be a great help. For example, for visualising the brain disorder at the basis of autism, you could show them a drawing of a wire that is poorly connected or missing.

Lists of all kinds are a great practical help too. People with autism love sorting things, labelling them and putting them in lists and compartments, in short, they love to systemise. This systemisation clarifies the world. This is why *I am Special* contains sets of lists, for example an inventory of what a person can or cannot do, an overview of the difficulties of autism and helpful solutions and aids.

Even people with autism with average intelligence experience difficulties with verbal communication. Ordering their own ideas and placing them in proper perspective pose the great difficulties. In order to help with these two problems, it is important to have them *write down* as much as possible. Writing things down is much slower than talking. Through the writing, visual feedback appears and they no longer need to focus their attention simultaneously on the reactions of their interlocutor. Experience has shown that if people with autism know how to write, they are clearly better able to express their ideas and feelings on paper that in discussions. This is why *I am Special* is a workbook that attaches great importance to completing written exercises, to writing things down and filling things in.

Conversations with people with autism need to unfold in a structured way, with a definite goal, and according to a set plan. Responsibility for the content, duration and unfolding of the dialogue should not lie with the person with autism. In the hands of a person with autism, chances are that a conversation would become interminable, very changeable (flitting from this subject to that, due to thought associations) and purposeless. It will certainly not be very result-oriented. Our conversations with people with autism should be directive but unfold in a positive atmosphere. If the person with autism gets onto new topics of discussion during the conversation (due to concrete associations), these must be channelled, for example, by saying, 'We'll talk about that at the end of the discussion, we'll finish with this first' or 'I'll write that down for next time.' The facilitator needs to keep a clear direction in mind.

Working in a directive and structured way in no way means that we are not going to take into account the contribution of the person with autism. On the contrary, we are trying to give the person with autism the information they are asking us for, even when this request is not explicit. For this reason, the facilitator needs to probe the thoughts of the person with autism frequently, and preferably at the end of each session. It is for this reason that the workbook consists of exercises that give the participant an opportunity to pose questions. Working in a directive way and working in a way that is oriented towards questions are by no means mutually exclusive methods.

8 Reactions to the diagnosis

Many of the reactions expressed by people with autism when they are told what is wrong with them are very recognisable: denial, sadness, anger. These are, after all, human reactions, not specific to people with autism. They try to assimilate this news about their autism and attempt, in their way, to devise ways of living with this news. But in this area, too, their different way of thinking plays a part. They will compare themselves to others, which is a normal reaction. However, they also focus very strongly on concrete details. Thus they will link autism to the physical, concrete behaviours they encounter in other people with autism. For example, 'People with autism only ever talk about trains,' or 'People with autism don't speak with other people' or 'People with autism don't have any friends.' It is important to show that there are differences in the characteristics common to autism, for instance: 'OK, this person with autism talks continually about trains, but you always talk about that girlfriend of yours, and that's just as stereotyped.'

It is important to approach an individual with autism first of all as a person and not as 'an autistic'. He or she should be seen as an individual with their own difficulties and limitations that differ from those of other people, with or without autism. Last but not least, it is essential to see an individual with autism as a person who has more to offer than just his autism. When we are working with *I am Special*, autism does have to occupy the main place in thematic discussions, but sufficient space also needs to be given to the individual's other characteristics, such as their character, their interests, their attempts to compensate, their camouflage techniques, their skills and their desires.

People with autism, especially those with an above average level of intelligence, will compensate for their lack of 'intuition' by 'calculating' all sorts of things. For them, autism is also something they want to measure, quantify and compare. They ask questions such as, 'What is my autism percentage?' or 'How long can I talk about a subject, exactly, before it becomes stereotyped?'

These 'calculators' also consider themselves to be different from other people with autism. Sometimes, they make statements such as, 'I have milder autism,' or 'I have less autism, it's just Asperger's Syndrome I've got.' In this case, it is again advised to stress the differences between people with autism and to individualise: 'What is important for you to know about yourself?' One can also stress that, in autism, it is not a question of more or less, but of difference. In this sense, introducing the term 'autism spectrum' may shed light on the matter.

In a few cases, people will 'panic' when they find out about their autism. It then becomes a focus of stereotypical interest, a real preoccupation. A risk analysis must be carried out on this, particularly before beginning the sessions on autism. If it does become a stereotypical subject, it is then important to limit the length of the sessions, and if need be, to agree on when, where, for how long and with whom they can talk about it. We need to clarify again and provide guidance, since these people experience enormous difficulty with striking a balance by themselves.

Sometimes, people with autism use their autism as an excuse for things turning out badly, or to escape certain situations. One often hears it said, 'Don't ask me, I have autism.' This is why it is worth going over what is a result of autism and what is not; talk about whether certain unachievable things are related to autism. If they are unable to perform a task, ask them how you may help, so that they can do it in the future and also so that they can do it by themselves.

This 'use' of autism is sometimes a strategy put in place by those who are only following others' examples and is thus a kind of echolalia. If the parents and/or professionals frequently say things such as, 'You can't go out because you have autism' or 'You don't understand because of your autism', then there is obviously a greater risk that the person with autism will use the same strategy or make the same statements via their echolalic or echopraxic behaviours.

Many of the reactions above are really strategies for *coping with their autism and seeing the positive aspects of their disability*. People with autism are trying to survive, to develop a positive self-image, and, in a sense, they are no different from us all in this regard. Thanks to these strategies, they can try to keep their head above water and feel better about themselves.

Some people with autism are, however, exactly the opposite and have a very negative image of themselves. They often say: 'I have autism, I don't know how to do anything, I'm no good for anything.' Research has shown that people with high-functioning autism, especially, have an increased risk of developing a negative self-esteem. Due to the fact that they are very intelligent, they reach significantly higher levels of perspective-taking. They notice more of how other people react in their presence and what they think of them, and as a result, they better understand their own shortcomings.

They are at risk of depression. This happens frequently with the onset of adolescence, when they see their peers doing things they are not capable of or are not allowed to do: driving a car, living independently, having a boyfriend/girlfriend… Again, their self-image is based on comparisons of very concrete facts.

It is important to establish with them lists of things they can do, not only an inventory of their shortcomings. Sometimes, they need to be forced to write only positive things about themselves and to be restricted for a moment in their discussions about their problems. If it is a protracted and serious depression (more than three months), a referral to specialist help (psychotherapy and possibly medication) is certainly advised.

Some people deny their own autism. In itself, this phase does not pose any problem: denial is a normal stage in the process of assimilation. However, denying or ignoring one's own limitations for a long time can have negative consequences. Trying to convince with words, entering into a debate or making continual reference to their autism certainly does not help people who are denying their disability. Trying to accelerate the information process does not advance matters more, nor does persuasion. On the contrary, it usually increases the opposition of people with autism. The best tactic to adopt is to adapt yourself to their pace. People with autism need much more time to assimilate information than so-called 'neurotypical' individuals. Mention the positive aspects of autism (memory, perception of details, the ability to see in fragments) regularly. If you wish all the same to confront the person with autism with their own limitations, above all do not do it verbally (in a discussion). Leave it to the person with autism to find out what they can do well and what they are unable to achieve. Let them experiment and try out things (even if you think they are not capable) and teach them how to evaluate the results. This method makes things much more concrete than 'hollow' words. Ensure that the risks taken are calculated risks and also be sure to have a safety net in place to deal with the potential consequences of failure.

Finally, for people with autism, nuances are not their cup of tea. They tend to think in an absolute way, straightforwardly and in black and white. A person with autism rarely has a realistic image of himself or herself. Then again, that is rare for any person. Obviously we all have illusions about ourselves. However, compared with others, people with autism are less capable of seeing things in context and seeing themselves in a broader perspective. We cannot expect the image they have of themselves to be identical to the image we have of them, even after the exercises in *I am Special*. We must not overvalue the exercises in the workbook. *I am Special* is just one of many steps to take in helping people with autism give their disability a place in their lives.

Chapter 6

Working with *I am Special*

Informing someone about their autism is not something to be done hurriedly. Experience has taught us that anyone who presents a selection of the workbook exercises to a child, adolescent or young adult with autism without due consideration will soon face problems. Explaining autism demands thorough preparation. The success of the programme depends more on this preparation than on the practical exercises. Before beginning to use the workbook, it is necessary to ask, among others, the following questions:

- Is the person with autism ready (conditions and indications)?
- Are those around the person with autism ready (collaborative preparation)?
- Am I ready? Who will be in charge (the facilitator)?
- What are the arrangements (time and duration, in a group or individually, place and equipment, etc.)?
- What information am I going to provide and what information will I not provide?
- How am I going to frame the information (inductively or deductively)?
- How am I going to tell the person with autism about these things?
- What is my aim and how am I going to gauge the results (evaluation)?

1 Conditions and indications
1.1 General indications
Using *I am Special* is advised as soon as the person with autism or those around him or her feel the need to know (more) about this disability.

The chapters 'I am unique' and 'My body' can also be used without this need, as preparation for later receiving information about autism and its implications. These first two chapters can also be used as an assessment (see the previous chapter), in order to gauge whether *I am Special* may be used with a particular child or young person.

If the time lapse between these two parts and the rest of the workbook is too long, the effects of progress related to the worksheets will be lost.

1.2 General conditions

The person with autism needs to have the following skills and aptitudes:

- the ability to concentrate sufficiently to work on a task for between 30 and 60 minutes

- adequate reading and writing skills (if necessary, the facilitator can help the person when there are writing difficulties or he or she can also write for them)

- the ability to think about oneself and others; in the first instance, to reflect on their own body and on their inner self.

1.3 Additional conditions for the chapter on 'autism'

- The person must be aware of the fact that they are different, even if they are not yet able to make sense of this difference.

- They should not have too negative self-esteem.

- They must have enough motivation to be open to the workbook.

- The parents and carers must be available for following things up and helping the participant assimilate the information – some chapters involve a high degree of confrontation.

- Collaboration with those around the person (parents, carers, tutors and social network) is necessary.

These conditions can be verified during a preparatory discussion with, for example, the professional team or a carer in an organisation. It is also possible to draw up a list where the indications and conditions are put into question form.

2 Collaboration with the environment

The fact that we cannot describe the indications and conditions criteria precisely and that furthermore, they can vary enormously between individuals, makes close collaboration with those around the person with autism indispensable –

before, during and after the sessions. With children and young people, these are the parents in the first instance. If a young person or adult is living in (residential) care, close collaboration with the main carer is also essential. Consulting the support network of a person with autism before the sessions is recommended (with adults, it is of course also necessary to have their agreement).

2.1 Before the sessions

The indications and conditions for *I am Special* are discussed with the person's support network. For children and adolescents, parental permission is essential before autism is explained to their son or daughter. Indeed, *I am Special* opens doors that will be difficult to close again. The facilitator needs to question those around the person about their attitude towards autism. If, for example, the parents have strong doubts about the accuracy of the diagnosis (autism) or reject or deny it, the risk of confusion for the child is great, as he or she receives contradictory information (with the facilitator saying it certainly is autism but Mum and Dad saying it is not).

The questions that need to be gone over in the preliminary consultation are, notably, the following:

- Why do you wish to give information about autism to your son/daughter?
- What are your expectations of the process?
- What negative consequences should we take into consideration? How can these be alleviated?
- Who is going to provide information to the child or adolescent?
- What sensitivities of the child or adolescent do we need to take into consideration?

Before starting the sessions, the facilitator needs to ask those around the child or young person with autism about the diagnosis: when did they ask about a diagnosis? What does the young person already know? What is their attitude towards autism?

Those around the person are an indispensable source of information, particularly for preparing the sessions on autism. Parents and carers are able to provide concrete examples concerning their son or daughter's impairments. Those around the person can provide information necessary for adapting one's style of communication, for example, 'She finds it easier to write things down than to say them.' Finally, the facilitator discusses with those in the support network who is going to ensure there is follow-up: who can the person with autism go to with their questions, once the sessions with *I am Special* are finished?

2.2 During the sessions

With children and adolescents, the facilitator keeps parents and other professionals fully informed about what has been discussed. This may also be done via the person with autism. The facilitator can assign showing the workbook (or certain chapters) at home, at school or at the carers' organisation as homework. We point out to the participants that it is their workbook, but that they can also show it to their parents, teachers or carers; thus they can teach something to their parents or carers, etc. Another opportunity for collaboration lies in the tasks where the cooperation of parents, teachers or carers is necessary, for example, for completing certain worksheets.

Parents can also be contacted in between sessions to see whether their child is making use of the sessions at home: does their child tell them things spontaneously? If so, what do they tell them? Do they enjoy the sessions? Have they been more tense, aggressive or depressed since the sessions started? Or more relieved, more relaxed?

2.3 After the sessions

Immediately after the sessions have finished, the facilitator carries out an evaluation with those around the person with autism. In consultation with those in the support network, the follow-up to the sessions is drawn up in practical terms as follows:

- If necessary, provide an extra question-and-answer session.

- Who can the young person go to with these additional questions? Where and when?

- Where, when and to whom can the parents turn if their child starts showing a particular reaction that they can't quite understand or can't cope with on their own? The same question applies to other professionals, as well as to carers of a group in an organisation.

- If necessary, the person with autism can be referred for psychological support.

To gauge long-term effects, the facilitator should also carry out an evaluation discussion with the parents or carers some weeks or months after the sessions have ended.

3 Facilitating

I am Special needs to be carried out by someone with sufficient experience in the field of autism. Preferably, this is someone who is unknown to the person with autism. That is, someone who is not part of their everyday life or immediate circle of carers. This anonymity has the following advantages:

- Someone unknown often has more authority than someone from one's everyday surroundings.

- The person with autism is not hampered by any previous (negative) experiences with the facilitator. They can start with more of a 'blank slate'. This applies the other way around, too: it is easier for the facilitator to adopt a neutral, positive position towards the person with autism.

- Once trust has been gained, the person with autism can open up more easily, without fear of being tackled later about certain things they said during the sessions.

The need for an unfamiliar professional makes it even more necessary to pay particular attention to transfer, as well as to close collaboration with the learning environment (parents, educators). For children and young people staying in residential care, the facilitator can be:

- the psychologist, psychotherapist, speech and language therapist or specialist teacher for the organisation or for another establishment

- a tutor, therapist, teacher or team leader who is not part of the permanent support team for the person with autism (for example, a tutor from another team).

The facilitator adopts a positive attitude in relation to the people with autism. Their style must be accepting, directive, positive and empowering. It is additionally advantageous for the facilitator to evaluate him/herself and the impact of his or her work, so that the person with autism is not up against too high expectations. Using a certain amount of humour helps participants face the most confrontational moments. The most important requirement is that the facilitator has a thorough understanding of an autistic style of assimilating information. This understanding is only acquired after years of experience. The risks associated with errors made by the facilitator when informing someone about their autism are much greater than those associated, for example, with failings in the process of training someone how to tie their shoelaces.

4 Frequency and duration of the sessions

I am Special can be easily adapted and individualised according to the needs and capabilities of the person with autism, the facilitator and those around the person.

The workbook can be presented in its entirety, although the facilitator may also choose to use only certain chapters. However, *I am Special* as a whole is constructed logically and this logic will be lost if only certain parts are used.

I am Special can be spread out over several weekly sessions. Leaving a gap of more than 15 days between any two sessions is especially not recommended, as the facilitator will have to repeat too much to establish the link with the previous session. Homework, such as completing an additional worksheet or rereading certain pages, helps to bridge the gap between sessions. We also need to take into account the planning of the meetings. Starting a series of sessions just before the long holidays is not advisable, since after only a few sessions, there will be a break of at least six weeks. After the holidays, all the work will have to be done again.

Going through the whole workbook (minus additional exercises) takes from 10 to 20 hours, both for individual and group work. At least eight sessions are therefore necessary. There is no set number of hours per chapter. According to the age and/or developmental level of the participant, the facilitator may decide to adapt the frequency, quantity or duration of the sessions. Repetitions can be fitted in, too, as necessary. They may indeed by indispensible with individuals whose developmental age is relatively 'young'.

To maintain attention, concentration and motivation, we advise against too long a series of sessions. With more than 15 sessions, the person with autism may lose track of the overall view, become bored or lose their motivation ('I know that already!').

Experience has also taught us that a session should not last longer than 45 to 60 minutes, especially for children. For older participants or for groups, a session may be extended to one and a half or two hours. In this case, the facilitator must timetable in at least one break. This must be short: a break that lasts too long complicates the transition from free time to work. If you like, the person with autism could also have a STOP card to use when tired or when they wish to have a short break.

Another option for easing the tension linked to various tasks is to prepare a piece of work on the content that is quick and easy. We provide many suggestions in the *I am Special* chapter of the practical manual. The chapter on the version for young people with learning disabilities ('That's me?!') also includes numerous tips for exercises. 'Time to speak' frequently turns into 'time to do something', especially with children and adolescents, or with young adults with learning disabilities.

Each session ends positively, for example with a snack or a drink, a short group game or chatting about a participant's favourite subject.

For the person with autism, it is essential to be clear, beforehand, about the 'time' aspect of the sessions: start, finish, duration, frequency and breaks.

5 Location and resources

For working with *I am Special*, it is necessary to secure a space where the facilitator and participant(s) can work without being disturbed. It is best to use a room that is not used for anything else, so that it carries no meaning or erroneous associations for the participant(s). It is preferable that all sessions happen in the same place. Having a table and sheets of paper is indispensible for making things more visual. If the break takes place in the same room (e.g. with drinks, a short game), the nature and duration of the relaxation needs to be made clear, visually.

The resources needed for some of the adaptations are given in the respective chapters.

6 Group work

I am Special allows for both individual and group work. Sometimes, it is indeed beneficial to bring a group of people with autism together to talk about their autism. These meetings offer the following advantages and opportunities:

- People with autism see that they are not alone and that others have problems, too. This can be a real relief, especially for children and young people who have the feeling they are the odd ones out in a mainstream school. People with autism are often relieved to see they are not alone in experiencing difficulties.

- They learn that autism in others is at once very different and very similar. Everyone finds it hard to deal with other people, but everyone has their own ways of coping with these difficulties. In a group, the idea of an 'autism spectrum' requires less imagination. It is present, visually and concretely. Many people with autism focus on comparing themselves with others. A group enables this to happen in a more or less controlled way. In fact, we are then using the same method they use automatically: comparing themselves to others.

- Experience has shown that, as a result of their own experiences, they are often very keen to give their peers good advice. But because of their difficulty with adopting another person's point of view, their well-meant advice is sometimes inappropriate. This is where the facilitator's role is much more important than in individual sessions. Even if people with autism sometimes do not understand a situation very well, they can still have the feeling of being understood by others. And, in our experience, people with autism love to hear how other people with autism cope.

- Our experience also suggests that participants in a group session about autism or another sensitive topic are more willing to 'accept' views contrary to their own when these are expressed by their peers, rather than when they come from the facilitator.

- As a facilitator, you can also use the group or some of the participants as catalysts. Sometimes in a group, a participant speaks very openly about certain subjects (through lack of embarrassment, or through naivety but also because they not hampered by the neurotypical shame to talk about difficulties and shortcomings). The facilitator can then use this to address certain themes. Good facilitators are recognisable from the way in which they use the group as a tool, and make the most of the potential contribution of each participant.

- In a group, the facilitator receives more information than would be possible in individual sessions, because what each person with autism says contributes to the process. For example, in a group you get more examples of different personalities than with only one person.

- For the participants who claim they don't have any problems, the facilitator can take advantage of the social aspect of the group in order to illustrate the difficulties that can occur in the areas of social interaction and communication. As the young people are in a social event where skills such as listening to each other, taking turns and communicating adequately come into play, they will not be able to camouflage their difficulties as much as they would in an individual discussion with a tutor, therapist or facilitator – a situation that is safer, more structured and more artificial.

- With confrontational topics, participants can take cover within a group. This is a technique we use regularly. We make a remark or an important point that concerns only one of the participants, as if it were intended for all. This technique is much less threatening.

- Finally, group work is more economical. With more or less the same investment of time, one can reach more participants.

Group work can also have a certain number of disadvantages and limitations:

- The sessions can lead to unduly favourable comparisons being made and thus contribute to a denial of problems ('the others are affected more severely than me'). Incidentally, a positive comparison is not always entirely a bad thing. It can be a real boost for someone who has previously developed a negative self-esteem ('my situation isn't so bad after all').

- Bringing together people with autism sometimes causes conflict. They unwittingly tread on one another's toes, they tell each other a few home truths (very straightforwardly and frankly). A competent facilitator can make the most of these conflicts as useful and productive material, for example as a starting point for a discussion on differences between people, each other's feelings, etc. The situation differs according to whether the participants know each other (e.g. they go to the same school, are in the same class or in the same group) or not. If the participants know each other, they will also bring to the group their stories about mutual acquaintances, their conflicts, their experiences and memories, which present both advantages and disadvantages. Nevertheless, such incidents demand more of the facilitator's time. Sometimes after the sessions, one needs to review or rectify some of the contributions from several participants.

- A group offers fewer possibilities for individualisation and adaptation. As the facilitator, there is a risk you will pay less attention to some of the participants as individuals. There is also the risk of one or several participants monopolising the group. Skilled group facilitation, as well as the ability to keep track of individuals within a session, reduces these risks. The belief that working in a group prevents individualisation is a misconception. A facilitator with enough experience in and knowledge of group work can also create space for individualisation.

- People with autism are not always capable of good listening. That is why the premier condition for group conversations is good facilitation.

Not all participants want to be in group sessions. There are a number of conditions. It is certainly necessary to assess whether *I am Special* should be offered in a group or individually, based on the person with autism's difficulties, the experience of the facilitator and other practical aspects.

6.1 Conditions for participants in a group
In addition to the criteria already cited for *I am Special*, participants also need:

- to be able to rely on a tutor, an educator or a parent who, if necessary, will provide individual follow-up on a number of subjects

- to have minimal listening skills

- to be able to wait their turn

- to be able to or have the courage to say something about themselves in a group.

6.2 Conditions for group facilitators

The group facilitator must be properly prepared. He or she needs:

- To consult parents and others who will potentially be affected (tutor, teacher, specialist teacher, etc.).

- To gather information about the group participants' communication and learning style and about their group skills (activity level and pace, social background, etc.).

- To gather information about participants' diagnoses: how long have they known about their diagnosis, what do they know and what is their attitude towards autism (do they have fears? Are they ashamed? Are they proud of their autism? Do they not believe it or are they opposed to it? Do they blame someone for their problems? Who?).

- To organise a preliminary information session for parents and/or educators, during which the group facilitator gathers information and outlines the programme.

- To have sufficient knowledge of autism spectrum disorders.

- To have sufficient experience of groups, in particular those composed of people with autism. The numerous advantages of working with a group of people with autism will be realised only if the facilitator runs the group well and knows how to make the most of each participant's unique contribution.

- To be able to handle the Socratic method in a group.

- To show a great deal of flexibility. A group facilitator needs to be able to react to more interactions than a facilitator in individual work. We often say jokingly, 'When you begin working with a group of people with autism, you always know where you're going to start but you never know where you're going to end up.' It is better for facilitators with a high need for control and predictability not to start out with a group.

- Furthermore, a group facilitator needs to have enough ideas in reserve to be able to work towards the planned goals in a flexible way. This calls upon the skills necessary for leading a group. The worst thing that can happen for the participants is that the group leader, like them, loses the thread of the conversation.

If the group is composed of participants who come from the same environment (school, community, care home), having two facilitators is recommended. One of them is the group leader: he or she directs the whole process. This is an unfamiliar person, someone who is not part of the professional group working with the children or adolescents on a daily basis. This helps people with autism to retain some consistency amongst all the people who support them. In this way, the group also has a clear boundary. Also, as stated above, unfamiliar people are often given more credit and authority by people with autism than the more familiar people working with them (or their parents), whom they see every day.

Second, there is a facilitator in a supporting role, someone who knows the participants and can possibly correct or clarify some aspects.

Two facilitators can also be useful in a group comprised of children who do not know each other. This duality offers many opportunities for individualisation or for extra support to be given in certain tasks.

The separation of roles between two facilitators needs to be made clear. It is inadvisable to constantly swap roles in an unpredictable fashion (one facilitator leads the group one time, another time the other takes over). This alteration causes confusion among the participants. They do not really know whom they should address if they want to ask questions or say something in the group. This is why it is important to have a clear separation of roles. If a participant addresses the supporting facilitator about something he or she wants to say to the group, the second facilitator should respond by saying he or she needs to ask the group facilitator.

6.3 Selection, composition and size of the group

An ideal size for a group varies, from five to eight participants. These are selected on the basis of the previously cited criteria. In an ideal group, there is a perfect balance between the heterogeneity and homogeneity of the participants. Taking into account group dynamics and the explanations of the autism spectrum, we do not select too many participants who are similar. For example, a group composed only of passive, shy and reserved participants will not be very energetic. A group composed only of hyperactive participants will be ineffective due to an excess of energy. Nevertheless, bringing together participants who are not completely different in age, temperament and loquaciousness is recommended. It is advisable to opt for a certain amount of heterogeneity across the spectrum of autism and for a certain amount of homogeneity with regard to age, intelligence and activity level.

To avoid having sessions that constantly degenerate, for example, because the group is comprised of six participants with autism and ADHD (attention deficit hyperactivity disorder), it is also important that information has been provided beforehand about the disorders and any multiple difficulties. A group consisting only of participants with poor self-esteem and a negative attitude towards autism does not bode well either.

Whether the participants know each other or not, each of these circumstances has advantages and disadvantages. When participants do not know each other, the facilitator will need to devote sufficient time and activities to forming the group. The structure of *I am Special* provides for this. The worksheets on 'My outside' and 'My inside' lend themselves perfectly to familiarisation. Giving each element clarity and predictability is a great source of security for participants unknown to each other.

When participants do already know each other, existing relationships and associations need to be taken into account in the composition of the group. For example, there is a risk of the session on 'My not so strong points' leading to bullying of a participant if he is in a group with another young person who bullies him. Positive relationships must be in the majority in the group.

Placement of the participants is also important. For example, it is better not to place a participant who is easily distracted in front of a window. Often, after the first or second session, it is necessary to give the participants different places. If two participants get along well with each other, it is best to place them together so they can support each other. A participant who needs more individual support can be placed right next to the facilitator.

6.4 Establish clear agreements with the group beforehand

Because of their social difficulties, participants with an autism spectrum disorder do not always have the experience necessary to participate in group discussions. For them and for the facilitator, establishing clear agreements beforehand is a great help. For example:

- we have to listen to each other
- we do not interrupt each other
- we will put up our hand if we wish to speak or ask a question
- we won't make each other angry
- we won't blame each other for anything

- during the week, we will write down any questions that come up and take them to the facilitator.

We can make these agreements visual, for example, on a large card.

With adolescents and young adults with autism, it is inadvisable, for the first session, to 'assail' them with a whole list of things that are allowed or not allowed. Doing things in this way does not promote a positive atmosphere. Often, it works better to draw up a list of agreements or rules *together*. This list can be added to or amended over the sessions, in response to different incidents.

Our experiences, both in Belgium and abroad, have shown that group sessions are the first choice when using *I am Special*, especially with adolescents and young adults; providing there is competent facilitation, the advantages outweigh the disadvantages.

A decision for individual or group application need not be irrevocable. It is possible to combine the two, with basic information being given in a group, while individual sessions, either in between times or after the group course, make it possible to answer specific personal questions and to individualise the information provided.

7 Introduction to the individual with autism's workbook
7.1 Aim of the workbook: learning about myself and learning about my autism

I am Special is a workbook developed for people with autism. Thanks to the workbook, the person with autism can, in the first instance, learn more about him/herself. The workbook will be the person with autism's own personal workbook. It is a book that the person with autism helps to write, so to speak. It is designed to be kept up to date and does not have to be handed in. When the sessions have finished, if the child or adolescent wishes, they will be able to reread some of the chapters.

The workbook or its chapters can also be used by other people as a way of getting to know the person with autism. In the case of children or adolescents with autism, very often it is the parents, especially, who provide information to a new school, a new group home or summer camp. Children or young people with autism do not always find this very pleasant, but at the same time, they experience significant difficulties with speaking for themselves. We explain to them that with their book, they can introduce themselves more easily. By reading the workbook to someone else, they can provide very relevant information about themselves, without having to use a more direct kind of verbal communication.

People with autism need to be told clearly that *I am Special* is not going to tell them everything about themselves, nor everything about autism. Indeed a certain number of children and young people with autism may think, 'If I finish this work quickly, I'll have my diploma in autism and I'll be a specialist in the subject.' This is why we explain that with the workbook, they can learn a great deal, but to 'know yourself' is an endless process. It is the same for learning about and understanding autism.

We also tell them that *I am Special* will supply them with information, but the work does not stop there. They will have to put this information to use in their lives. From then on, they must also apply and use the knowledge gained, in real life. In other words, *I am Special* is only the beginning.

7.2 Overview of the themes

People with autism love predictability. This is why, at the beginning, we provide an overview of the different themes we will be reviewing in *I am Special*.

Some participants expect us to start talking about autism right away, in the first session. This is why an overview session should take place. If this does not happen, the participants are not going to understand, for example, why a discussion is about the brain and not about autism, and they might switch off.

In order to justify the sessions preceding the chapter on autism, it is best to use an image, for example, one that symbolises the construction of a house. It is possible to sketch out this image and, as a result, to visualise the construction of *I am Special*. It follows that the sessions explaining about the body, the outside, the inside and other disabilities are the foundation elements, on which we can build our knowledge of autism. Below are two examples of possible visualisations.

It is even possible to actually construct this house, for example, with a piece of furniture or set of trays representing the stages. The worksheets and resources needed for each stage of *I am Special* are located in the relevant drawer. For a concrete example, see the version of the worksheets adapted for young people with learning disabilities, 'That's me?!'.

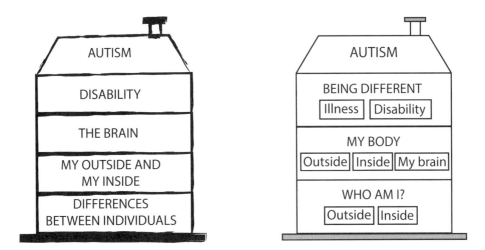

Figure 6.1: Two possible visualisations of the construction of I am Special

The alphabet is another image that may be suitable. We explain that the first sessions are the letters, thanks to which we will be able to read, write and understand the information about autism.

In addition to providing clarity and predictability, giving an overview at the beginning of each chapter is not a bad idea. These summaries are included in the workbook.

7.3 Giving the workbook a place

For us, this title means that we must explain the workbook and the sessions in such a way that the person with autism will be able to find a place for them in his or her life. People with autism experience difficulties with coherence and, as a result, we need to help them to connect *I am Special* with their everyday life.

First of all, we can achieve this by giving an overview not only of the content but also of the frequency, duration and location of the meetings or sessions. This gives them clear-cut answers to the questions: what, when, how often and for how long? Furthermore, we also provide information and clarity about the people involved in the programme. This is comprised of much more than simple information about who will be conducting the sessions. It is also advisable to provide answers to the following questions: Who knows about/can/should look at my workbook? Who can I talk to about it? If I have questions about the content of the workbook, who do I ask?

The involvement of parents and/or carers should also be made clear. If the child or adolescent's network consists of people with whom he or she discusses things regularly, such as a carer, an educator, a tutor or psychologist, then *I am Special* must have a place in this support network, also.

Depending on their experiences and expectations, the participants will interpret *I am Special* sessions in particular ways.

If they are in group sessions, some will liken these to social skills training. Depending on their experience of this, their associations can be negative or positive. Some young people or adults also regard the sessions as academic courses, especially those concerning the human body. Experience has shown us that the word 'course' was generally received positively by the participants and evoked an accurate enough image of what was going to happen.

If they are in individual sessions, it is necessary to situate these within educational and therapeutic discussions as a whole.

8 Moving, removing or adding sections

I am Special is designed for very flexible and individualised use. Although the worksheets are organised in a logical order according to the construction previously described, the facilitator does not necessarily need to use all of them or make use of them in that order. It is possible to move, skip or add sections. Thus, you can do the worksheets on the body's outside ('My body: the outside') together with those on a person's outer appearance ('My outside' in 'I am unique') then go on to the inside (worksheets on character, etc. in 'My inner features').

This is why there are no page numbers in the workbook. This allows you to add, remove or swap pages without running the risk of confusing the participant(s) because 'the page numbers aren't right'. A space has even been provided for pagination. The facilitator can fill in the page numbers or ask the participant(s) to do this.

As this edition of *I am Special* includes several versions, it is also possible to make a new workbook with worksheets from different versions. For example, the worksheets from 'The big book about me', plus the original workbook, along with supplements on specific topics can easily be put together to form a new, personalised version of *I am Special*.

Although with some people, especially young adults, it is desirable and feasible to drop some sections from the workbook, for example the chapter on the body, nevertheless it is inadvisable to take this decision lightly.

Most participants will have already learned about the human body at school, but their knowledge is not always sound or suitable for this context. A brief revision is not wasted. These worksheets will refresh the participant's memory and, for the facilitator, they can be a kind of assessment of how much the participants know about themselves. Since many young people have already done this at school, this chapter is also easier and can be a break from more demanding worksheets.

Naturally, with adults with average intelligence, we do not review this chapter. Instead, worksheets on communication or social interaction can be added. Later, we give an example of the way in which *I am Special* can be used with adults with average or above-average intelligence.

That said, we often overestimate people with autism, especially those with a very good facility with language. This is why we should not be too quick to assume that certain areas of knowledge and/or skills have been acquired. During our courses, we noticed that many aspects were completely new to a group of adults with average intelligence: the fact that every person with autism possesses an inside and outside, what belongs to the inside and what belongs to the outside, the fact that every human being is unique, etc. Most of them regularly use terms such as 'character' or 'personality' for 'inside'. Before the course, we thought they would find this kind of exercise too simplistic, but this was a mistake. What seemed obvious to us was a revelation for them…

For some of the more difficult chapters, especially with young people who have below average intelligence, the facilitator can introduce 'as a relaxation activity' some easier, fun activities, for example, games about the horoscope and their astrological signs, or colouring in a drawing.

If worksheets are added, moved or not used, it is also necessary to adapt the contents page for each chapter.

9 Inductive and deductive use of the worksheets

There are two kinds of worksheets in the workbook:

1. Worksheets with little or no text. These are found especially at the beginning of the workbook, in the chapters about the differences between individuals and about the human body. After a short introduction, the worksheets are given to the participant(s) for completion.

2. Worksheets with more text. These consist primarily of information participants need to concretise or put into practice themselves. The chapter on autism is composed mainly of this kind of worksheet.

For the second kind of worksheet, there are two possible ways of working:

1. Deductively: the facilitator briefly summarises the information on the worksheet and lets the participants read the contents. Then, the facilitator asks questions about the worksheet and provides further explanations.

2. Inductively: the facilitator asks targeted questions, so that participants arrive at an understanding of what is discussed on the worksheet, on their own. Then, the facilitator distributes the worksheets, so that the participants can read the summary.

We are in favour of the second method, since it is in keeping with the Socratic method.

Furthermore, choosing an inductive or deductive approach is applicable not only to individual exercises but also to the workbook as a whole. For example, at the beginning, you can tell the participant he or she has autism and that together you are going to look at what that means (deductive approach) or through a process of discovery with the workbook, you can let him/her come to the conclusion that they have autism.

10 Evaluation and monitoring of aims
10.1 Evaluating the sessions
In Part 2, the 'Practical Manual', we list the objectives of each section. After each section, it is advisable to monitor what and how the participants have understood the contents. This monitoring can be carried out via a list of questions (written or oral), a kind of test (but look out for children and adolescents who hate school!) or in the form of a quiz for group sessions.

This monitoring is illustrated with an example in the workbook: a 'true or false' worksheet about autism spectrum disorders. You can also ask questions to find out what the young person has learned that day. At the end of each chapter there is a worksheet where the participant can write down what they have learned. This exercise has a double objective. The person with autism summarises what is important for them, and the facilitator has an opportunity to assess what the child or young person has retained from the preceding session.

10.2 Taking transfer into account
To be certain of the impact of the sessions, it is not enough to check the participants' understanding after each section or at the end of sessions. A good memory along with behaviours connected with a specific context can

make us believe, wrongly, that people with autism have learned something or that they are capable of carrying out a particular task.

For this reason, the facilitator needs to pay particular attention to transfer. This can be done, for example, through a piece of homework (in any case, work for outside the session) consisting of recounting the sessions. Many children and adults will not do this spontaneously. This is why parents are often advised to ask questions through which they can check what their child has understood, how and to what extent he or she understands it. With children and adolescents, it is made clear from the beginning that the topics are also going to be discussed at home. Because of their autistic way of thinking (and sometimes also due to other reasons, such as feeling ashamed or resistance to the diagnosis), some participants want to confine the contents of their workbook exclusively to the sessions, in an extremely strict and rigid way.

To verify whether the information provided has lasted, it is also advisable to monitor this after the sessions have come to an end, for example after six months.

With regard to the chapter, 'How do I deal with difficulties caused by my autism?', the transfer aspect is even more important. In this chapter, our aim is not only to provide theoretical knowledge about coping strategies, but above all to have these strategies actually being used. For example, with the use of aids, the child or young person can make practical plans for coping better with the consequences of their autism. With the consent of the participant, these plans will also be shared with parents, carers and teachers, in order to ensure follow-up. Agreements can be made about where, when and with whom these plans will be evaluated.

10.3 Monitoring informative aspects

In keeping with the aims of *I am Special* (see Chapter 2, 'Self-image'), the following questions are guidelines and can help in carrying out an evaluation of *I am Special* and measuring its impact:

- Is the person with autism capable of giving a general definition of autism? For example, 'Autism makes it hard for me to understand what others are thinking or feeling.'

- Can they give examples of their autistic characteristics? For example, 'I don't really know how to start up a conversation with someone.'

- Can they give examples of the consequences arising from autism for their own functioning and their own life? For example, 'I'm in special education because of my autism' or 'My autism played a role in my choice for staying single.'

- Can they say which situations are (can be) difficult for them (because of their autism)? For example, group conversations, waiting for a bus, going swimming.

- Can they identify strategies to be used for managing these situations, as well as new strategies and new skills they still need to learn? For example, 'I use an answering machine to be less upset by unexpected phone calls' or 'If I'm on edge in class, I ask to leave, in order to let off steam a bit.'

- Can they identify aspects of their autism that are an asset or even a talent? For example, 'I have an excellent memory for dates, so I never forget someone's birthday' or 'I have a keen eye for details: I always help my sister with her written assignments, picking out the spelling errors.'

10.4 Monitoring effect on self-image

The suggestions above concern the whole content of the workbook, its specific themes and 'autism'. The aim of *I am Special* is not only to increase knowledge about autism. Besides the four informative aims, *I am Special* also aims to increase self-esteem and self-image.

In order to assess self-esteem and self-image, different information sources can be exploited:

- parents (to what extent does your child feel good about himself? How does he speak about himself, in mainly negative or positive terms? How does he describe himself?)

- the professional team can also give their impressions of the self-esteem and self-image of a pupil with autism (How does he cope with academic failure? Does he ever use expressions such as 'I'm an idiot!', 'I can't do anything, anyway!'? What about his self-confidence with new tasks?)

- a tutor, home support worker or professional responsible for psychosocial help.

Apart from the information sources around the person, it is also possible to ask the person with autism questions about their self-image, directly.[83] For example, there is the *Self Understanding Interview* by Damon and Hart.[84] This interview consists of six sections relating to self-image, namely:

- self-definition (for example, what kind of person are you?)

- self-esteem (what are you especially proud of about yourself? What do you like least about yourself?)

- self in past and future (do you think you'll be the same or different five years from now?)

- continuity (do you change at all from year to year?)

- influence (how did you become the person you are now?)

- distinctiveness (what makes you different from the people you know? In what ways are you different?).

The questions in this interview are very general and quite abstract. This poses problems, especially for children and/or young people or adults with learning disabilities. It is not necessary to ask questions from each of these areas, to be in accordance with the aims of *I am Special*. The most important questions, closely linked to the aims of *I am Special*, are the questions targeted at self-definition, self-image and differences with other people.

An example of more concrete and more structured questioning can be found in the 'Self-Description Questionnaires' (SDQ) by Herbert Marsh, professor of the SELF Research Centre at the University of Western Sydney. As the questions are more concrete and more structured, these lists are easier for people with autism to use. They test various aspects of self-image, notably:

- physical aptitudes (for example, 'I'm good at sports')

- outside appearance and physique ('I look healthy')

- relationships with others ('I have lots of friends')

- relationship with parents ('I get along well with my parents')

- courses: reading and mathematics ('I like reading')

- general functioning at school ('I find schoolwork easy')

- general self-image ('I'm not inferior to others').

There are three versions[85] of this list, one for young children (ages five to eight years, but which can, in our opinion, also be used with children a bit older), one for secondary school students and one for young adults. These lists of questions have been translated into and standardised in many languages.

A list of questions almost identical to Marsh's is the Self-Perception Profile for Children by Susan Harter[86] of the University of Denver. This measures the self-concept of children aged 8 to 12 years and consists of 36 questions in six different domains: academic ability, social acceptance, athletic ability, physical appearance, behaviour and self-satisfaction.

Harter and her colleagues have also developed versions of this list of questions for other age groups: adolescents,[87] adults[88] and also for students with learning disabilities.[89]

For very young children (four to seven years), Harter developed a version incorporating images, the Pictorial Scale of Perceived Competence and Social Acceptance for Young Children.[90] Here, for each item, the participant is presented with two images, usually one in which a child is very good in an area and one in which a child is not. The tester then reads two short descriptions, one positive and one negative, and asks the child which of the two images corresponds to each description. The child is then invited to say which image is like them.

10.5 Participants' evaluation

In addition to an assessment of the desired effects of *I am Special*, it is also possible to ask questions about the satisfaction and impressions of the participants. An effective participants' evaluation yields precious information for corrections to the content and work methods of *I am Special*. The CD ROM contains examples of evaluation forms:

- The evaluation form we tested out in our group sessions.

- The evaluation forms developed by Ella Buis, educational psychologist in public health at *Vizier*, an organisation in the Netherlands which offers services for people with learning disabilities. There are three versions: two versions for participants (one for children/adolescents and one for adults) and one version for parents and/or carers of participants.

Participants' evaluations should be carried out in writing, in a structured way. Contrary to what some people think, people with autism are capable of giving their views, and sharing sometimes surprisingly astute comments. The process works better when they receive detailed questions and when they have enough time to formulate their ideas. A questionnaire with multiple choices also provides a wider view of all possible responses than would open questions, although these are not ruled out. In all cases, a clear form is of more help than a simple discussion that begins with much too vague, open questions, such as 'What do you think of it?' After having completed such a form, an evaluation discussion can take place, also. In this conversation, the completed form serves as a guide and unifying theme.

11 Additional training and development

For theory, the user can refer frequently to the manual. However, practice and real life can never be translated onto paper. The country is always different from the map… This is why everyone who wishes to work with *I am Special* will undoubtedly be faced with questions and comments that are not included in the manual.

For this reason, *Autisme Centraal* organises workshops on *I am Special*. There are two types: an introductory workshop and a follow-up workshop. In the first, the workbook is presented in a very practical way. Participants are made aware, through accounts of our experience and from demonstrations and exercises, of the methodologies that constitute the workbook's foundations. They can also learn how to develop their own sessions and worksheets. In the follow-up workshop, participants have the opportunity to share their experiences of *I am Special*. Actual experiences are discussed and they can ask questions that have arisen from their practice or from a particular case study.

In addition, *Autisme Centraal* organises workshops on the Socrautic method. Following a short introduction, this session enables participants to prepare themselves for using the Socratic method, through role play and application with people with autism.[91]

I am Special is not a finished product. *Autisme Centraal* continues to be interested in your experiences arising from use of the workbook in practice and still pays special attention to suggestions for supplementing, improving and adapting the workbook. All suggestions are welcome.

Part 2

Practical Manual

Chapter 7

I am Special

The target group of the worksheets of *I am Special*, as described in this chapter, are children (+10 years) and adolescents with an autism spectrum disorder who can read and write. For younger children, there is 'The big book about me' (Chapter 8); for people with a learning disability, there is 'That's me' (Chapter 9) and Chapter 15 describes how one can inform adults about their diagnosis.

In this part, we explain the various worksheets. For each of the chapters within *I am Special*, we describe in turn the aims, practical work methods and the main points of the different worksheets, along with some suggestions for variations and additions. This practical manual for *I am Special* also applies to 'The big book about me' version.

Anyone who has studied the manual in depth and adopted the work method of *I am Special* will, without further explanation, know how to use the new worksheets and the worksheets of the other versions now included in this revised edition of *I am Special*. Further instructions have been newly added only to the new part, 'What can I do myself, about my autism?' ('The world in fragments') and for the version for siblings.

First pages

Some children and adolescents do not want to put their photo here. You can suggest they draw a self-portrait and paste it on the page later. Other solutions: make a drawing of them yourself, describing their physical appearance. The participant needs to write their name in the box indicated.

The second page consists of explanations of the workbook. It is optional. If the child or adolescent already knows the workbook deals with autism, you can add the term 'autism' to the list of contents. Adolescents allergic to the term 'workbook' (especially 'work') perhaps prefer the expression 'readings and exercises folder' or 'portfolio'.

MY PERSONAL DETAILS

People with autism prefer concrete and factual information, such as data, numbers and labels, to more instinctive and abstract information. Most people will find the page on their personal details easy to complete. Starting off with an easy, concrete page to fill in also gives encouragement and motivation to complete the workbook. If the young person does not know all the answers, this page can be taken home and he can ask his parents for the missing information. For children belonging to newly formed families, there is clearly a need to adapt (for example, provide a space for the stepfather or stepmother).

1 I am unique: my outside
1.1 Aims of these sessions

- to get to know the session participants: facilitator(s) and participant(s)
- to become familiar with the work method
- to identify and name their own external features (body parts)
- to know that all people differ from each other in their outward appearance, but that there are similarities too
- to be able to name their own external differences and similarities in comparison with other people
- to know that every person's appearance is unique.

1.2 Method and essential elements

It is mainly younger children and people with a learning disability who struggle with the abstract distinction between our inside and outside. Therefore, introductory and supplementary to the worksheets in 'I am unique' it can be useful to give a more in-depth explanation of the two notions, in a more concrete way. To this effect, worksheet examples (developed by Marjan Deleu of *Het Anker*) are included in the CD ROM documents (for instructions see pp.193–195, section 4).

My outside

We begin with concrete, factual and measurable information. Some people with autism have difficulties completing the diagram of their body. Should this be the case, we give more attention to this, asking them first, for example, to name or point to different parts of their body. A drawing of the human body can help.

Many people with autism have difficulties with touch, especially when it is unexpected. We recommend you take care in this area, in this session. This caution applies especially if the facilitator is male and the participant is female (and *vice versa*).

Some people with autism do not like to look at themselves in a mirror. If this is the case and if, for example, they don't know the colour of their hair, someone else can provide this information.

It is common knowledge that some individuals with autism have difficulty with making eye contact. For naming their eye colour, using a mirror is therefore preferable to having someone look in their eyes.

The 'special features' mentioned on the worksheet can be: a pair of glasses, earrings, a moustache or a beard, a dental brace, or skin colour.

I look different from other people

This worksheet is very suitable for use in groups. It's possible to make a concrete, physical comparison, without having to rely on imagination.

For many people with autism, it is particularly difficult to make mental comparisons, even when these are about physical characteristics. If this page is used in an individual session, it can be given as homework, so that the person can do the actual comparing outwith the session.

Another idea is to ask the child or adolescent to compare photos of himself with those of other people. The facilitator can then ask the child to find five differences between his photo and that of a peer. To illustrate further differences between people, you can make a book of photos (see 'That's me?!' version – in the CD ROM documents).

If certain comparisons are rather delicate, for example, about the weight of an obese person who is bullied for that reason, it is preferable to choose another physical characteristic.

My outside is unique!

There are two possible ways of using this page and the other worksheets with text and explanations:

1. Guide the person towards the desired conclusions using Socratic questions, then have him or her read the page as a summary.

2. Read the page to the person with autism and then ask questions or explain further.

In any case, it is important to ask enough questions to check whether the person has a good understanding of the text. The term 'unique' is rarely used, hence the additional information.

- A tip: have the person look up the meaning in a dictionary.

- Alternative wording can be used just as well, such as 'there's no one like me!'.

Some people will need visual supports to experience the uniqueness of fingerprints. If they don't believe or understand that no two people have the same fingerprints, the facilitator can print his or hers next to the person with autism's. When working in a group, it is possible to compare everyone's fingerprints.

1.3 Resources

- passport-style photo
- glue
- ballpoint pens

- bathroom scales

- tape measure

- mirror

- paint and a sponge, or ink pad

- a ring binder

1.4 Variations and additions

Have the person lie down on a large piece of paper. Draw his or her outline using a pencil or felt-tip pen (resulting in a life-sized profile). The various body measurements can be added, or features such as a pair of glasses or freckles can be drawn in.

This part of the workbook is well suited to many group games that are a lot of fun. Some suggestions:

- The participants line up from shortest to tallest, then from lightest to heaviest, smallest shoe size to largest, lightest hair to darkest, etc.

- 'Simon says' game. Select two corners of the room. The facilitator calls out a physical difference, for example, 'Simon says, everyone wearing shorts go to the corner by the window; everyone wearing trousers, go to the corner by the door.' The participants are to run to 'their' corners as quickly as possible – only if 'Simon says'!

- 'Who is it?' All the participants write down three of their own characteristics which distinguish themselves from others. For example: 'I'm wearing a blue jumper, I wear glasses and I have long blonde hair.' All the pieces of paper are then folded and gathered in the middle of a table. In turns, everyone opens a note and says who fits the description.

- 'Who is it?' A variation on the previous game. One of the participants leaves the room and someone is chosen from the rest of the group to be 'it'. Then the person comes back in and has to guess who 'it' is, by means of questions about physical characteristics (Is it a girl or boy? Does he have black hair? Is he wearing a green jumper?).

- 'Guess what's different.' One of the participants leaves the room. All the others change something about their appearance, for example, exchange jumpers or shoes. The person comes back in again and he or she has to guess what's changed with everyone.

These sessions and those on 'my inside' can be supplemented by all kinds of texts, photos, cartoon strips on the differences between individuals.

I am unique: my inside
1.5 Aims of these sessions

- to be able to name (in general) the various aspects of a person's inner self: interests, character, abilities

- to get to know and be able to name one's own interests, character traits, talents and shortcomings

- to know that in this regard, each individual is different but there are also similarities between people

- to be able to name the differences and similarities between one's own personal interests, character traits and abilities, and those of other people

- to know that everyone's inner features are unique

- to gain in self-knowledge and understanding of one's own personality.

1.6 Method and essential elements

In contrast to the part about one's outside, where things were physically observable and comparable, this section is more difficult because it requires a certain level of insight and self-reflection. It is advisable to make things as concrete as possible and to illustrate everything with telling examples.

MY INSIDE

The information on this page can, again, be presented in either a deductive or inductive way.

- Deductive: the facilitator names the different aspects and explains.

- Inductive: let the person with autism name all kinds of personal characteristics of him/herself and the other participants and group these on a whiteboard or on a sheet of paper. Let the person label the different groups and categories. If this is too difficult, the facilitator can name the different groups.

With high-functioning participants, who often know a whole string of theoretical definitions and synonyms, it is best to avoid endless discussions on the words and terms used. Some of them can talk for hours about terms such as 'temperament', 'feelings', 'character' and the differences between them. Instead of continuing the debate, it is advisable to come to an agreement on the content of these sessions and meanings of the different terms.

MY INTERESTS AND PREFERENCES

If you wish, you can also ask the participants for reasons for their preferences. Under each theme, they can then write 'because…' Naming one's preferences is generally easier than explaining why one likes something. Often, younger participants and/or those with a lower level of intelligence will say little more than 'because I think it's nice' or 'because I like to read, see, listen to', etc.

MY CHARACTER

Since most people with autism experience difficulty with naming character traits, two lists bringing together a number of character traits have been provided. Choosing characteristics from a list is easier. The person with autism pastes (or writes) character traits applicable to themselves in the boxes on this worksheet. More boxes can be drawn if necessary.

The first list consists of opposing and contradictory traits, such as 'open-minded' versus 'closed-minded'. The second list has traits without their opposites (the opposites are often negative: dishonest, unhelpful, antisocial, etc.).

Experience has shown it's harder to choose from the second list than to choose between two opposites. If anyone has real difficulty with naming their character traits, it will be easier to let him or her choose between two opposing characteristics. For example, 'Are you more funny than serious?' In groups, it is again possible to employ a variation on 'Simon says', where the facilitator names two opposing traits and the participants run to a corner of the room accordingly.

Note that although choosing is easier than naming, for people with autism, having to choose is still quite hard. Some cover up or avoid this difficulty by adopting a middle position. 'I'm a bit open but also a bit closed.' 'I'm a bit of both.' Adding the word 'rather' can be helpful, or asking directive or very clear questions: 'Which do you think applies to you most?'

People with a poor self-image or those who are always defensive will tend to choose only positive characteristics. Here are some suggestions for dealing with this situation.

Explain that everybody has both positive (nice, pleasant) and negative traits. Tell them that this doesn't matter, as nobody is perfect. Positive and negative traits both have their advantages and disadvantages. For example: a fearful person is unlikely to cause an accident through rashness, but neither will they have very exciting experiences. An open person is also more vulnerable than someone who is quite closed.

The person with autism can also be asked to write down their positive qualities on the left and their less positive qualities on the right.

The facilitator then fills in a worksheet herself for the participant, or lets someone else do it, for example a parent, teacher, brother or sister. The two worksheets are then given different titles: 'My character as I see it' and 'My character as [name of other person or the word 'others'] see/s it.'

Younger children and people with learning disabilities will not always understand all the words or terms, or they may give them a very concrete or associative meaning. It is typical of people with autism not to indicate spontaneously when they haven't understood or when they understand something differently. It is advisable to check their understanding of character traits by having them describe them or, even better, by asking them for concrete examples.

The CD ROM includes some adapted versions on character. A simplified version for young children is available in 'The big book about me'.

MY TALENTS

This is an easier and less threatening worksheet than the ones on character. Here, the person with autism can mention their strong points, for example, an ability to perceive details. You can also ask them, next time, to demonstrate or to show something that will illustrate these, for example, bring along a drawing, a book about their favourite subject, or a musical instrument. For those who have significant difficulties finding an example of their talents themselves, you can compile a list of activities yourself and they can check off the ones they are good at. An example is available on the CD ROM for young children and adolescents with learning disabilities ('My strengths and weaknesses').

WHAT OTHERS FIND SPECIAL ABOUT ME: MY TALENTS
ACCORDING TO OTHER PEOPLE

Often, because of their autistic thinking, people with autism view the world differently. This also applies to the way in which they view themselves. The objective of this worksheet is to give them some understanding of what others think of them. The worksheet should serve as homework to be completed by their parents, teacher, tutor, brother, sister, etc. With some participants, it will be necessary to draw up a list during the session of all the people who should complete the worksheet. This gets around the problem of choosing and it avoids the situation of either asking everyone, including strangers, to write something, or of not asking anyone at all.

The person with autism can gain enormous satisfaction from this worksheet, especially when he or she has a poor self-image.

MY NOT-SO-STRONG POINTS

For some people, this can be a real threat. Some avoid this challenge or hide their weaker points by citing minor, concrete things like 'I'm not very good at speaking other languages, but that's not so bad because I don't like going abroad.' At this stage of *I am Special*, which serves more as an assessment than as a means for revealing information, it is not necessary to confront the person with autism with their limits or to try to convince them of some of their weaknesses. However, one possibility is to give them a list enumerating their talents and not-so-strong points. The facilitator can then ask them to sort these ('I'm good at these things, I'm not good at those'), as well as having them sorted by someone amongst their friends. The discrepancy between what the two persons involved think can then lead to a discussion. Avoid arguments about who is right.

MY NOT-SO-STRONG POINTS ACCORDING TO OTHER PEOPLE

This worksheet is complementary to and/or a rectification of the one filled in by the persons with autism themselves. It provides another chance to refer to the differences between the views of the person with autism and those of others. With this worksheet, it is important not to fall into the trap of skirting around the subject. Additional explanations could be given about having different points of view and of concepts such as 'everyone has their own truth'. The stance of denying what others think can be due to a defensive attitude (often a result of poor self-image), but can also be due to lack of ability to take another perspective or a 'theory of mind' deficit.

In preparation for the various topics to be discussed later, the facilitator can mention some characteristics of autism here, without however using terms like 'autism', 'stereotyped' or 'resistance to change'. Those who have not already done so may fill in this worksheet now.

MY PERSONALITY: MY INSIDE IS UNIQUE

Particularly with children and less able people with autism, it is sometimes necessary to make these points visual and concrete. For example: if everyone could run, swim or cycle equally fast, who would ever win a race? If everyone knew as much about the weather as the Met Office, who would ever listen to the weather forecast? If everyone wanted to be a doctor, who would still be there for them to fulfil this role? If everyone liked the same music, there wouldn't be very many CDs and the Top 40 chart would disappear.

Instead of a signature at the bottom of the page, a written name can be used. Just as with the fingerprints, it can be fun to compare different signatures or handwriting.

I AM UNIQUE

There's a risk that since a person with autism can take things very literally, he or she may think he or she alone ('I') is unique. Therefore, it is best to explain that everyone is unique!

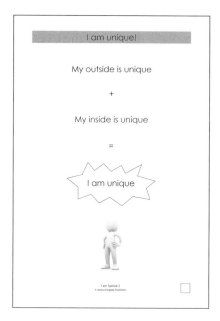

1.7 Resources

- scissors
- glue
- ballpoint pens

1.8 Variations and additions

- Describe personal characteristics using proverbs.

- Symbolise character traits, for example with drawings or animals (check first whether the participants have sufficient imagination and that, where necessary, they can make the distinction between symbols and reality!)

- An activity based on the horoscope. What is my zodiac sign? Does the description of my star sign correspond to the character traits I wrote down about myself?

- A quiz on the inner and outer self. Examples of questions:
  - John is 10cm taller than Eric. Inner or outer self?
  - Laura likes fish. Inner or outer self?
  - Sophie is afraid of spiders. Inner or outer self?

- A collage of 'my inner self'.

- An individual's personality is also determined by their experiences. Past experiences shape a person's character, interests, knowledge, skills, potential and limitations. This is an aspect which can be added to the inner characteristics already mentioned. The children can be asked to identify events in their life that were important to them, such as a trip abroad, a new school, the birth of a sibling, etc.

2 My body
2.1 Aims of these sessions

- to be able to name the different parts of the body and their functions
- to know the location in the body and the functions of the brain
- to know how the brain functions and processes information
- to understand the different kinds of intelligence and to be able to apply these to oneself.

2.2 Method and essential elements

In this session, it is important that special attention is paid to any possible fears or bizarre ideas that may come up. The session appeals to the imagination and it is well known that people with autism are not always at ease in this area, and that their imagination can run wild. The illustrations of the organs, especially, may evoke sordid or frightening associations.

For this session, only some basic worksheets are included. There is sufficient interesting and appropriate material on the human body in medical encyclopaedias for adolescents, books for children and even fun CD ROMs that enable one to take a virtual journey through the human body. This subject is taught to all children at school. The worksheets serve as a means of checking their recall and the accuracy of their knowledge.

MY BODY: THE OUTSIDE

The participant needs to stick the small strips with the names of parts of the body in the right place. There is a male version and a female version. On the female version, the ear is not visible.

MY BODY: THE INSIDE

The participant needs to draw lines from the parts of the body to the right place. It is useful to have a medical encyclopaedia to hand, so the participant can look up a part of the body they don't recognise. The illustrations of the skin and the eye in particular are difficult to recognise. The proportions are not all correct. It is best to point this out to the person with autism (if they have not already done so themselves, of course).

FUNCTIONS OF THE DIFFERENT PARTS OF THE BODY

This is a bit more difficult than the previous worksheet. The participant can, if necessary, look up the functions of different organs.

MY BRAIN

Scientific research has shown people with autism generally have good knowledge of the input and output functions of the brain, much less so of the information processing function. Illustrating the processes of receiving, processing and sending information with several concrete examples is advised.

Autism is a brain disorder: the brains of people with autism process information differently from those of so-called normal people. This is therefore a key part of the workbook. It is vital to check whether this part has been properly understood. If not, it will have to be repeated later.

Here are the answers to the true or false statements on one of the brain worksheets:

1. true   2. false   3. true   4. false   5. true

Here are the answers to the worksheet which includes the questions on 'What is the brain doing here?'

I see a car coming: receiving

I think my sister will be late today: processing

I give the ball a good kick: sending

I say my name: sending

I read a book: receiving and processing.

Here are the answers to the worksheet of the man who is thirsty and takes a drink from the fridge: receiving, processing (and receiving), processing, sending.

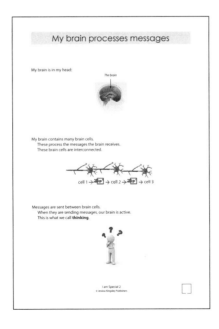

The distinction between the three processes, receiving, processing and sending, is not always clear-cut, because the brain carries out these three actions simultaneously. Furthermore, observing and processing are indivisible: as the man sees the fridge, then the very fact that he sees this image on his retina as 'a fridge' constitutes a certain processing of his observation…

The 'Various worksheets' folder on the CD ROM includes worksheets developed by Howard Childs in the UK and adapted for our use. These illuminate this complicated subject in a very concrete way for young children and adolescents with learning disabilities ('How the brain works (simplified version)'). There are also worksheets on the brain in 'That's me?!'

For those with a young developmental age, it is sometimes advisable to replace the terms 'receives – processes – sends' with 'observes – thinks – does'.

Other examples like the computer analogy are: mobile phones, 'regular' mail or e-mail. In these cases it is also a matter of receiving, processing and sending information.

KINDS OF INTELLIGENCE

Once again, these sessions are not meant to confront the participants with the consequences of autism, for example on social intelligence. However, it is important to provide sufficient exercises on the different kinds of intelligence. Try to avoid having the participants see these examples as points on which they should score. Some children and adolescents have a tendency to emphasise they are, in fact, very good at every example.

For people with high-functioning autism, it is an idea to first let them look up the different kinds of intelligence and then provide examples themselves.

Other forms of intelligence can be added to the list, such as musical intelligence, emotional, kinaesthetic, etc.

The CD ROM includes an appealing, simplified version for young children and adolescents with learning disabilities in the 'That's me?!' version.

MY DIFFERENT KINDS OF INTELLIGENCE

The participant's list of different kinds of intelligence can, again, also be drawn up by another person. This can be a way for the facilitator to monitor how the person with autism sees himself and how realistic their self-image is.

The final remark should also be given due attention. People with high-functioning autism often overestimate the impact and importance of intelligence (or of certain types of intelligence). The term 'common sense' requires additional explanation and it is necessary, in any case, to monitor whether the participant sufficiently understands this notion. It is recommended that you add that it is impossible to measure common sense.

WE NEED OUR BODIES

This worksheet forms the transition to the chapter on 'Being different' – about illness, disorder and disability.

2.3 Resources

- scissors
- glue
- ballpoint pens
- a children's medical encyclopaedia.

2.4 Variations and additions

- There are a lot of clear, illustrated books about the human body to be found in libraries. There are also a lot of educational CD ROMs on the subject. Nowadays, there are also innumerable internet sites of very good quality, providing attractive, concrete information on the body and the brain.

- The functioning of the brain could be illustrated with various mind-puzzle games, such as a game of memory, a game of seven differences between two pictures, visual illusions, drawings with mistakes in them, etc.

- The section on intelligence could be enlarged upon by discussing intelligence tests, the definition of IQ and its distribution over the population (Gaussian curve).

3 Being different

3.1 Aims of these sessions

- to know and be able to distinguish between the terms *disorder*, *illness* and *disability*

- to understand the idea of disability in its relative sense, that is, in relation to one's environment
- to know about the different types of disability
- to gain a general view of the positive and negative aspects of disability
- to know that a disability does not disappear, but that there are ways to minimise the negative consequences arising from it
- to be able to give examples of different aids and forms of support for people with disabilities.

3.2 Method and essential elements

This section causes more confrontation. It all depends, in fact, on how the participant understands the terms *disorder*, *disability* and *limitations*.

The difference between illness, disorder and disability is difficult to explain, especially to younger children and young adolescents or to participants with a learning disability. With them, it is better to omit the worksheets on disorder. However, a worksheet on the differences between illness and disability can follow on from one on illness. Then, different kinds of disability can be discussed just after this. The worksheet on different disabilities needs to be adapted if you omit the worksheets on disorder: delete the first paragraph and do not use 'as a result of a disorder' in this case. The worksheets on the different kinds of disability can also be adapted (the column on disorder in particular must be deleted).

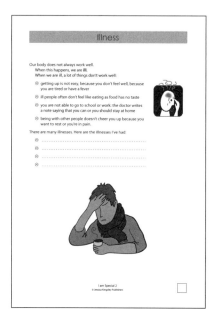

For participants who are a bit older and more able, this part is too short and incomplete. The term disability, above all, deserves more explanation and special attention (see below).

ILLNESS

The difference between curable and incurable diseases often needs more explanation, especially given the following worksheets on the difference between disability and illness.

DISORDER

This is a difficult part. This worksheet need not be used if it is not appropriate or necessary (see above). Moreover, some adults with autism do not consider their autism as a disorder, but as 'being different'. It is best to accept their point of view. These adults are, in our experience, open to an explanation about the social model of disability, in which a disability or handicap is defined also in terms of opportunities and restrictions to be found in the environment (see below).

DISABILITY (VERSUS ILLNESS)

Generally, it is not easy to explain difference. Some participants will have trouble with the imprecision and relativity of the terms 'mild' and 'severe'. Indeed, people with autism need to be presented with measurable, clear and incontestable criteria and terms. These worksheets could conceivably lead to an interminable discussion about what is or is not a disability, or which disability is more significant than another. In fact, a definitive line should not be drawn between disabled and non-disabled.

The following explanation may help when dealing with older or more able participants: illness and disorder are objective and physical terms. It is possible to observe and establish whether an illness is present, even if very complicated instruments and techniques are sometimes necessary. Illness and disorder are also absolute: throughout the world, paralysis is paralysis, regardless of the person's age, skin colour or where they live.

On the other hand, disability is a relative and socio-cultural term. That is, in a given situation, a disability may not constitute an impediment, yet in another situation it may. Someone who has only two fingers will not be hindered in some activities (for example, attending a conference, taking a history class) but it may become a real disability at other times, for example, when playing the piano, using a computer keyboard, or opening some packets.

A disability is not, therefore, a direct consequence of a disorder. The environment plays an equal role, more particularly, the demands of the environment, the aids and forms of support it offers, the opportunities it creates, or not. Before the advent of glasses, severe myopia was a disability. This is no longer the case, or is much less so. Furthermore, a person can also compensate for one or another limitation. For example, a blind person can learn to identify others by paying close attention to body odour or scent.

Figure 7.1 helps explain certain elements:

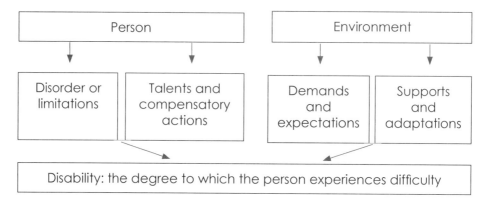

Figure 7.1: Disability model

A disability is not a personal characteristic. The degree to which a person experiences difficulties is related to the balance, or rather the imbalance, between one's own potential and limitations, and the environment.

The model immediately shows the possible actions for reducing a disability: make the disorder or limitations disappear (usually impossible), compensate, adapt expectations, support the person concerned or offer forms of assistance.

DIFFERENT TYPES OF DISABILITY

You may need to fill in the most common types of disability in the left-hand column yourself, but most of the time, a number of 'Socratic' questions which provide clues will prompt the participants to find the answers: physical disability, visual, auditory, learning disability.

If the participant already knows about his autism (as a disability), this can be added as a fifth possibility. What they put in the columns on the right-hand side (part of the body which does not work well, restrictions and examples) gives an overview of what they already know about their autism.

Solutions and aids, Special education and support, Environmental adaptations

Again, it is possible to work in a deductive or inductive way.

Deductive: the facilitator mentions these three categories of aids and support, after which the participant thinks of examples and completes the worksheet.

Inductive: the facilitator asks an overt question like 'what help is available for someone with a disability?' The information given by the participant is written on a paper or a whiteboard, and divided into the three groupings (solutions and aids, special education and support, environmental adaptations). The facilitator then names the three categories and the examples are copied onto the worksheet.

Table 7.1 Some possibilities for disability worksheet

Disability	Supports and aids
Physical disability	• wheelchair • adapted car • lift mechanisms for the bedside or toilet
Visual disability	• Braille • guide dog • white stick • magnifying monitor on the computer
Auditory disability	• finger alphabet • sign language • hearing aid • flashing-light doorbell • vibrating alarm clock
Learning disability	• symbols • big tricycle • communication board

The disorder or deficit that results in a disability is often permanent. For some participants, it is necessary to add the following clarification: 'As long as science fails to cure the disorder.' Indeed, a certain number of people with autism are very interested in science and read a great number of scientific journals that regularly announce progress in state-of-the-art technology, such as electronic devices where someone who could barely hear recovered their hearing (or can hear much better).

In view of the immutability and the seriousness of restrictions, most disabilities are similarly permanent. Even though a person compensates and his environment supports him and is adapted, a good number of situations remain more difficult for someone who has a disability than for someone who does not. The message is the following: a person with a disability can, in principle, just like others achieve a great deal, but this demands more effort, both from the disabled person and from the environment.

PEOPLE WITH A DISABILITY HAVE TALENTS

Here, the facilitator can ask the participant(s) to think of other examples. There are a number of people with disabilities who were or are celebrities: President Franklin Roosevelt was in a wheelchair, Einstein was dyslexic, as is John Irving. At the end of his life Beethoven was deaf, etc. A book of photos of celebrities with disabilities can be very illustrative (see 'That's me?!' in the CD ROM).

PEOPLE WITH A DISABILITY ARE DIFFERENT

This worksheet serves as a summary of and conclusion to the section 'Being different'. To check whether the participant has understood this section, it is possible, before reading the worksheet, to use questions to verify whether the main conclusions are (well) understood. For example: can people with a disability become like people without a disability? What can one do to cope with a disability?

3.3 Resources

- pens
- if necessary, to illustrate: all kinds of aids, such as Braille.

3.4 Variations and additions

- Libraries and publishers have full lists of books on different disabilities and we recommend you visit their websites, especially as we are seeing an increase in publications for young people as well as the production and distribution of films or DVDs.

- There are different experience-oriented games and activities for adolescents and children to understand what a disability is like. Some examples:
  - Blindness and partially sighted: have the participants carry out all kinds of tasks blindfolded, or wearing special glasses.
  - Deafness: have them attempt to have a conversation wearing headphones.
  - A physical disability: have them move with their feet tied together, try to open a door in a sitting position, write something without using their hands (with the pencil in their mouth or between their toes), etc.
  - A learning disability: one of the children leaves the room, while three others invent a new (non-existent) card game. The first child comes back in the room and plays the game but the others don't explain the rules.

- Demonstrating how different aids are used can make the situation more real. Having the children try out some aids themselves can be part of a fun game to lighten the seriousness of this session. Some examples:
  - a short text in Braille and a Braille alphabet card
  - navigate an obstacle course blindfolded, using a white stick
  - a hand-out with the finger alphabet; participants can spell out their names using sign language
  - a wheelchair race
  - combine Arabic, Cyrillic or Chinese writing with symbols, to show how symbols help someone who doesn't understand (written) language.

4 Autism: a special disability
4.1 Aims of these sessions

- to understand that autism is a brain disorder
- to be able to name the two main areas of impairment in autism spectrum disorders (social communication and interaction, flexibility) and be able to give examples relating to each

- to be able to explain why autism is described as a disability
- to understand no one is to blame for their autism and that it has (still unknown) biological causes
- to know the meaning of the concept of a spectrum of autism and to know that all people with an autism spectrum disorder are also different from one another
- to know that an autism spectrum disorder cannot be cured, but that there are various ways of minimising its negative effects
- to be able to give examples of these means and forms of support for people with autism spectrum disorders, as well as examples relating to oneself
- to be aware of the positive and negative aspects of autism
- to not/no longer see autism as something inferior, but as difference.

4.2 Method and essential elements

Again, there are two ways of informing someone about their autism: inductive or deductive.

Inductive: we start by enumerating concrete things with which the participant has difficulty, then placing these into two groups (social communication and interaction, and flexibility). Then explain to him/her that everyone who finds difficulties in these areas has an autism spectrum disorder. This is the bottom-up approach.

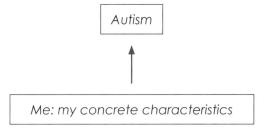

Deductive: we start with the following comment: 'You have autism.' We then explain what this is and what it consists of. Together with the participant, we then attach personal significance to this concept: the participant thinks of examples from their own experience. This is the top-down approach.

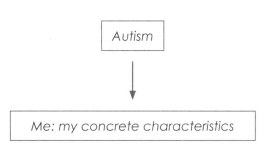

The deductive method is the one applied in the workbook because most children and adolescents have already heard the word 'autism' and usually know it applies to them. However, they often do not know what the term means and they cannot always see in which ways it applies to them. For those who know their diagnosis but do not know really know how it affects them, the deductive method is recommended.

When the participants do not yet know the term 'autism spectrum disorder' and they are also unaware they have the disorder, the inductive method is recommended. Sometimes this also works best with people who doubt their diagnosis.

If the inductive method is used, it is advisable to conclude with, 'And all this is called autism', and to illustrate again the concept of 'autism spectrum disorder' with concrete examples. Furthermore, you must also address the aspects relating to cause, invisibility, a spectrum, aids and the positive and negative consequences.

For participants with 'Asperger's Syndrome' it is necessary to give information on where Asperger's Syndrome belongs on the autism spectrum, from the beginning. A visual representation of the spectrum can be used but risks giving rise to mistaken ideas, such as 'Ah, I am on the side of normality, so I'm much less severely affected than others.' The workbook contains a supplementary worksheet for placing Asperger's Syndrome.

One should also provide complementary information for those with other diagnoses within the spectrum, such as atypical autism, pervasive developmental disorder – not otherwise specified (PDD–NOS), etc.

For some participants, these sessions bring a wealth of information. For some, this is also new information. People with autism are very sensitive to information overload and the speed at which they assimilate information (correctly) is usually slower than that of people without autism. This applies equally to people with high-functioning autism. The facilitator must accordingly pay particular attention to the amount of information given and to the speed at which it is provided.

AUTISM (OVERVIEW)

Depending on the needs of the participants, their prior knowledge and the associations autism has for them, this worksheet can either be done at the beginning of the session or it can be used as a summary at the end.

If it is used at the end, the next worksheet with important questions about autism can be used as an overview.

If necessary, an explanation of the use of the word 'autism' can be given. In this worksheet and the next, it is used as a general term for the autism spectrum. If necessary or desirable, one can replace the word 'autism' by 'autism spectrum disorder' in all the worksheets of *I am Special*.

AUTISM (QUESTIONS)

In addition, the facilitator can ask the participant(s) to write down any other questions. Depending on the nature of their questions, the answers can be incorporated into the worksheets or gone over in a round of supplementary questions at the end of the sessions on autism.

AUTISM IS THE CONSEQUENCE OF A BRAIN DISORDER

Giving examples relating to oneself is not always easy. The link between external behaviour and a brain disorder requires more imagination than people with autism may have. Here, the facilitator should provide help. Additional explanations about autistic thinking, preferably through concise, concrete remarks, can provide greater exactitude and clarity. For some children and youngsters, it is enough to tell them that they have autism because they have a special brain, a brain that works differently.

THE CAUSE OF AUTISM

For some people with autism, news of an hereditary cause can be understood as 'the parents' fault'. It may also raise the question of which of the two parents is to blame. It is recommended that the difference between cause and fault is explained. A concrete example may be: there is a difference between hurting someone by accident (you are the cause of the pain, but you could not do anything about it because it was 'an accident') and deliberately hurting someone (in this case, you are guilty). In the case of hereditary disorders, the disorder comes from (grand-) parents, but they are not guilty. It is impossible to deliberately transmit hereditary disorders.

AUTISM IS A DISABILITY

Here, the aim is not at all to address the impairments caused by autism. The worksheet provides a chance to check again what associations the participant has with autism. The participants may find examples in the previous worksheets on their and others' weaker points.

The social model of disability, used as a preliminary to the session on disability, can be adapted according to the situation. If they wish, the person with autism can draw up a supplementary list of situations where autism is a disability and situations where it is not. The conclusion can be: 'I have autism all the time and everywhere but this does mean that all the time and everywhere I have a disability.'

COMPLICATIONS RESULTING FROM AUTISM

1. Interacting and communicating with others.
2. Thinking and acting with ease and flexibility.

People with autism notice other people's autism and shortcomings quickly and much more easily than their own. They experience difficulties with self-reflection. This is why it can be useful for the facilitator or someone who knows the participant well (a teacher, an educator or a tutor) to add concrete examples.

Sometimes, because of their autistic thinking or their resistance to their diagnosis, some people with autism think of this list of examples as a kind of score sheet: having more marks means having more autism, or more serious autism. It is important to stress beforehand this is not the case.

This will be addressed again when they are given information on the autism spectrum.

OTHER COMPLICATIONS

Apart from the two main areas of impairment already mentioned, people with autism are also affected by certain sensory stimuli. Complete sensory overload is, for instance, a common difficulty. Also, someone with autism can have other restrictions or disorders as well (for explanations on learning disabilities, see the worksheets in 'That's me?!' on the CD ROM). This page of the workbook is optional.

ASPERGER'S SYNDROME

This worksheet is for participants with Asperger's Syndrome. For other participants, it can be omitted. For those with another diagnosis (for example, PDD-NOS), a similar worksheet can be developed that goes over the same information.

EVERYONE WITH AUTISM IS DIFFERENT AND UNIQUE

Here, additional information on the concept of a spectrum of autism can be provided. A description of the spectrum that uses qualitative terms (such as the different colours of the spectrum or different positions in a room) is preferable to using a quantitative term. Thus, a different colour can be attributed to each of the two main areas of impairment, a third colour to sensory difficulties, and group participants can make up their own 'palette'. From a comparison between these, it can be seen that the final colour is different for each.

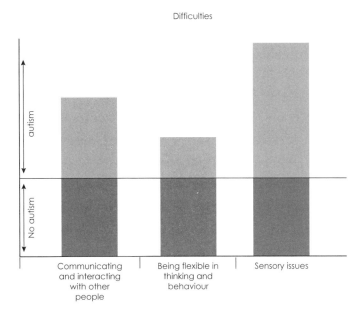

Figure 7.2: Complications due to autism

However, it is sometimes necessary to present something in a quantitatively visual way, in order to illustrate the difference between those who belong on the spectrum and those who do not. Indeed, some participants may argue that everyone can experience difficulties interacting, with communication or when dealing with changes. In this case, this can be visualised by graphs or bar charts which illustrate the main areas of impairment and show the boundary between autism and 'normal variation' (see Figure 7.2 for an example of a possible chart).

Example
If one version is created for each group participant, together the versions clearly show the diversity within the spectrum: one person experiences more difficulties in the field of social interaction and communication, while another may have more difficulty with flexibility.

AUTISM, AN INVISIBLE DISABILITY …BUT NOT ENTIRELY INVISIBLE
The facilitator can ask the participant(s) to give examples of situations in which others showed a lack of understanding towards them or when it was an advantage for them that their autism cannot be seen.

The list of 'erroneous' statements about the person (mad, stupid) can be expanded: 'What other things are said, that are wrong, about you?' An example: 'That I'm stubborn.'

AUTISM CANNOT BE CURED

The facilitator can expect questions such as, 'And what if they do find a drug?' Here, it is advisable to say that the discovery of a remedy cannot be ruled out, but this is not going to happen tomorrow or even next year and it is better to find other ways of coping with autism.

Furthermore, if desired or necessary, the facilitator can warn of the risks of experimenting with all sorts of medication or so-called miracle cures and therapies.

With older or high-functioning persons, it is possible to engage in a philosophical approach, to find out what is behind the idea of being cured. Here, you can quote people like Jim Sinclair,[92] who explicitly say or write that they do not want to be cured of their autism, because they would no longer be themselves. Such statements in which the person rejects the view of autism as something inferior are also very useful in the worksheet on talents.

...BUT THERE'S A LOT WE CAN DO

It is important to stress that the person with autism can do something themselves to deal with their autism. Examples are an open attitude, being motivated to seek support, asking for help, or a personal search for all kinds of aids as well as the will to use them. It is useful to mention these things to children or adolescents who consider their autism to be a good excuse, for example, 'I can't help forgetting to do my homework, it's because of my autism.'

The social model of disability introduced earlier can now be altered to take autism into account:

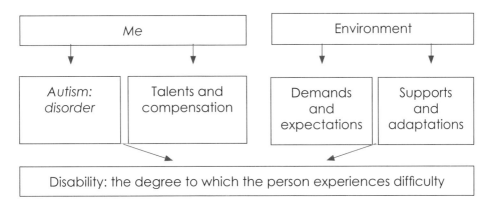

Figure 7.3: Is autism always a disability?

The degree of difficulty experienced by the person or the extent to which they're held back in certain circumstances (disability) is not only the consequence of their autism and is certainly not a direct consequence of it. The person with autism can get round or reduce certain restrictions caused by their autism thanks to their talents or their compensatory strategies. Autism is a personal characteristic but the disability it causes is not. We cannot take away the autism, but it is possible to find solutions by working on three factors (compensatory actions, environmental demands and supports). The worksheets on 'How do I deal with difficulties caused by my autism?' provide further explanations.

PEOPLE WITH AUTISM ALSO HAVE TALENTS

Sometimes, autism has its advantages. Although it is not easy and with some participants this runs counter to their personal experiences of their disability, the facilitator can still ask them to think of examples of disadvantages, advantages and assets of their autism. And the facilitator can always make the following statement: 'Your different way of thinking includes some originality, because other people don't think like you.'

The positive sides to autism

Due to autism, it is impossible to accomplish certain things. Likewise, some activities are more difficult to carry out because of autism.
 In certain situations, therefore, autism is a **handicap**, a burden.
 For example: autism can be a handicap when someone with the disorder plays or works with other people. He/she has difficulties in these activities because of their autism.

> *My example: when is autism a burden for my brother/my sister?*
> *For him/her, autism is a handicap when:*

In other situations, autism is **not a handicap**. The person with autism is capable of carrying out some things just as well as so-called normal people.
 For example: some people with autism are not affected by their disorder when they ride a bike, go for a walk or get dressed.

> *My example: when is autism not a burden for my brother or my sister?*
> *For him/her, autism is not a handicap when:*

And sometimes, thanks to autism, my brother/sister can do some things better than others! In some situations, autism is even a **talent**.
 For example: some people with autism have an excellent memory and can easily retain all sorts of facts. Thus, compared to others, they can be better at remembering dates of birth.

> *My example: what is easier for my brother or sister, thanks to their autism?*
> *For him/her, autism is a talent when:*

I am Special 2
© Jessica Kingsley Publishers

WHAT I FIND IS ALL RIGHT ABOUT MY AUTISM, POSITIVE ASPECTS TO AUTISM

The participant can complete this whether or not they can think of things that really are alright about their autism. Making a much longer list of 'not all right' things is not necessarily a bad sign. Autism imposes a number of restrictions and difficulties. When the participant fills in mainly negative elements, the facilitator can introduce the worksheet on the positive aspects of autism. People with autism can complete the worksheet themselves as well as ask others to do it.

With older and high-functioning persons, a list of 'strong points' of people with autism can be drawn up and can be a starting point for a discussion on 'My strong points thanks to my autism'.

TRUE OR FALSE?

These questions enable the facilitator to check whether the information given has been truly understood.

Here are the answers:

1. false 2. false 3. true 4. true 5. false

6. true 7. false 8. false 9. true 10. false

4.3 Variations and additions

- To conclude, a text on autism or Asperger's Syndrome can be added. Another idea is to suggest a FAQ (frequently asked questions) session on autism. The 'Various worksheets' folder on the CD ROM has an example of FAQs.

- For (young) adults: read and discuss books written by people with autism, for example Liane Holliday Willey,[93] Gunilla Gerland,[94] Temple Grandin,[95] Donna Williams.[96] In the discussion, the person with autism can say what they recognise (or don't recognise) in these books. The facilitator can prepare a sheet with two columns: what I recognise in myself and what I do not recognise. Take care that this task is not taken as confirmation or invalidation of the diagnosis: everyone with autism is different!

- For young people, the book by Luke Jackson,[97] written when he was 13, is very instructive. The detective novel by Mark Haddon[98] is equally great. The book introduces autistic thinking perfectly, without even explaining autism directly.

- Likewise, there are a number of books on autism for children. Most of the time, they are written for siblings, but some can also be used for children with autism.

- Some high-functioning adolescents and most high-functioning adults likewise read books on autism, such as *Autistic Thinking – This is the Title*.[99] The books can be a starting point for possible discussions on these persons' autism.

- Besides books and texts, videos available on the internet are another option for adults.

- Make a collage about the positive and negative aspects of autism.

- Write a comic strip about autism.

- Have the young person write a booklet explaining autism to others.

- Prepare a PowerPoint presentation on autism and its characteristics.

- To finish, the person can summarise what they have learned about themselves (in the different sections). The 'That's Me?!' version ('Who am I?') gives an example for adolescents with a learning disability. For young people and adults with average intelligence, this can even take the form of a 'portfolio' in which they keep personal information. This could consist of information they wish to share with others and could be used for transition to a (new) place of work or residence. With this kind of portfolio, they do not have to read or show the entire *I am Special* workbook.

- Once the sessions have ended, preferably a few weeks after the final session, it is recommended that an extra question and answer session be organised. Experience has shown that, for people with autism, it generally takes a few weeks to truly assimilate new information, especially information as complex and abstract as that regarding autism. Therefore it often happens that questions arise some time later. It can help enormously if, at the end of the sessions, they are given a sheet of paper on which they can write down their questions as they arise. In this way, they do not have to worry they'll lose or forget their important questions. Such a sheet can also serve to channel their questions and give them a place. It may also avoid the situation where they go to just anyone with questions about their autism. This sheet can be used to complete the worksheet on Frequently Asked Questions found on the CD ROM.

- The facilitator can also speak about the significance of autism for a person's future. In this way, *I am Special* ends with a sort of personal project for the future. 'That's me?!' includes a clear example for adolescents with a learning disability.

- For young people of average intelligence, 'What can I do about my autism?' is ideal as a follow-up to this chapter on autism.

Chapter 8

The Big Book about Me

1 Context

'The big book about me' is an original adaptation of the workbook, for young children. It was developed by Lisbet Van Gijzeghem of *Het Anker* ('The Anchor') in Bruges, Belgium. For the supplements and amendments, she was assisted by Marjan Deleu and Sylvie Carette.

Het Anker is a special school offering ongoing support for children, adolescents and adults with autism spectrum disorders, but without a learning disability.

2 Target group

'The big book about me' is geared towards primary school children, who are of (nearly) average intelligence. The minimum age is around nine years; the child must have sufficient command of language and communication skills and among other things, be able to read and write. The worksheets which include more concrete information (the human body, its inside and its outside) can also be used with younger children (from six or seven years), as long as enough attention is given to further simplification of the information.

Since the layout and content are adapted for younger children, 'The big book about me' can also be used with older children (12 to 15 years) who have a mild learning disability or whose level of intelligence is lower.

3 Description

'The big book about me' is based entirely on the *I am Special* workbook. The sequence and content of the chapters are practically the same as in the original workbook.

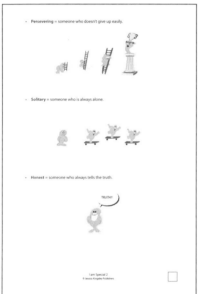

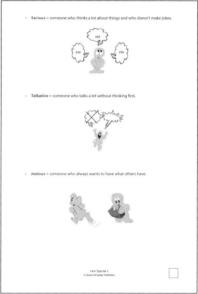

In 'The big book about me', the information and language are even more concrete. The worksheets are also more visual (with drawings, use of colour) and there are more activities. Furthermore, the link between the different chapters is made more explicit and there are more repetitions and summaries.

For some children, the illustrations and additional activities may represent more of a burden than they succeed in giving clarity; they could divert attention away from the essential information. With these children, using 'The big book about me' in its current form is strongly inadvisable. It is therefore recommended the worksheets are 'simplified' (fewer colours, fewer illustrations, less information on one page) before they are used with children who are quickly affected by visual overload.

Studies with the target group of children in primary schools have shown, often, that more emphasis should be given to the distinction between the inside and outside of the body. Supplementary worksheets are provided for children who experience difficulty with understanding this difference.

Despite all the adaptations, it cannot be said that 'The big book about me' makes explaining these complex subjects 'simpler'. Individualised adaptations (removing or adding some parts) as well as providing further details remains indispensable. Just as with the original *I am Special* workbook, 'The big book about me' is only a glimpse into this way of working. The well-being of the child, along with constant attention to motivation, remains essential.

4 Manual

The manual for *I am Special* is also applicable to 'The big book about me', taking into account, naturally, the fact that the actual worksheets for the two different versions vary. With sufficient knowledge of the manual for *I am Special*, most of the worksheets here speak for themselves.

CD ROM documents

The documents on the CD ROM comprise a complete version of 'The big book about me':

- Contents
- Introduction
- My personal details
- My outside
- My inside
- My body
- My brain: a very special part of my body
- Being different
- Autism

Author: Lisbet Van Gijzeghem

Chapter 9

That's Me?!

1 Background

'That's me?!' was developed by six students at Limburg Catholic University College's (Katholieke Hogeschool Limburg, Netherlands) department of social work, in collaboration with the social welfare centre, *Ter Engelen*, in Maaseik, Belgium. The social welfare centre *Ter Engelen* provides care and support for people with disabilities. The centre consists primarily of a residential school for children with mild, moderate or severe learning disabilities, often combined with emotional and/or behavioural problems.

Experience had shown that the original version of *I am Special* was not always suitable for the children and adolescents who had mild learning disabilities combined with autism. That's why the *I am Special* workbook was adapted for this specific target group.

2 Target group

'That's me?!' is intended for children and young people (from the age of 12) with a mild learning disability. With its plain language, layout and especially its numerous exercises, this adapted version is also ideal for children and young people with an (almost) average level of intelligence (9 to 11 years) as well as for young adults with a learning disability. Although writing and reading are limited as much as possible in this adaptation, the ability to read and write (if necessary with someone's help) is also a prerequisite for this version, as well as being able to attend sufficiently to the exercises.

3 Description

3.1 Title

'That's me?!' was chosen, instead of '*I am Special*'. The question mark indicates that the workbook tries to find answers to questions posed by adolescents about their disability. The exclamation mark highlights the idea that everyone is unique. The young person should feel proud of who he or she is and not feel inferior to others.

3.2 Additions and adaptations

In view of the fact that language skills and an aptitude for abstract thinking are limited in adolescents with a mild learning disability, the most important changes to the original workbook are the adaptations to the text and layout of the pages. Complex words, as well as complicated phrases, have been simplified. Abstract terms are explained more or are given a visual representation. In general, the worksheets contain more drawings and pictures than in *I am Special*. The worksheet on hobbies is an example: a number of hobbies are visually represented and the young person can simply tick their own hobbies (see CD ROM document). The layout of the pages has also been adapted so that the worksheets are clearer.

For children and adolescents with autism and a learning disability, teaching activities (oral or written) that are too lengthy are not a positive experience. That's why, at very regular intervals, worksheets alternate with short games or activities the participants can complete themselves. This variety makes the sessions more enjoyable for children and adolescents. In the original workbook, Peter Vermeulen had suggested choosing one image that would symbolise the construction of the workbook, such as a house. In 'That's me?!', this house is not represented by a drawing but well and truly exists: it consists of a wooden playhouse or chalet about a metre high, with three floors. It also has a removable roof. Each floor of the chalet corresponds to a chapter in the workbook. As one goes along, progressing through the exercises, the participant also ascends through the house, to arrive by the end of term in the roof, which symbolises autism. Together, we look for a variety of engaging materials to introduce into the 'home'.

In addition to the adaptations made to the workbook exercises, each floor of the chalet contains material related to their experience, a visual tool, preferably some form of support (see below).

Other complementary exercises have likewise been prepared. In view of the fact that children and adolescents with autism and a learning disability have a 'dual disability', two supplementary exercises have been added to explain a learning disability. Adolescents with disabilities often ask questions about their future. That's why at the end of this workbook, a topic on their future has been added. Thus work, housing and relationships are covered in new worksheets.

The transfer to real life of what has been learned during the sessions is also given particular attention. Children and adolescents do not always spontaneously generalise what they have learned to situations outside the learning environment. At the end of each chapter, there is not only a worksheet summarising the main conclusions, there is also an illustration of a tree available (see, as an example, the last worksheet on intelligence; the CD ROM documents also include the tree on a blank page, for use with each chapter, as long as the title has been completed appropriately).

> #### What I've learned about my intelligence
>
> What I am proud of:
> ....
> ....
> ....
> ....
>
> What I can learn more about or improve:
> ....
> ....
> ....
> ....
>
> I am Special 2
> © Jessica Kingsley Publishers

The tree symbolises opportunities for growth in every human being. In life, there are highs and lows. Each year, a tree loses its leaves, yet new ones appear with each spring, and the tree continues to grow. (For a young person with a dual disability, this figurative use of the term 'tree' is not easy to understand *prima facie*. Using clear explanations, it is the facilitator's task to get the meaning of this symbol across to the young person.)

At the end of each chapter, the young person notes at the side of the tree the important information they've learned about themselves, by looking over the chapter: a positive attribute (something of which they are proud) and a less positive attribute (something on which they are going to do more work). The young person and the facilitator can find a task corresponding to each point – homework to be done for the following week. The young person can, for example, show someone one of these positive attributes, or apply it in a certain situation. They can give more attention to the less positive attributes. For example, at the end of the first chapter, the conclusion may be to play with LEGO® as a hobby (positive attribute). An example of homework: the young person can show another child how to make a house out of LEGO®. In the chapter on character, when a student realises he argues a lot with a certain student (less positive attribute), he can select the following homework: to try to complete at least one activity with this student without bickering.

Finally, this adaptation also takes into account the significant amount of support required for a young person with autism and a learning disability to have a positive self-image. During all the work carried out in the workbook, the young person constantly meets their own image head-on. This confrontation influences the image they have of themselves. Often, people with autism and a learning disability have already suffered many setbacks in their lives. That's why they can be very sensitive to criticism and negative remarks. As they are sometimes confronted head-on in the workbook with themselves and their disability, they risk developing more of a negative self-esteem (again). We want to avoid this. That's why, in this adapted workbook, we have opted for a playful approach. Through the use of play materials and appealing activities, we try to make the sessions as enjoyable as possible. Likewise, we try to portray as much as possible the positive, delightful aspects of the person. This can be done particularly with a smiley face. The facilitator has a set of smiley face stickers (the well-known small, yellow faces) for use in different ways. At the end of each session, the young person can, for example, put a smiley face sticker on a finished worksheet. Giving out the stickers is thus synonymous with a compliment from the facilitator. Another way of working: each time the young person discovers something positive about themselves, something of which they are proud, they put a sticker in the margin. If the facilitator wishes, they can also, at the end of each session, thanks to the smiley faces, prepare a page going over all their positive attributes again, under the title: 'What I am proud of'.

The workbook uses symbols. For young people, these increase the predictability of the work method during the sessions.

 The crayon refers to a writing exercise.

The house refers to an activity linked to the educational material in the chalet (see below).

The tree refers to a personal conclusion and to a transfer activity.

The smiley face refers to a compliment.

3.3 Educational (play) material

'I am special' contains four chapters (I am unique, My body, Being different and Autism) and for each chapter, a certain number of engaging activities are incorporated into the house. The material used to this effect is described below. For most of these activities, you can make the materials yourself. The CD ROM contains pictures of some of these materials.

CHAPTER 1: I AM UNIQUE (GROUND FLOOR)
My outside

- *Book of photos*: this scrapbook containing all sorts of magazine photos is used to point out that the appearance of all human beings is comprised of both similarities and differences. For instance, on one page of the book, only people with brown hair are depicted. Nevertheless, each person's other characteristics are different.

- *Large sheet of paper*: to shed light on the outline of the human body, there is a large sheet of white paper in the first drawer of the wooden house. A life-size drawing of the young person can be traced on this sheet. The young person lies down on the paper and the facilitator traces the contour of his or her silhouette. Then, the young person can draw in their physical characteristics: eyes, freckles, glasses, etc.

- *'Families' and 'Everyone is Unique' books of photos*: in order to show that everyone is unique and there are no two people alike, two books can be used. In the 'Families' book there are twins who closely resemble each other, but nevertheless, are unique. There are also families whose members resemble each other yet who are at the same time very different. In the 'Everyone is Unique' book, there are different kinds of people. There are small people, big people, people with blond hair, brown hair, etc. There is also a diversity of ethnicity. The books are made from photos from magazines and the internet.

- *'Guess Who?'*: thanks to the Hasbro game, 'Guess Who?', where the aim is to discover as quickly as possible, through questions about appearance, a card the other player holds in their hand, the young person learns about different physical characteristics in a fun way.

My inside

- *Book of photos of skills*: this scrapbook brings together different magazine photos to show all sorts of skills. The concrete presentation can help the young person to discover activities in which they he or she is gifted or less gifted. If the young person is agreeable, they can show their skill or find an example for the following session. For example, a young person who draws very well can do a drawing during the session or make a painting for the next session.

CHAPTER 2: MY BODY (FIRST FLOOR)
My body: the outside

- *Poster*: this floor contains two posters drawn and coloured by the participant, one of an adolescent girl and one of an adolescent boy. The participant identifies themselves from the two drawings and receives different cards with the names of parts of the body. They place these in the right place (with Velcro or adhesive).

My body: the inside

- *Large images of the body*: A quick search will yield many publications available in the UK and US, with everything children want to know about this wonderful structure.
- A *doll* can be used to show the inside of a person's body, along with visual identification of the location of certain organs in the body. To simplify things, not all the organs are represented. The facilitator can also encourage the participants to indicate on themselves where the various organs are placed.

- *Games*: there are some fun board games available on the theme of the human body.

My brain: a special part of my inside

- For understanding how the brain works, some *mind-puzzle games* are advised before completing the worksheets. The house includes, in particular, Hasbro's 'Guess Where?' (but any other game of memory can also be used and it is easy to make your own) and a game of observation (guess what I'm feeling, Kim's game (a memory game for which you collect on a tray a number of objects – knife, pencil, pen, stone, plastic jewellery and so on)). Cover the objects with a cloth then uncover them for one minute. The players write down everything they remember. (For people who cannot write, they can 'whisper' it to a support person, or you can give them a set of cards with pictures of the items on the tray and you add pictures of other items, so they have to choose.) The one who remembers most wins the game, etc.

The brain receives, processes and sends information

- *Book of the five senses*: thanks to this scrapbook of images of the five senses, the abstract term 'senses' becomes concrete and visual.

- *Posters*: for each of the three stages (receiving, processing, sending), there is a large image glued onto an A3 size card. On different cards, there are example of these stages of observing, thinking and doing. The young person has to stick these onto the most appropriate large card (using Velcro). For example, a card saying 'I taste something sour' belongs on the 'receiving' card.

Intelligence

- These worksheets are adapted in such a way that each time an activity is completed, it is used in order to illustrate the different kinds of intelligence. If the facilitator wishes, these supplementary worksheets can be added to 'the home'. The page on technical intelligence refers to building a robot. The robot (LEGO®) and the corresponding plan can be put in the house. Naturally, any other object which involves technical understanding can be used instead of the robot.

CHAPTER 3: BEING DIFFERENT (SECOND FLOOR)
Solutions and aids

- *Posters*: a large poster is prepared for each kind of disability. All kinds of aids are represented on cards (pictures from magazines or the internet). In this task, the young person sticks the cards on the right poster (using Velcro). A card depicting a guide-dog for the blind, for example, is stuck on the poster for visual disability.

Environmental adaptations

- *Book of photos*: this scrapbook contains all kinds of pictures of adaptations for people with a disability (for example, areas of tactile paving).

People with disabilities also have talents

- *Celebrities who have a disability*: this hand-made book brings together photos of famous people who have a disability, such as Stephen Hawking, Andrea Bocelli, etc. The same book, or a complementary book, can also contain photos of famous people who have autism.

CHAPTER 4: AUTISM (ROOF)
Autism is an invisible disability

- *Book of photos*: to impress upon the young people that autism cannot be seen on the outside, we ask them to indicate which individuals have autism in the book of photos on the ground floor (see 'My outside').

Naturally, other tasks can be integrated as well. The aim is not to make the workbook a tedious or academic tool. With adolescents who have a learning disability, it is recommended one uses activities related to their experience as much as possible, with resources that are fun, educational and attractive. Psychoeducation is oriented more towards the process than the results, which promotes a relaxed atmosphere.

4 Manual

The manual for *I am Special* (Chapter 7) also applies to 'That's me?!' For this special version, the expanded or adapted worksheets speak for themselves – as long as one is familiar with the manual for *I am Special*.

To complete the worksheets on autism, the facilitator can ask the young person to fill in the 'Who am I?' page, as a sort of summary or final evaluation.

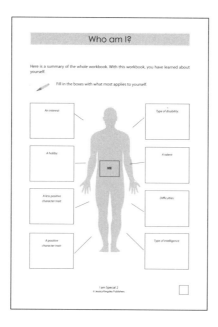

My future

The exercises on 'My future' can serve as another supplement. They give the participant the opportunity to ask questions about their future (where will I live, work, etc.?). The worksheets allow the facilitator to verify to what extent, after the sessions, the young person has adopted a 'more realistic' view of themselves and their future. Thus they can serve as an assessment, as it were. They also provide information for the young person on the different kinds of housing, work and relationships for people with (learning) disabilities. This information can lead to a Socratic dialogue about the topic concerned.

The worksheets are:

- My future (Contents)
- What questions do I have about my future? (list of questions)
- Housing (draw the house of your dreams)
- Different kinds of housing (two explanatory pages and a space where the young person notes down their options)
- Work (draw or describe the job of your dreams)
- Different kinds of work (explanations and a space where the young person notes down their options)
- Relationships (my questions about relationships and different kinds of relationships are enumerated).

In this version, the results of the 'My future' theme are very cursory. The worksheets serve above all to draw up a list of ideas for the young person and to open up a dialogue about their future. To continue with the topic in depth, the methodology and material from literature about personal future planning can be used.

CD ROM documents

The CD ROM documents do not contain the complete version but only the exercises addressed in the text and the newly developed exercises:

- Contents
- My hobbies
- The senses and how the brain works
- Intelligence
- Learning disabilities
- Autism
- Who am I?
- My future: housing, work, relationships
- The tree

Authors:

Elke Gilissen Gudrun Janssen Sophie Maris Chris Put Bert Vanderheyden Karolien Vermaelen	Limburg Catholic University College
Rose-Linde Breels Els Buntinx	Dienstencentrum Ter Engelen

Chapter 10
I am Special for Siblings

1 Background

Originally, *I am Special* was meant for use with people with autism only. However, the brothers and sisters of someone with autism also need clear, comprehensive explanations of autism. They face autism every day and questions on the subject undoubtedly arise, even if they do not ask questions directly. Sometimes siblings have distorted ideas about autism, for example that the disorder is going to go away or that their brother or sister deliberately behaves in an annoying way. Evidence from research and practice has shown that the difficulties experienced by siblings due to the presence of a child with a disability decrease sharply if they receive detailed information explaining the behaviour of their brother or sister.

In the first manual for *I am Special*, we mentioned that the workbook could also be used with siblings. To do this, we had yet to adapt some of the exercises. These adaptations, made in 2000, were available as an appendix for everyone registered with *I am Special*. The version for siblings is now fully rewritten in the CD ROM documents.

2 Target group

In its current form, the workbook can be used with siblings aged eight to ten years. For younger children, some aspects of the current version are too difficult, particularly the chapter on how the brain works and certain parts about autism.

Nevertheless, answers are available for younger children, such as in books with text and pictures: *All About My Brother*;[100] *Brotherly Feelings:*

Me, My Emotions, and My Brother with Asperger's Syndrome;[101] *My Brother is Different*.[102] (See also 'Literature Suggestions' below.)

3 Aims

The aim of the workbook is the same as that for an individual with autism: to give clear explanations of the disorder. The aim is not only to give explanations of the disability but above all to increase understanding.

On this point, we repeat that *I am Special* provides information but the work does not end there. The information then needs to be applied to real life. In other words, *I am Special* is just the beginning. Books written specially for siblings as well as meetings provided specially for them can serve as supplements.

4 Description

The themes of *I am Special* for siblings are the same as those in the original workbook. We have expressly chosen to make the topics 'my outside' and 'my inside' applicable to siblings and not to talk about the child with autism in this chapter. An understanding of their own individuality as well as an awareness of their own limitations and talents allows them to identify more easily with the individuality of their brother or sister with a disability. However, for talking about a brother or sister with autism, these worksheets can also be adapted a second time.

The topic about autism has been adapted: the words 'I', 'my', 'myself' are replaced with 'brother' or 'sister', 'he' or 'she' and 'him' or 'her'. As well, the chapter on autism is followed by a section that specifically addresses the position of siblings: 'What does it mean to have a brother or sister with autism?'

Finally, we also provide exercises to help siblings when they need/want to explain their brother or sister's autism to others: to their friends, family, at school, to strangers. When they've finished the workbook, they can make a small card with which they will be able to explain their brother or sister's autism (or Asperger's Syndrome).

4.1 The whole workbook or only the part about autism?

Depending on the age and past history of the siblings (how much they already know, their experiences), one can use the whole workbook, certain parts or only the chapter on autism.

It is recommended, especially with younger children (under ten years), that the whole workbook is used. Younger children often still don't know enough about topics such as the personality, differences between individuals and brain function. Just as for their brother or sister with autism, this knowledge is necessary for a complete and accurate understanding of the chapter on autism.

Initial trials of the workbook with some children without autism showed that the autism friendly ways of working (structure, simple language, measured use of information, variation between reading and writing) suited them, as well.

5 The worksheets

The explanations for the original workbook apply also to the topics 'I am unique', 'My body' and 'Being different'. The supplements, play activities and the suggestions for reading can equally be used with siblings. For the chapter on autism, the explanations in the original version are used in large part. It is advisable to familiarise yourself with the manual of the original *I am Special* workbook, because below there are only the specific suggestions and adaptations for using *I am Special* with siblings.

AUTISM: A SPECIAL DISABILITY

Besides the objectives already mentioned in the manual for the original version, the worksheets in this part, adapted for siblings, are also designed to help the participants:

- better define and understand the behaviour of their brother or sister with autism
- understand the effects of having a brother or sister who has autism
- understand the positive and negative aspects of having a brother or sister with autism
- express their emotions about having a brother or sister who has autism
- have an idea of how autism can be explained to others.

Depending on the siblings' prior knowledge, autism can be approached inductively or deductively. If the participants already know the word, the existing order of the worksheets can be followed. If they do not already know the word, then it is preferable to use an inductive method (for further explanation of these two working methods, see the explanations in *I am Special*, pp.115–116).

The text uses brother/sister, he/she throughout, so that the workbook can be used by both sexes. The siblings can delete as appropriate. Sometimes, there are dotted lines: the participants can fill in the name of their brother or sister.

AUTISM (INTRODUCTORY PAGE)
For siblings, it is preferable to start by responding to their questions. Only later or at the end of this series of worksheets will a summary sheet be given.

ESSENTIAL ISSUES IN AUTISM
In comparison with the original workbook, here we mention some questions which are more typical of siblings, such as 'Can I catch autism, too?' The facilitator can also ask them to write down other questions about autism. Depending on the nature of the questions, answers can either be addressed during the exercises, or during a new questions session, once the sessions on autism are finished.

AUTISM IS THE RESULT OF A DISORDER OF THE BRAIN
Just as in the original workbook, supplementary information on autistic thinking, a preferably concise and concrete explanation, can provide further clarification and shed light on things here. The idea that people with autism 'act differently' needs further clarification, especially for younger children. The facilitator can help them by asking them to come up with some of their brother or sister's 'strange' or 'odd' behaviours. This exercise assumes that the participant is familiar with the functions of the brain (receiving – processing – sending). Siblings, particularly younger ones, have not always acquired this knowledge. The facilitator is then faced with two options: either he or she goes over the worksheets on how the brain works, using one of the versions available on the CD ROM, or he or she does not use these worksheets and replaces them with other activities, explaining that children with autism behave differently or oddly sometimes, or that they are more challenging than other children, but that they do not do so and are not like this on purpose.

THE CAUSE OF AUTISM
Siblings may ask whether it is possible for them to get autism, when you mention the hereditary causes of this disorder. From here on (the exercise on 'autism is incurable'), it is made clear that autism is not contagious. If the

brother or sister does not have autism at the moment, he or she will not have it later on.

It is important to clarify, because children can think that later on, they too may eventually have autism. Depending on their age, siblings may also ask if their own children might have autism. Older children, especially, ask this question. It is not an easy one to answer. Due to the hereditary nature of autism, the risk is not absent; it is even relatively significant. However, it is impossible to determine the magnitude of the risk. Nevertheless, the response given must be honest and statements such as 'don't worry' or 'your children may well not have autism' are not. Supplementary explanations about *genetic counselling* can be given to siblings who are a bit older. Although this gives no definite answer on the amount of risk, this type of medical advice, however, can support them in their decision to have children or not.

Just as in the workbook for people with autism, the facilitator must place sufficient emphasis on siblings' issues of guilt.

AUTISM IS A DISABILITY

With older siblings (from 14 years), it is advisable to use an adapted worksheet which includes the implications of the social model of disability (see the explanation in the *I am Special* version, important points in the chapter on 'Being different').

DIFFICULTIES DUE TO AUTISM

1. Communicating and interacting with others
2. flexibility of thought and behaviour.

To supplement remarks on these impairments, a supplementary exercise (optional) can be given on other characteristics such as sensory hypersensitivity, perception of detail, splinter skills or mental blocks and blockages of action.

PEOPLE WITH AUTISM ARE ALSO DIFFERENT FROM
ONE ANOTHER, THE AUTISM SPECTRUM

If the participants know other people who have autism, apart from their own brother or sister, the facilitator can create another table in which they can record the names and characteristics of other people with autism, in order to compare them with their brother or sister.

Asperger's Syndrome

If the brother or sister has Asperger's Syndrome, the supplementary worksheets on this topic from the original workbook can be used. With some adaptations, this worksheet can also be used with siblings of a child who has a diagnosis other than autism, for example PDD-NOS.

Autism is an invisible disability ...but not entirely invisible!

Unlike in the original workbook, here the table about the advantages and disadvantages of autism is not filled in. The participants can record both the advantages and disadvantages of this invisibility for their brother or sister and the advantages and disadvantages for themselves. If they choose the latter option, the facilitator can ask them to think of positive and negative aspects for their brother or sister, as well. In this way, they are encouraged to put themselves in their siblings' place.

The following information can be added to the list of 'mistaken' descriptions of the person (crazy, stupid): 'What do others say about your brother or sister that is totally wrong?'

Autism is incurable...

To finish off the original version, it is necessary also to mention the fact that autism is not contagious.

But we can do something about it

Here, the subject deals only with what others can do about autism. What the siblings can undertake will be addressed later in the chapter 'Having a brother or sister with autism'. The facilitator can, if he or she wishes, reverse the order of the two worksheets.

People with autism also have talents and My brother/my sister is special and unique!

On the dotted lines, the participants fill in the name of their brother or sister who has autism.

True or false?

Here are the answers:

1. false	2. false	3. true	4. true	5. false
6. true	7. false	8. false	9. true	10. false

A certain number of supplementary worksheets are now added to the originals, about the experience of having a brother or sister who has autism:

HAVING A BROTHER OR SISTER WITH AUTISM IS NOT SO GREAT, SOMETIMES

This worksheet can open up a discussion, particularly about the following subjects:

- having to take care of an older brother or sister
- withstanding the pressure from parents on the 'normal' children to show a good example – not being allowed to do certain things because of their brother or sister's autism
- feeling responsible for their brother or sister who has autism
- needing to or wanting to intervene and defend their brother or sister or autism when he/she is being made fun of or teased
- missing out on things other children can enjoy or activities that others are allowed to do.

If the participants mention activities they cannot do because of their sibling's autism, it can be important to help them find solutions. A supplementary worksheet with two columns can be used. In the left-hand column, they record what they cannot do or do not know how to do because of their sibling's autism and in the right-hand column what they might do or conceivable solutions. For example:

> *In the left column:* 'We can't go to an amusement park because it's too crowded for my brother.'

> *In the right column:* 'I could maybe ask my cousins to take me when they're going to an amusement park.'

HAVING A BROTHER OR SISTER WITH AUTISM IS GREAT SOMETIMES

These worksheets simply serve to underline the fact that, if you have a brother or sister who is special, you are special too!

HAVING A BROTHER OR SISTER WHO HAS AUTISM, SOMETIMES I FEEL DIFFERENT

If the participants find it difficult to enumerate the feelings they have, they can use the given list. They can cut out the emotions they experience and paste them onto the worksheet.

The facilitator needs to mention that it is normal to have these feelings. The participants do not need to be ashamed of experiencing negative emotions in relation to their brother or sister with autism. Furthermore, the facilitator can add that even the brothers and sisters of a child who doesn't have autism can feel angry, embarrassed, sad or jealous about their brother or sister, too.

I CAN HELP MY BROTHER OR SISTER!

Here, the facilitator can clarify that the participants do not have to become the support workers or even therapists for their brother or sister. He or she can emphasise the fact that the many small things they do in this respect, without a doubt, mean a tremendous amount to their brother or sister. These things also make them special, compared with other children and adolescents who don't have a sibling with a disability.

EXPLAINING AUTISM TO OTHERS

These worksheets were inspired by Julie Davies' books (see 'Literature suggestions' below). So that siblings do not feel ashamed if they experience difficulties explaining to others what's going on with their brother or sister, we start with the principle that explaining about autism is not easy.

At the foot of the worksheet, the siblings can write down the situations, and to which people they would like to explain their brother or sister's autism. With younger children, it is easier to work with names than with situations.

The facilitator can also open up a debate about situations in which the children do not want to talk or in which they do not dare to, and what they can do about this. The reasons for such hesitation can also be addressed. The facilitator can reassure them by telling them that above all, there is no need to be ashamed of their brother or sister's autism.

The next worksheets give an outline of the five steps that constitute an explanation of autism:

1. The name (e.g. autism, Asperger's Syndrome).

2. A description of the way in which autism manifests itself in their brother or sister. To make a clear distinction between this and the next step, the facilitator can, in this case, use the title 'The outside of autism'. These are the things that others can observe (see and hear), namely the behaviour of the brother or sister.

3. A description of the 'inside' of autism; the way in which their sibling sees the world, and the difficulties he/she experiences. The inside serves as an explanation of the outer side and encourages perspective-taking or empathy with the sibling.

4. We explain this part as follows: even when other people know the name for your brother or sister's disorder, they still do not know how they should react. Most people don't know a lot about autism or even don't know anything at all. Or they have stereotyped and false ideas about autism, such as that all children with autism are not able to speak. From your experience, you know better than strangers how to help your brother or sister. If you explain these things to others, they too can help and act.

5. We explain this part as follows: most of the time, other people only see the negative side of autism. It is a huge helping hand for your brother or sister if you tell other people how special he or she is and what talents he or she possesses.

In the next worksheet, the siblings create a personalised version about their brother or sister with autism. There is one worksheet for brothers and one for sisters. Of course, the participants can also create their own version, illustrated with their drawings or with a photo of their brother or sister.

These worksheets also provide the facilitator with an opportunity to assess whether the siblings have understood the chapter on autism.

These exercises serve, so to speak, as 'scripts' for the participants, so that they can provide – if necessary or desired – explanations of their sibling in various situations. The facilitator can also vary the scripts: different scripts for different situations. What do you say at school? What do you say to a close friend? What do you say to strangers?

Some participants give presentations at school about their sibling with autism. These worksheets can lead onto such a presentation or even serve as a basis for writing the presentation. The other worksheets in the chapter can be used too, if necessary.

6 Adaptations and additions

- To finish off the worksheet exercises, a book on autism or Asperger's Syndrome can be added. There are books written especially for siblings of people with autism (see 'Literature suggestions').

- Make a collage of the positive and negative aspects of autism.

- Write a cartoon strip on autism.

- Create an album or a collage of photos about autism.

- Prepare a presentation on autism.

7 Literature suggestions
7.1 Explaining difference to young children

- *Elmer*. A herd of elephants lives in the jungle, all different from one another yet the same colour, all except Elmer, who is a multi-coloured patchwork elephant. One day he disguises himself in order to be the same as the others and no one recognises him. He is very satisfied. Alas, he sees how sad his friends are that day, realises they miss him and that they had laughed at him not because he was different but because he's the most appealing, lovable elephant in the world. David McKee, Andersen 2007.[103]

- *The Ugly Duckling*. A classic tale of difference, in which a young bird, before knowing who he is, experiences rejection from other ducklings, then comes to the realisation he is in fact a beautiful swan.

7.2 Books on autism for siblings

- *The Curious Incident of the Dog in the Night-time*. This is not really a book about autism, but a very well-written detective novel about a young adolescent of 15 years who has autism. The book introduces perfectly the autistic way of thinking. For young people over 14 (also for adults!). Mark Haddon (2004).

- *The London Eye Mystery*. Another excellent mystery story, for a younger readership than above, with particularly good treatment of sibling relationships. The mystery is ultimately solved thanks to the talents of the young protagonist whose brain works in unique ways. Siobhan Dowd,[104] David Fickling Books (2010).

- *Children with Autism: A booklet for brothers and sisters*. Designed specifically for siblings of children with autism from the age of seven upwards, this booklet explains what autism is and explores some of the difficulties which siblings may experience. Julie Davies (1998).[105]

- *Able autistic children with Asperger's Syndrome: a booklet for brothers and sisters*. Julie Davies.[106]

- *My Sister is Different*. Sarah Hunter.[107]

- *My Special Brother Rory*. Ellie Fairfoot.[108]

- *You Are Special Too: A Book for Brothers and Sisters of Children Diagnosed with Asperger's Syndrome*. Josie Santomauro.[109]

7.3 Websites

www.sibs.org.uk: website of Sibs, a UK charity representing the needs of siblings of children and adults with a disability.

www.autism.org.uk: website of the National Autistic Society, the leading UK charity for people with autism (including Asperger's Syndrome) and their families.

Chapter 11

I am Special for Peers

1 Background

More and more children with autism are being educated in mainstream schools. Likewise, many also participate in a wide range of activities (Cubs, Scouts, Brownies and Guides, holiday camps, sports clubs). One of the cornerstones of full inclusion is that other children accept the child with autism. In order to enhance peers' understanding of autism and above all to encourage a positive image of the child with autism, an adapted version of *I am Special* can be used.

One study[110] pointed out that a brief information session, such as a short video or an hour's discussion, was not enough to change classmates' attitudes towards the child with autism. Creating a positive environment towards autism, for example in the classroom, requires much more than concise explanations of autism at the beginning of the school year.

Moreover, neither is a positive attitude enough to change the behaviour adopted by those facing a pupil with autism. Autism can be so overwhelming and confusing for classmates that, often, they do not know how to behave toward the pupil concerned. At times, the latter seems to understand other people, the next minute he seems lost. He takes part in one game but not in a similar activity. One minute, he seems normal, the next minute, he behaves very strangely. There is no physical disability and he appears to be very intelligent. And where do the sudden outbursts come from? Because of the odd, incomprehensible behaviour of the child with autism, his classmates are completely baffled. The only way to dispel this bafflement is to have a good understanding of autism. Indeed, we do not like the unknown (it is also threatening).

Informing classmates has other advantages, too. For example, it makes an explanation of the special status of the pupil possible ('How come Pierre can leave the class?'). Naturally, the other pupils do not always like this preferential treatment, but at least they will understand the reason for it. An information programme for children also makes putting in place various support activities, such as teamwork, possible. The other youngsters can support the child with autism to take part in various activities. For example, the child with autism can have a buddy in his youth club who can explain individually how to follow the rules of the game, when he doesn't understand explanations given to the whole group.

Some parents and teachers are hesitant with the idea of informing peers. Nevertheless, we must not delude ourselves. Children are not blind and, most of the time, they can see that the child with autism is different, but they do not know what his problem is and like uninformed adults, fall back on their own frames of reference in explaining difference ('he is stupid, mad, pedantic, shy', etc.).

Some parents and teachers are afraid that the information will lead to bullying and exclusion. It constitutes a risk, in effect, but given the fact that this aspect is addressed in the information programme, experience shows this kind of behaviour rarely happens. The information given to classmates should not be limited to calling autism a disability. A good information programme also puts some emphasis on interacting with the child with autism (dos and don'ts). Furthermore, new information can be integrated and be part of a project on bullying.

2 Target group

The original workbook of *I am Special* may be used with children from nine to ten years on. For younger children, 'The big book about me' can serve as a model. However, younger children have no need for detailed information on autism. With them, it is preferable to address their experience of their peers with autism and it is advisable to limit explanations to the fact that the child with autism is 'excusable': 'He can't help it, he doesn't really understand.' There are alternative resources in the form of illustrated books, just as there are for siblings.

3 Aims

The aims of the sessions are the same as for individuals with autism: to give understandable explanations of autism. The principal aim is always to give explanations of the sometimes odd, incomprehensible behaviour of the child with autism. Also, we hope to increase their understanding of disability and to provide children with concrete advice about how they can relate to the young person concerned.

4 Description

The description below deals with information given to children in an educational context. It is based on an experimental project in a centre for children with special needs, for fourth year primary pupils (of around nine to ten years), where *I am Special* was adapted for a class project on 'difference'. With some adaptations, this method of work can also be applied to other contexts, such as providing information for peers in cubs or scouts.

Thanks to the introduction to *I am Special*, the resistance that often exists when faced with a separate explanation of autism was overcome ('there are children with other disabilities in the school, too…why single out this child?'). Indeed, *I am Special* does not only address autism but also the individuality of each person and disability in general. This is why the title of the class project did not mention the term autism, but encompassed 'difference' in general. In summary, the project was about differences between people and the ways in which this can be managed. The skills and attitudes which can prevent bullying were a particular focus. Autism gave concrete expression to the information because the content was applied to one child in the class. One can also think of other children who have one or other disability, such as ADHD (attention deficit hyperactivity disorder) or dyslexia, and the project can very well place emphasis on these topics.

Ideally, information given to classmates about a pupil's autism should form part of a wider information session than one on autism alone, where school staff and parents of other pupils are involved as well.

The information project can be organised as a specific project or it can form part of lessons on citizenship or social skills.

Naturally, an information session cannot take place until after consultation with the parents. This consultation picks up the same questions as those asked of a child with autism before starting the *I am Special* programme: 'Why do we want to educate a child's peers? What are we expecting from this session? What are we hoping for and what are our fears? What do we say? Who will do it?' Moreover, parents can be actively involved in the process: they are usually very able to spell out their child's autism very clearly. Anecdotes and concrete examples sometimes say more and tell us more than a strictly theoretical explanation.

Sometimes, although parents are not against discussions on autism, they oppose describing autism as a disability. Most of the time, this opposition disappears when the concept of disability is made clear and the way in which everything will be explained is addressed. However, if the parents are still against it, the project must be changed. Autism can be described as one of many forms that constitute 'difference'.

From a certain age, besides the agreement of parents, the agreement of the pupil is also required before informing classmates. Throughout the process, he or she can be prepared and supported by parents, his or her teaching assistant or another significant adult. If he wishes, he can contribute to the information sessions, for example, by giving a talk on autism. Clearly the information contributed on autism is strongly dependent on the child already knowing and already having been informed about the disorder himself. It is a prerequisite to the organisation of an information session for his peers that the child with autism is previously informed.

For the lessons or specific sessions, we use worksheets from one of the various versions of *I am Special*. The advantage is that the child is a step ahead of his peers. Indeed, he has already gone over the worksheets in his *I am Special* sessions. In this way, the information is not new for him and he already knows the answers to the questions. He can thus give a good impression and this encourages the formation of a positive image (beneficial for both the child and his peers).

Each child receives their own workbook, with worksheets. During art lessons (one hour), the children can create their own cover for the workbook, whether at the beginning or the end of the lesson.

Take for example a project of four sessions. Each session lasts a morning or an afternoon, with a breather or a break between each activity. The four sessions cover:

1. Everyone is unique.
2. Illness and disability.
3. Different disabilities.
4. Autism.

In principle, the teacher can lead the series of four sessions, but the pupils often prefer 'invited speakers' to cover some themes. In the eyes of the pupils, guest speakers represent not only an authority on a particular area, but their contribution lends variety and a change from 'ordinary lessons', as well. Thus, the school psychologist or a different teacher can introduce certain topics, such as 'everyone is unique' or 'different disabilities'. And the school nurse or doctor can provide the sessions on illness and disability. Other people can be invited for the section on autism: a specialist teacher, a school support worker, a home support worker or an associate from an autism organisation. Naturally, the class teacher is also present during each session.

To keep the project going and to increase the pupils' motivation, all kinds of complementary activities can also be organised. Thus, the session on illness and disability can lead to a class trip to a hospital or a support network. After each classroom session, books and pamphlets on the theme discussed can be displayed in the school library. The children can write up a report about the sessions in the school newsletter or organise a display in their class on the themes arising from the project.

4.1 Session 1: everyone is unique

This session consists of all the worksheets of the original *I am Special* workbook. Given that this session is presented in class, the facilitator can use various activities for the children to carry out independently, clearly showing how each is unique, despite some similarities: a game of 'Simon says' with different emotional and physical characteristics that determine to which part of the classroom the participants must run. Another idea is the game 'Who is it?' where the children must identify a pupil in the class by asking yes/no questions about his physical appearance or character. As a concrete end result, each pupil can make a drawing or a collage of their own personal, unique characteristics.

4.2 Session 2: illness and disability

The first part of this session is about illness. Every child has already had an illness and this experience makes an excellent starting point for a class discussion. The original worksheets on illness can be used.

The facilitator can bring in complementary worksheets: what does one do if there is someone in the class who is seriously ill (send a card with wishes for a speedy recovery, keep his school notebooks up to date, visit him, etc.), or worksheets which highlight the importance of healthy living and a healthy diet.

At the end of the session, the facilitator introduces the theme of disability (the term disorder does not have to be explained) and, thanks to the workbook exercises, the pupils will grasp the difference between illness and disability. In preparation for the next session, the pupils can do an 'assignment' on disability (interview someone who has a disability, find information in the library, collect newspaper clippings or photos of disabilities).

4.3 Session 3: different disabilities

The facilitator can start with the worksheets on different types of disability from the original workbook. For each disability, a large sheet of paper can be hung up in the classroom. The children can stick on their newspaper clippings or photos they've collected.

To complete the description of different disabilities, we discuss the solutions and aids for alleviating the problem. The facilitator can make this part very interesting by presenting in concrete terms all sorts of solutions and letting the children experiment with them. *I am Special* has several activities such as 'a blind pupil' or 'a journey in a wheelchair' which the pupils can carry out themselves. Most pupils appreciate this type of activity. The children who know someone with a disability in their family or in their community can talk about their experiences. Then, the facilitator can relate a story about contact with people with a disability. For example: how do we talk to someone who is deaf? Finally, the facilitator can emphasise the talents of people with disabilities, in keeping with positive images of people with a disability.

Often, other disabilities and limitations come up during these sessions, some of which are included in the worksheets from *I am Special*, such as ADHD (attention deficit hyperactivity disorder) or dyslexia, since some pupils in the class present with these disorders. The worksheets can be adapted, but the facilitator may also decide to treat these separately, during a subsequent, special session (in the same way that autism is treated during a later session). The decision depends above all on whether there are children in the class who present with the disorder and whether the disorder has been explained to the other pupils.

To prepare for the session on autism, the facilitator can introduce the difference between visible and invisible disabilities: with some people, it is impossible to see immediately that they have a disability.

4.4 Session 4: autism

This session can be introduced in two ways. First of all, we can introduce the child with autism and add that he or she, also, has a disability, which will be explained. This method of work is possible when the previous session had clearly shown that this child has a disability (or more specifically, 'autism') or when this situation is already understood. When no one knows about the child's autism, it is preferable to talk of autism as a general theme and to illustrate as you go along, using some behaviours of the child with autism in the class as examples. Generally, this way of working is recommended because the child with autism is thus not always identifiably at the centre of the whole class's attention, which would not be nice for him.

The facilitator starts by explaining the difference between visible and invisible disabilities, thanks to the preceding session. If autism has not already been mentioned in the list of invisible disabilities, it is added at this time.

For this session, the facilitator must choose between a number of worksheets on autism from the original workbook. Not all the worksheets have to be done. For example, the one on a disorder of the brain does not necessarily have to be used. The information on the location of autism in the brain, its causes and its treatment are far less important than the characteristics of autism and the ways in which other pupils can get along with the child concerned. In general, the 'facts' of autism can be summarised in a single page.

The facilitator can outline the characteristics of autism. All the characteristics in *I am Special* need not necessarily be mentioned. The facilitator chooses to emphasise the typical characteristics of the child with autism in the class. In our experience, most of the time children guess very quickly that there is a pupil with autism in the class and soon know who it is. If this is the case, they can add other characteristics (the child with autism must be prepared beforehand). The facilitator should ensure that the information is positive for the child with autism, correct misunderstandings and give further details when necessary. If the pupils do not associate the information on autism with the child with autism right away, the facilitator can clarify: 'There's someone in class who has autism, namely…'

At this moment, the pupil with autism can bring in their contribution. It can take very different forms: presenting a short talk on autism, handing out a book, having the facilitator read out a text the pupil has written himself. For example, a boy with autism wrote the following text and it was read out by the facilitator:

WHAT I WANT TO SAY TO THE CHILDREN

- That I have autism.
- That because of this, there are things that I cannot do well:
    - I do not play much with other children and this is the reason why I run around mostly on my own in the playground.
    - I do not understand maths right away.
    - Sometimes, I do not like being alone.
    - I can't take part in every game, I think this is because there are some things I can't do very well. Nevertheless, sometimes I would really like to participate.
    - Sometimes, I like to play alone.
    - I feel better when I know what's going to happen.
- There are also lots of things I can do:
    - I am good at talking.
    - I am good at skipping.
    - I am good at working on the computer.
    - I often win certain games.
    - I almost never lie.
    - I set up my computer myself.
- That I found this project great; and I really like so many people coming to visit us.
- That I am able to play more.

Naturally, the contribution of the child with autism is prepared in advance with the facilitator. The worksheets in the version for children can serve as inspiration for this intervention; it consists of worksheets siblings use, such as a model for talking about their brother or sister's autism (see the version for siblings in the CD ROM). By making minor changes (for example replacing the words 'he'/'she' with 'I'), these worksheets can be equally used by the child with autism.

Remaining on the same subject, the facilitator will address the ways in which it is possible to help a person with autism, what to do and not do. Through a Socratic conversation, the facilitator can transform the experiences of classroom peers with the pupil with autism into a list of practical advice for interacting with this pupil. In this context, it is possible to introduce a digression on 'teasing'. Also, class routines may be employed for interactions with the child who has autism, or agreements may be established to implement a buddy system in order to assist the pupil in the playground or with storing school supplies at the end of the day (who helps John to put away his things in his school bag at the end of the lesson?). The arrangements agreed must of course tie in with what the child wants from his classroom peers.

The pupils can summarise the information on their peer's autism on a separate page.

During this session, the facilitator links the information on autism with what has been learned in earlier sessions. For example: everyone is unique, everyone has limitations and talents, people with a disability also have talents.

To conclude, the pupils can also read a book (for suggestions, see those cited in the version for siblings) or watch a video.

If agreements were made regarding interacting with the pupil with autism, the facilitator is also looking for the transfer of these to everyday situations. The list of agreements can be put up on the wall and can be evaluated during weekly class discussions and – if necessary – updated. Indeed, informing classroom peers has a positive effect on the inclusion of the child with autism only if concrete agreements are kept. Not merely words, but actions…

Jaris has autism

Jaris is in my class.

He has a disability: autism. We can't see it because it is in the brain.
His brain works differently from other people's.
So he sometimes acts differently from others:

- he thinks differently
- he has trouble changing rooms.

For Jaris, some things are as difficult as they are confusing or unpleasant:

- accepting change
- understanding what others say
- interacting with other people.

I can help Jaris by:

- explaining things very clearly.

Jaris also has talents:

- drawing
- working on computers
- maths.

Chapter 12

Various Worksheets

1 How the brain works

The chapter on the functioning of the brain (receiving – processing – sending) is one of the most complex in *I am Special*. Many people took up the challenge of simplifying this information and making it more concrete.

Additional information on the five senses is a common characteristic of the different adaptations developed. A concrete description of the five senses constitutes an excellent starting point. Information on the five senses makes the concept of 'receiving information' much more concrete and, in this area, it is easy to find appealing images and activities.

 An example of the worksheets on the senses appears again in the 'That's me?!' workbook, in the CD ROM documents.

Howard Childs sent us a good example of simplification of this *I am Special* chapter. Howard is a Behaviour Specialist who works for Surrey and Borders Partnership NHS Trust in Guildford (UK). This organisation provides various services in the field of mental health care, as well as support for people with learning or developmental disorders, in the Surrey area situated south-west of London.

The worksheets developed by Howard illustrate the functioning of the brain, starting with the five senses: the senses send messages to the brain (receiving). The brain cells process the messages: they send messages (processing). In turn, the brain sends messages to the limbs (sending).

Howard's worksheets were adapted for integration into the present version of *I am Special*. We have added a supplementary worksheet on receiving, processing and sending messages. For this, we opted for a mobile phone analogy. In the original version of *I am Special*, we had made a comparison with a computer, as a model for the functioning of the brain. This image did not suit all children. By contrast, there is no doubt that a mobile phone receives, processes and sends information – and even messages, in a literal sense (SMS/texts). For this reason, we believe the mobile phone constitutes the ideal alternative to the computer comparison. Children familiar with sending text messages certainly understand this analogy better than that of the computer.

The complete set of worksheets is found on the CD ROM ('How the brain works').

2 Character

In the manual for the original workbook, we have already mentioned that character is a very abstract notion and therefore difficult to explain, most of all to young children and people with a learning disability. The first worksheets were evidently too difficult because the character traits mentioned were too abstract and only described verbally. 'The big book about me' provides a more concrete approach to the topic but other people have also drawn up a simpler version. One such person is Ella Buis, an educational psychologist in public health services and a member of the Netherlands' Ambulatory Autism Team. She has looked into the subject for *Vizier*, an organisation in the Netherlands which offers services to people with learning disabilities (housing, employment, family support). *Vizier* intended to do *I am Special* in the form of classes for children and adults. Ella adapted many of the worksheets for this course. We have used the ones on character. They are available on the CD ROM (in 'My inside').

Anyone making a brief internet search will find appealing, attractive illustrations showing different character traits and personality traits. A worksheet on different character traits using drawings has been developed, with which to finish the character sections in the workbook ('My character 1 – for children and young people').

A worksheet is included in the CD ROM ('My character 2 – for adolescents and adults') which is mainly for adolescents and young adults with average intelligence (for children, the concepts as well as the drawings are too vague and abstract).

3 My strong points and my not-so-strong points

Most of the worksheets in the main workbook contain mainly text. For younger children and adolescents with a learning disability, this often poses problems. Similarly, when the young person is asked to fill in personal information, these are often written tasks which are likewise very difficult.

The task is made easier and more concrete when:

1. the text supports the image, rather than *vice versa*

2. the child or young person does not have to do a lot of writing but simply ticks or underlines their responses.

The latter option is also advised for children and adolescents who experience difficulties thinking up their own responses. 'Recognising' is much easier than 'remembering'.

At a workshop on *I am Special*, we asked the participants to come up with an application of the two principles mentioned above. They had to adapt a workbook topic so that it could be used by a target group of people with a young developmental age. The participants came up with the idea of simplifying the worksheets on 'My talents' and 'My not-so-strong points', leaving the child or young person to choose from a series of photos or drawings. At this workshop, we did not have a computer, so the participants had to cut out photos and drawings from magazines. The CD ROM documents include a digital version of their idea ('My strong points' and 'My not-so-strong points').

4 My inside and my outside

Many young children and adolescents with a learning disability find it difficult to understand the difference between the outside and the inside of an individual. Terms such as 'interests', 'character' and 'abilities' are rather abstract. To make them concrete, we need to refer to behaviour and therefore to what is found on the outside.

Often, a supplementary explanation of the difference between the outside and inside is recommended for this target group. It is preferable that this explanation is provided before the 'I am unique' worksheets. If, while working on this section, it appears that the child or young person has difficulty making the distinction between the two concepts, it is advisable to give a fresh meaning to it.

Feel	Hot	Perfume	Acidic	Glasses
Smell	A white cane	Eiderdown	Noise	Music
See	Hearing aid	Listen	Beautiful	Delicious
Taste	Blind	Ice	Green	Ugly
Hear	Look	Hot soup	Salt	Sun cream
Eyes	Odour	Eye patch	Wet	Burned
Ears	Deaf	Lemon	Stink	Bitter
Tongue	Braille	Drum	Calm	Whisper
Skin	Sense of smell	Call	Sweet	Hard
Nose	Alarm	Colour	Dry	Rotting fish
Gentle	Paint	Cold	Dark	Refrigerator

Marjan Deleu, who put together 'The big book about me' in collaboration with her colleague at *Het Anker*, Lisbet Van Gijzeghem, has developed a number of worksheets on the CD ROM called 'The senses, My inside, My outside' to make the difference between the inner and the outer self clear.

It is preferable to begin with a topic that many children and young people know: the senses. The five senses are listed. To see whether the child or young person has acquired knowledge in this field, one worksheet contains all sorts of words related to the senses (e.g. hot, sour, beautiful, hearing aid). The words are cut into strips and sorted into the senses or marked with a colour (each sense being given a specific colour).

The outside of an individual is observable through the senses. On a worksheet collating examples, the person with autism ends up with the senses with which he or she can perceive things about an individual's outside. Then follows a description of the outside: the appearance and behaviour of a person.

The inside cannot be seen and is described as follows: interests, feelings (more concrete than character), skills. A worksheet adheres to this description; for each phrase, the child or young person needs to indicate whether it refers to the inside or outside (marked on the worksheet or sorted by categories). If wished, the facilitator can also ask more specific questions: on the outside, is this 'behaviour' or 'appearance'?

The last worksheet needs to be filled in and can serve as a summary and/ or a test.

Furthermore, the facilitator may also discuss changes to one's inside and outside: what can we change and what can we not change about our outside/inside? Later, when we discuss the fact that there is no cure for autism, this worksheet can be gone over again.

A short version of this set of worksheets, without illustrations, is included on the CD ROM ('The senses', 'A person's inside', 'A person's outside').

5 FAQs

Even when the objective is to inform the person with autism, through worksheets on the principal characteristics of the disorder, questions may still remain. The questions asked most often (FAQ: Frequently Asked Questions) were put together on an information sheet. It was written first of all for children somewhat older (10 to 12 years) and for young people (12 to 14) with average intelligence. For other target groups, such as adolescents, adults or individuals with a learning disability, the questions as well as the answers can be adapted. For example, if a discussion arises around the question of whether Asperger's Syndrome and autism are the same, some participants may be interested to know that in the revised *DSM-V* diagnostic handbook a distinction is no longer made between the two.

The worksheets serve only as examples. They are included in the CD ROM documents ('FAQs').

Chapter 13

I am Special – Board Game

As part of a weekly *I am Special* course for young adults, we created a game entitled *I am Special*. The aim is to become familiar, in an enjoyable way, with the main areas of impairment arising from autism.

The game board is a simplified snakes and ladders board. By means of dice, the participants make their way along the board and arrive at squares where there is a mission to accomplish. These are related to autism characteristics.

1 Resources

- game board
- ordinary dice
- dice coloured with three colours (each colour appears twice)
- as many tokens as there are participants
- three packs of questions or tasks to be accomplished, in three different colours:
  - green: social communication
  - red: social interaction
  - yellow: flexibility and imagination
- resources corresponding to tasks to be accomplished (depending on the task).

2 How to play

Each participant takes a turn to throw the ordinary die. They advance the same number of squares as shown on the die. Thus, they can land on six different squares.

☐	A plain square. Nothing happens. The next player throws the die.
☺	The player has to pay a compliment to one of the other players. He or she then advances three spaces.
⇨	Green arrow: the player advances the number of spaces indicated on the die.
➡	Red arrow: the player moves back the number of spaces indicated on the die (in other words, he or she returns to where he or she was).
🛑 STOP	The player misses a turn.
🎲	An autism characteristic square. The player throws the three-coloured die. He or she takes the top card corresponding to the colour of the die. If their response to the question is correct or if their task is accomplished correctly, the player throws the ordinary die and advances the number of spaces indicated. If their answer is incorrect or the task is not carried out correctly, the player stays where they are. The next player throws the die.

3 Tasks to be accomplished

The game can have two objectives: to familiarise the players with autism in general (what is social interaction/social communication/imagination?) or to become familiar with the characteristics of their own autism. Depending on the aim being pursued, the game could contain two kinds of cards:

1. Cards by means of which the participants, as they play, learn about the concepts of social interaction, social communication and flexibility/ imagination. The aim is not in any way to talk about autism and certainly not about the characteristics of the players' autism.

2. Cards showing the characteristics of autism. The task to be accomplished is the following: do you recognise this characteristic in yourself? If yes, can you give an example or recount a story about a time when this was the case?

 The CD ROM documents offer an example of a game board for the *I am Special* game. Also, there are some examples of cards for enjoyable, unusual missions.

When the aim of the *I am Special* game is to open up a discussion about their own autism characteristics, the cards will then have on them the characteristics of autism as found in the worksheets in the *I am Special* workbook.

Chapter 14
Evaluation Forms

The original manual for *I am Special* gave some suggestions for application and evaluation forms, but apart from a sample evaluation form, no concrete examples were included. Ella Buis, of whom we have already spoken, also developed a number of forms. We have included these in full on the CD ROM, with only some minor changes to page layout or use of language.

The following forms are on the CD ROM:

- referral form
- invitation to the course (it is also possible to add a column for applying)
- evaluation form for participants (children and young people)
- evaluation form for participants (adults)
- evaluation form for parents and carers.

The CD ROM documents also include an evaluation form for groups.

Chapter 15

I am Special for Adults

1 Explaining autism to an adult

In recent years, the diagnosis of autism has progressed enormously, particularly with regard to the recognition of autism in individuals with average intelligence. Autism is being diagnosed earlier and earlier. However, there are still many adolescents and adults who have not yet been diagnosed. Some amongst these will receive a very late diagnosis. This diagnosis often provides answers to numerous questions that have been lingering over many years. Nevertheless, for this category of people with a late diagnosis, autism requires explanation. It is not that they do not know the term, but that they do not know what it means for them, personally: where it is encountered, and what are the consequences for everyday life? Furthermore, diagnosis necessitates a readjustment of self-knowledge. As a result of the diagnosis, ideas one held about oneself are seen in a different light.

The information content about autism does not differ for adults, compared to that for children or adolescents. The approach, however, is different: adults, especially those with an average level of intelligence, face different issues from children or young people. A good number of them have a stable relationship or a regular job and want to know, for example, what influence autism exerts upon their relationships or their work. In addition, we also need to adjust the presentation of the information to make it age-appropriate.

These changes do not mean that the principles previously referred to are no longer applicable. Adapting one's communication for adults with autism (and average intelligence) is again recommended: concretising language and slowing down the flow of information are the essential points. Our experience has shown that presenting 'images' in the form of diagrams or models, for example of the different stages of communication, was much clearer and led more often to understanding: 'Ah, that's what happens! Now I understand why…'

Another principle, equally valuable, is that of the alternation between talking and doing. Even with adults, working with the worksheets and exercises is recommended. This also makes it possible to provide personalised information.

We will describe two forms of concrete information for adults with autism. They were developed by *Autisme Centraal* (Belgium). The first takes the form of a course for young adults with mild learning disabilities to those with higher levels of intelligence. The second is a course for older adults with average to higher level intelligence. Both courses were given in groups. In our experience, providing information in a group has many advantages over individual discussions. Usually, adults are very interested to hear others' narratives. The facilitator thus has the opportunity to concretise the concept of a 'spectrum' within the group, thanks to the differences which always appear between the participants. A group also allows the participants to support one another. They become allies.

Naturally, the following descriptions also apply to individual support and contexts other than that of a course, such as psychotherapy or mentoring.

In addition to the two courses described, other forms of information on autism are also conceivable. The information can, for example, form part of professional coaching or career support.

For each of the two courses, we will briefly describe the content and process, illustrated here and there with examples of worksheets. The latter can also be found in the CD ROM documents. Note that not all the worksheets are explained. Every course is different, especially those for older adults, as the starting point is their experience and no book or workbook can be prepared beforehand.

We will now describe some activities and sessions which differ from the initial workbook.

2 Evening classes for adults of average intelligence

Autisme Centraal (Belgium) offers this course as six evenings on 'Autism and Relationships'. Although some participants are unemployed or employed in a special capacity, this course is primarily intended for adults over 21 who have permanent and regular employment. Some are in a stable relationship (married or cohabiting), others live alone or with their parents.

The title, 'Autism and Relationships', was chosen deliberately. Adults experience difficulties mainly in their relationships. Most of them know more or less what autism means and are not really interested in traditional explanations of the disorder. Besides, this theme is also more concrete than the more abstract, general topic of autism. For general information on autism, other sources of information are available, such as books or the internet. Most participants have already read a number of books on the subject. Adults are particularly interested in the real consequences of autism for their own lives (in particular in the area of relationships) and this is why a course on autism and relationships is more suitable than a session just about autism.

Sessions are held every fortnight. The number of participants varies between five and eight people. Two facilitators are present: one leads the session and the other writes up the minutes for each session. The minutes are sent to the participants by post or e-mail. These notes enable them to go over the information again, and to assimilate it, calmly and individually. The participants do not need to worry about taking notes during the sessions, although they are free to do so (some take notes in order to concentrate better or to have an overview of the session's progress). At the beginning of each meeting, the minutes are reviewed and some points may be defined again or the facilitator can respond to new questions.

Each participant has a red card. This can be used when a participant does not want his comments minuted. In our experience, a visual support works better than oral communication when a participant want to exercise their right to privacy in the minutes; indeed, the card is always present as a visual reminder, while a verbal explanation literally evaporates.

The facilitator proceeds exactly in accordance with the principles previously described in the chapter on psychoeducation. Thus, the group discussions are always prepared in writing by the participants: they receive one or more questions on paper, and they have time for reflection and a few minutes to write down their responses. Thanks to this time for reflection and the visual support of paper, group conversations proceed much more easily. It is at this point the discussion begins. The main conclusions of the conversation are captured on a large sheet of paper or on a card, so that the participants literally have an overview of the topic. The sheets are put up in the room in the next session and are eventually completed, for example, with conversation rules. The facilitator's task is to structure the conclusions as systematically as possible into a logical whole. Abstract words are defined, explained concretely and made visual as much as possible.

2.1 Session 1: familiarisation and introductions

The course content is presented and is followed by a round of introductions.

The introductions proceed thanks to a six-colour dice. Each colour represents a topic:

1. Who am I (including name and age)?

2. My education and my childhood memories.

3. My daily activities (my job, my volunteer work, …)

4. My free time, my hobbies and interests.

5. Where I live and the people with whom I live.

6. My wishes regarding the group's conversation rules.

 Each participant receives a worksheet or can prepare their description in writing (see CD ROM documents). In turn, the participants throw the die and talk about the subject corresponding to that colour. They can ask the speaker additional questions. The die makes each person's turn visible and defines the role of each (to speak or to listen).

This getting to know each other is pursuing various objectives:

*   Participants are getting to know each other (group formation).

*   Bearing in mind that the 'content' of the course is a difficult subject, the course methods (worksheets, group discussions, the facilitator providing explanations, minute-taking) are presented in such a way that the participants are reassured regarding the predictability of procedure and form of the course.

*   The facilitators are getting to know the participants, not only who they are but also how they communicate, how they function in the group, etc. For the facilitator, the first session is in fact an important assessment exercise (in the same way as the sessions on the inside, the outside and the body are, in the original workbook).

In light of the round of introductions and the related discussion, participants also have the option of making known their wishes regarding group support and communication within it. Each person can formulate a number of 'rules', for example: 'Don't interrupt me, as I need time to formulate my thoughts and an interruption makes me lose the thread of my ideas.' These rules become group agreements and are listed on a large sheet of paper (a visual support) and, again, put up in the room.

2.2 Session 2: my relationships

Just as for each subsequent theme, this session begins with a worksheet on which the participants can formulate their 'definition' of the evening's theme: 'What is a relationship, for you?' The facilitator thus gets to know the participants' terms of reference and a shared definition can be established.

If necessary, a dictionary can be used to find such a definition. This exercise also serves as an assessment: the facilitator gains an overview of the participants' experiences in the area of relationships.

Then, the participants map out their relationships. On a large sheet of A3 paper they draw several circles, representing different relationships: partner/family, close relatives, friends, acquaintances, colleagues, and an empty circle. Each circle is divided into two: the upper part contains people's names and the lower part the troubling things, difficulties, problems encountered by the participants in their relationships with these people (see the CD ROM documents).

People's names (or a general description of the relationship, for example 'colleague') are written on a page that has 'ME' at its centre, surrounded by a number of concentric circles, in which participants can write the names of people according to the degree of relationship: from the most intimate to the most distant. The problems and difficulties previously expressed are then placed against the degree of relationship.

The conclusion is as follows: compared with individuals they do not feel very close to, participants not only harbour higher expectations of people with whom they are close, but these expectations are also less defined. For example, expectations of a work colleague are lower than those harboured towards a spouse, but they are also more explicit and more 'regulated' (particularly as a result of etiquette). This exercise demonstrates to us that people with autism do not experience the same difficulties in their different relationships, but encounter more problems in the area of close relationships, where most things are reliant on implicit rules and reading between the lines.

Implicit expectations are the biggest difficulty for people with autism. This leads on to the theme of 'communication'.

2.3 Session 3: my thinking

In principle, the theme of communication can be addressed after the previous session. However, we opt for the topic of 'thinking' before going on to communication, since the session on communication deals with the 'intentions' of others, which presupposes an understanding of the concept of 'meaning', linked in turn to the mind and to 'making sense of an event'. The topic 'thinking' also allows one to speak about autism – the ways in which the participants differ from other individuals.

We begin, again, with definitions given by the participants for 'thinking'. Each participant receives a sheet of A3 paper on which they need to draw 'how they think'. They can choose to make a drawing of a metaphor for their own thinking style, for example 'my brain works like a spiral: my associative thinking makes me drift away from the centre' or 'I am often overwhelmed by stimuli, as if I am being hit by a tsunami'. Or they can make a schematic drawing of how their senses and thoughts work. Participants who do not know how to draw well should not worry: it does not need to be a beautiful drawing and they will have the opportunity to explain their illustration. In our experience, visual representations of the abstract topic of 'thinking' generally say more to the other participants than a verbal explanation.

The drawings are discussed in the group and recorded by the facilitator under the functioning of the brain model (receiving – processing – sending/ entering – transformation – output/observing – processing – executing), as explained in the original workbook.

During this discussion, certain themes can be addressed: observing things in a fragmented way, processing things in detail, linear thinking and literal understanding.

2.4 Session 4: sense-making

The session on 'thinking' clearly shows that the stages of processing were equivalent to making sense of things. The 'sense-making' session is the most difficult because the subject is highly abstract. It is for this reason that, during this meeting, we are mainly providing information. This session is also the most 'academic' of the series, although we devote a space for discussion so that the participants can talk about their own experiences.

The facilitator starts off with a number of exercises to explore the topic, based on experience. He shows the participants photos of objects (for example a chair) and asks questions such as: 'How do you know that this is a chair?' 'How do you know you're able sit on it?' The participants understand that meanings are not properties of objects (or of reality) but that the brain adds this meaning during observation. The option of being able to sit on the chair is not a physical property or a directly observable characteristic, but is a specification formed by the brain. Sense-making requires 'imagination'. It is also clear that observing isolated details does not suffice to make sense: neither colour, nor texture, nor the number of legs on a chair enable one to say that it is possible to sit on this chair.

Then, the facilitator shows that meanings can be formed in different ways, that there are various kinds of representation (usually, the term representation is not used): for example there are drawings, but also words. The participants are then given words which have more than one meaning, such as iris (can be a flower or a structure in the eye). Thanks to the responses of the participants to the question, 'What do you think when you hear this word?', a discussion on the role of context in making sense of an event can begin. The meaning applied to observations depends heavily on the context. Depending on the other words in the sentence or the rest of the story, it is possible to tell whether a person is using the word 'iris' to refer to a flower or to an eye.

In this sense, the discussion may lead on to an explanation of autism as a kind of context blindness.[111] However, this observation could be deferred until the last session on autism (depending on the questions and prior knowledge of the participants).

So far, the examples given by the facilitator have referred only to objects. In the final part of the session, the facilitator refers to objects again but makes a connection to social situations. The part on 'sense-making' (receiving, processing and sending) can be repeated, starting with a photo of someone crying (see CD ROM documents). Another exercise consists of making sense of a social situation where only part of a photo is revealed and other parts are shown little by little. The role played by context in making sense of a social situation then becomes very clear.

We bring up the theme of communication again: communication entails an exchange of meanings. This is the next session's topic.

2.5 Session 5: communication

This session begins with asking the participants the usual question about definitions: 'What does communication mean, for you?' An example is included on a worksheet in the CD ROM documents. Other questions: 'Name different kinds of communication' or 'Name five essential features of communication.' Then, starting with the definitions and examples given by the participants, the facilitator introduces a visual model of the communication process.

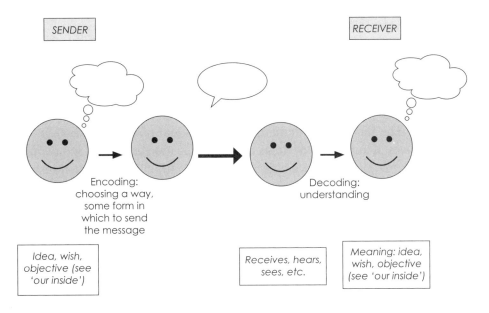

Figure 15.1 The communication process: a visual model

 The difficulties experienced by participants with regard to the receiving side of the cycle of communication are addressed. The participants can write down their experiences on a worksheet (see CD ROM documents for some examples) and these are discussed in the group. Following on from the theme of 'sense-making' previously addressed, it becomes clear that people with autism and average intelligence quite understand what is being said (the words, phrases) but experience difficulties in understanding what the person wants to express: the meaning of what he or she says (the sense). This meaning greatly depends on context – in the first place, on the 'way' in which it is said, which includes body language. In intimate relationships, precisely where most things remain implicit, the manner of communication, as well as context, is essential.

The same process applies to the expressive side of communication: the sending of messages. Participants draw up an inventory of difficulties they experience in making themselves understood and in providing others with information they need or which they deem necessary. A useful experiential exercise for approaching this aspect is, for example, to prepare a report of the first session. It emerges from this that the participants often give an enumeration of facts, only, and recount much less of their own experience. Yet it is exactly this experience that matters in relationships, above all in more intimate and personal relationships. The participants can relate this conclusion to what they said previously in the session on relationships.

2.6 Session 6: autism

In the previous sessions, autism has been addressed sporadically. All this information is now brought together and presented as a whole.

 Again, we begin by asking the participants what autism means for them, what they recognise in themselves of autism, and also what others recognise in them as such (see worksheets in CD ROM). This worksheet is discussed in the group. The facilitator summarises the facts and places emphasis on the consequences of autism in the areas of communication and social interaction, since these are the theme of this course. The difficulties in relationships identified earlier are linked to the characteristics of autism, above all to the different way of thinking.

We focus on the description of autism as a disability for a moment. The term 'handicap' is explained, and the social model of disability visualised (see the *I am Special* workbook for a representation of this model). It is then obvious that the social impairment in autism does not mean that people with autism have difficulties in every relationship and with every contact, also that they do not always encounter the same problems. Everything depends on what is expected of the person with autism and the degree to which these expectations are communicated explicitly (see the session on relationships and communication).

 Many participants ask the following question: 'When should I explain about my autism to others and how do I go about it?' (In the first course organised by *Autisme Centraal*, the idea for a visual presentation arose from this question, which led to us making a video – named *Automatically: 61233 images about autism* – with the participants of that course, in which they gave personal accounts of their autism.) A worksheet (see CD ROM documents) can serve as a starting point for discussion of this question, on which the participants can record their experiences. During the group discussion which follows, the facilitator particularly takes into account the negative reactions that sometimes follow an explanation of autism. The facilitator as well as the participants can offer suggestions or give support in order to prevent or compensate for such negative reactions.

These tips also help to make the transfer of what has been learned on the course. Participants have not only attained a better understanding or knowledge of their autism, but have also discovered how to explain their autism to others and how they can compensate for their autism and their 'difference'.

The session concludes with an evaluation, also prepared in writing. In this evaluation, participants have the opportunity to make suggestions of topics for future courses and the facilitator describes the options for possible complementary courses. At the moment, there are already fairly basic complementary courses, notably on: autism and relationships with spouses; autism and relationships with your children. These courses focus on a specific kind of relationship. Other topics are possible: autism and leisure time, autism and self-organisation or autism and anxiety. If they wish, participants can register for the basic course, 'Autism and Relationships', again. Many participants do. They say that this repetition helps them better understand and assimilate its complex information.

3 One-week course for adults

Autisme Centraal organises all sorts of courses and educational activities for adults with autism spectrum disorders. The choices are wide-ranging and courses on topics such as perception, parenthood, sexuality, stress management, and leisure time are all offered. Autism is one of these topics and we therefore developed a week-long course. The *I am Special* workbook was specially adapted for this course. Naturally, the content can also be delivered as a day course, spread out over several weeks.

The course lasts six days. The table below gives an overview of its contents. A class is given during the day and recreational activities are organised for the evening. These are linked to the day's topic. For example, for a class on disabilities, a partially sighted person and someone who is a wheelchair user could be invited to an evening reception. Participants may ask questions.

Since the sessions are very intensive, a free afternoon is timetabled around the middle of the week (after the part about autism in general), the aim being to relieve the pressure, rest or take one's mind off things. In consultation with the facilitators, participants can plan this activity as they wish.

Participants in the one-week course, usually between 20 and 30 people, are placed in groups as homogeneous as possible, of six to nine people. Some groups are composed of people with a learning disability and those with average intelligence who, due to their autism, experience as many difficulties in their functioning and processing of information as the former. With regard to the pace and style of communication in a group and their level of functioning, some people with autism and average intelligence fit in better with a group of people with a learning disability. Other groups are composed mainly of people with a learning disability or groups of only participants with intelligence broadly ranging from average to very high.

Table 15.1 Timetable of one-week course for adults

	DAY 1: I am unique	DAY 2: My body	DAY 3: Disability	DAY 4: Autism in general	DAY 5: My autism	DAY 6: I am Special
Morning	Introduction My appearance	Outside and inside	Illness and disability: limitations and solutions	Autism	Autism – my characteristics I am Special game	The autism spectrum: I am Special
Afternoon	My inside	The brain	Course on disabilities Talents and disability	FREE TIME	What can be done about my autism? Learning time: asking for help	That's me?!: unique and special
Evening	Board games	Quiz on the body	Talk-show: invited speakers on disability	Film: Rain Man or another movie	Surprise activity	

For participants with average to high intelligence, the course closely resembles the original workbook and the timetable shown. The workbook, on the other hand, has been thoroughly adapted for those participants with a lower level of intelligence or a learning disability. They will work with fewer worksheets and have more activities focused on their experiences. Several 'doing' activities are also given to the most able participants. Particularly during a week's course, it is inadvisable to work all week by means of worksheets and group conversations. The 'doing' activities are much more attractive and greatly increase the participants' motivation.

Personal details

Identity card: Participants create a 'new' identity card with their personal details (different exercises can be found on the CD ROM).

My appearance

Then and now: to simplify their description, participants compare two photos of themselves, an old photo (baby or infant) and a recent photo.

My inside

Interview on interests: participants become journalists and interview others about their interests. They present these to the others, after which the participant who has presented can give a concrete demonstration of their interests (such as showing photos of their hobbies, showing photos of a collection of objects related to their interests, showing the cover of their favourite CD and listening to a track, etc.). (In the invitation to the course, participants are asked to bring something related to their interests.)

Collage of a character: using the 'ghost' character depicted in 'The big book about me,' participants make a collage of their character traits. They present these to the rest of the group. The group has a large sheet of paper in front of them, with a table of all the participants' names (horizontally) and all the character traits (vertically). Each person has to tick the boxes corresponding to the character traits they possess, so it is visually apparent that there are differences and similarities in the character of each member of the group.

A game of 'Simon Says' can be organised. The facilitator indicates two corners of the room and each corner is associated with a character trait. Participants have to run as fast as possible to their 'own' corner. The large sheet displayed in the room serves as a visual reminder.

Talent hunt: each person has the opportunity to display their talents. The facilitator may additionally introduce tasks that illustrate the talents of the participants, for example a short numbers quiz (if there is a participant who has an excellent memory for numbers).

MY BODY

Making my own caricature: the facilitator explains what a caricature is (a drawing where certain parts are exaggerated, therefore often enlarged) and shows some examples of famous people, such as the pope, the queen or other members of the royal family. Participants draw a caricature of themselves (or if a participant is very good at drawing, he or she can do a caricature of all the participants). Participants who dislike drawing or who think they cannot draw can take a copy of a photo of themselves, cut out the head and paste it on to another body (cut out of a paper or magazine) or *vice versa* (paste a well known head on their body). A discussion on the topic can be linked to the previous conversation on 'my appearance'.

Body-related expressions: all sorts of sayings and proverbs which include a reference to a part of the body are captured on a flipchart. Who knows the meaning of the proverb? Can someone give a portrayal of it? Some examples: getting cold feet about something, having eyes bigger than your stomach, wearing your heart on your sleeve. Another alternative is to write the sayings and proverbs on a flipchart and leave gaps to fill in with parts of the body. Participants are given strips of paper with drawings or names of parts of the body and put these in the right place. For example: a photo of an eye for: 'Her daughter is the apple of her…'

Memory or observation games: the facilitator offers all kinds of memory or observation games. Some examples:

- *The bomb:* a participant leaves the room. The rest of the group selects an object from a set of objects in the middle of the group: this is 'the bomb'. The participant comes back into the room and removes the objects one by one. The group counts out the objects removed and must shout 'boom' when the participant removes 'the bomb'. The group must remember the object that has been selected as 'the bomb'. The participant who removes the most objects before the 'explosion' is the winner.

- *What's different?* A participant leaves the room. Then, the group changes some elements (two people trade places, clothes are swapped, someone takes off their glasses, etc.). The participant comes back in and has three chances to guess what's different.

- *Kim's Game* A number of objects are hidden under a cloth in the centre of the group. The facilitator lifts the cloth for a certain amount of time (30 seconds or a minute), after which the participants have to write down or recall as many objects as possible.

DISABILITY

Video on one or more disabilities: the group watches a video on one or more disabilities. Participants recount what they have seen. To give an overview, the facilitator gathers this information on a flipchart that has the name, limitations and solutions for each disability.

Disability course: participants, individually or in pairs, make an obstacle course with different stages. At each stage, they have to achieve a task linked to one or another disability. Some examples:

- *Wheelchair circuit:* complete an obstacle course in a wheelchair (eventually a course for two).

- *Finger-spelling alphabet (sign language):* two participants each have a card illustrating the finger-spelling alphabet. One person 'says' a word and the other has to recognise the word.

- *Feeling objects:* participants have to recognise objects by touch, with their eyes covered.

- *Obstacle course for the blind:* one participant has to verbally guide another, who is blindfolded, through an obstacle course.

- *Blind drawing:* a participant who is blindfolded draws a picture. Another has to guess what it is.

- *Lip reading:* the facilitator sings a well-known song for the participants, but without making a sound. Participants have to guess which song it is.

- *Mission incomprehensible:* the facilitator gives a mission to a participant in a language the participant does not know. The facilitator gradually makes it easier by drawing the instructions.

- *Without words:* one participant has to explain a task to another, without using words.

- *Without hands:* participants have to move all sorts of objects (for example put balls in a box, toss a ring over a wooden stick) without using their hands.

Participants then discuss this course: which disability was represented at which stage, what the difficulties were, how to approach things when you have a disability, etc.

AUTISM IN GENERAL

Statements game: each participant receives two cards, one red card with 'false' written on it and one green card with 'true' written on it. The facilitator reads out statements about autism and the participants show, with their cards, whether the statement is true or false. After each round of statements there is a discussion. The conclusions that follow are recorded by the facilitator on a flipchart. Five themes are as follows:

- The inside and outside. Examples of statements: everyone who has autism has brown eyes; there are people with autism who wear glasses; everyone with autism has long legs. Conclusion: you can't tell from someone's appearance whether they have autism.

- Causes of autism. Examples of statements: you can catch autism by watching too many violent films; you can catch autism by falling down the stairs; autism is the result of a bad education. Conclusion: in the main, autism is congenital.

- Disorder. Examples of statements: everyone with autism has poor heart function; autism results from a respiratory problem; autism is located in the brain. Conclusion: the brain of someone with autism functions differently (brain disorder).

- Processing difficulties. Examples of statements: people with autism are hard of hearing; people with autism have better vision. Conclusion: autism lies not in the reception of information but in the processing of information.

- A different way of thinking. Examples of statements: people with autism think in Chinese; people with autism prefer thinking bit by bit; people with autism think backwards. Conclusion: autism is characterised by a detailed and very concrete way of thinking.

Discovering the main impairments: participants receive a set of strips of paper, on which are written characteristics of autism relating to social communication and interaction, or rigidity of thinking and actions. Participants look over the characteristics of autism. They are read aloud. The facilitator sticks them on a large sheet of paper and sorts the first strips according to the main areas of impairment: social communication, social interaction, flexibility of thinking and actions. Participants can then look for the category where they would place the next strips. At the end of the activity, the facilitator asks the participants to think of a title for each of the groupings.

My autism

A painting of the autism spectrum. There are three pots of paint (one pot of white and two of other colours). Participants count the number of ticks they marked (characteristics I recognise in myself) on each of the three worksheets on the characteristics of autism (see original workbook). For each page, they receive as many portions of paint as ticks made. For example, for each tick in the list on communication, the participant receives one portion (for example one drop) of white paint. They mix the portions of the three colours and spread the resulting colour on a page. Then all the participants' pages are compared with one another. Thus, participants see that no one obtained the same colour, yet everyone has more or less the same hue. So it becomes clear that despite common characteristics, people with autism are all different from one another.

I am Special game. For a description of the game, see Chapter 13.

That's me: unique and special

Myself in pictures: each participant draws a person on a piece of cardboard (there is an example on the CD ROM in this section, on the 'Who am I?' document). The drawing is done on two pieces and the parts are placed one on top of the other. Small windows are drawn on the top part and cut out on three sides so they will open. A title is written beneath each window, for example, 'my character', 'my hobbies' or 'my autism'. A piece of card is pasted underneath. In the space behind the window (on the underside piece of card), the person writes the most important things they have learned on the course. It may be, for example, two character traits that the participant found were very important. Underneath the window with the title 'autism', the participant can, for example, paste the painting obtained in the autism spectrum exercise. On top of the drawing of the person, the participant writes the title, *I am Special*. Finally, participants present these to each other. The aim of the windows is to show that characteristics such as skills, character, interests and autism are not immediately visible on one's outside. Naturally, it is possible to open a window for someone else, which symbolises the participant wanting to reveal something of their character or their interests. On the same theme, the facilitator may initiate a group discussion about when someone can talk about their autism and with whom.

Chapter 16
The World in Fragments

1 Background

'The world in fragments' is a supplement to *I am Special*, developed by Marion Fuijkschot-Timmers and Bart Konings of *Pleincollege Antoon Schellens* in Eindhoven, the Netherlands. The *Pleincollege Antoon Schellens* is a secondary school providing special education (support for learning) for students with a level of intelligence ranging from near normal to high (verbal IQ above 80). Many of the students have psychiatric or neuropsychological problems (autism spectrum disorder, ADHD, non-verbal learning disability or co-morbidity of these disorders). Students with delays in certain areas of learning may present with social-emotional difficulties, as well. For the 'traditional parts of the curriculum', such as history, maths and language they attend general classes, and with regard to their problems, 'remedial classes' are offered. Also, depending on their social-emotional difficulties, classes on social skills are provided. In addition, each class has its own tutor and some students also have a personal tutor.

Students for whom the traditional lessons on social skills do not suffice can attend specific small group sessions (six to seven students and two teachers) and sometimes even individual sessions. This way of working applies particularly to students with autism spectrum disorders. A special course was developed for them, adapted to their specific needs and learning style: 'The world in fragments.' This training is based on *I am Special*. Each chapter (interests, character, talents, etc.) has a summary, which results in one panoramic, individualised chart: 'ME.' This not only gives the student an insight into what they have already accomplished, but also a clear summary of who they are as a person. Sometimes, to finish with, a 'social map' is added: this provides information about the young person's environment and may in particular provide information about who they can talk to about their autism or whom they can go to, to ask questions.

'The world in fragments' includes additional sessions which provide suggestions for achieving better social interactions, which can be used to conclude the original *I am Special* workbook. Besides some of the more familiar subjects (recognising emotions, understanding and using familiar social skills, coping with criticism, asking for something), 'The world in fragments' includes a specific section on the management of autism. This chapter is included in the updated version of *I am Special*.

The main aim of 'The world in fragments' is to find *strategies and possible solutions* to difficulties deriving from autism. 'The world in fragments' begins where *I am Special* ends, that is to say, with an understanding of what autism is and the way in which autism manifests itself in each young person in question.

2 Target group

In principle, the worksheets were designed for (young) adults and adolescents of (almost) average intelligence, with a minimum age of 12. The content and the language of the worksheets are a bit more difficult than in the initial version of *I am Special*. The lower limit of 12 years therefore applies to young people who are more gifted. The language and layout should be adapted and simplified for young people between 12 and 16 who have a below average level of intelligence or for young adults with a lower level of intelligence or mild learning disability. For more gifted young adults, the repetitive information can be merged into a much reduced number of worksheets.

3 Conditions and indications

One of the conditions for working with the worksheets in 'The world in fragments' is that the young person has worked through one or other version of *I am Special* and therefore knows, for example, what their talents, their not-so-strong points and their autism characteristics are.

An additional condition is that the young person wants to work on himself and believes in his own ability to change with regard to the difficulties resulting from his autism.

Furthermore, the role of parents is essential since the young person's self-image is influenced by what they learn at home; moreover, in a number of tasks, parents are invited to collaborate, to enable comparisons to be made.

4 Structure and content

The structure of 'The world in fragments' is as follows:

- First of all, the young person makes an inventory of what he finds *difficult or troublesome*. These are listed according to the main autism characteristics: social communication, social interaction and thinking and acting flexibly (if this inventory has already been made in previous sessions, it is not necessary to repeat the process). The young person chooses their priorities and opts for three situations they find particularly difficult and for which they would like to find a solution.

- The drafting of a summary includes a 'decision tree', namely whether to take the decision to tackle a difficult situation or leave it.

- The next information page outlines different ways of *approaching a difficult situation*:
  - using talents
  - using aids and asking for help
  - applying compensatory tactics
  - acquiring or improving skills.

- In the next series of worksheets, there is an information page which introduces each of the above strategies. Then, for each of the three main difficulties, the young person looks for solutions based on the use of these strategies (using talents, aids, etc.).

- To facilitate the transfer of the processes applied in the three situations, a number of worksheets are provided for planning how to deal with specific problems or difficult situations. An information sheet shows a task analysis for *solving a problem*. The following worksheets are completed during different stages of resolution of the problem.

- A final section focuses on a specific problem often experienced by people with autism: blockages. A number of worksheets give details about *blockages of thought and action*, when they occur and what happens during them. In the worksheets which follow, the young person can personalise these points: 'What should I do during a blockage of thinking or action?' Thanks to an information page, the young person receives explanations about the kinds of reactions that are socially desirable (or not). In the light of these appropriate reactions, a plan incorporating personal advice for better ways of managing blockages can be developed. Finally, the participant can draw up a number of tips for those around him: 'How can others help me when I have a blockage of thinking or actions?'

5 The manual

5.1 Introductory remarks

The aim of the exercises in 'The world in fragments' is that the person with autism acquires necessary strategies and assimilates advice for coping with situations which are difficult or troublesome as a result of their autism. The worksheets 'How do I deal with difficulties caused by my autism?' provide a brief summary. These may be presented to the young person as follows: 'We've learned what autism is, now let's look at what you can do in order to be troubled as little as possible by this disorder.' In the original version of *I am Special*, the worksheets 'Autism is incurable ...but something can be done about it!' place emphasis on adaptations and environmental supports. The worksheets in 'The world in fragments', above all, are about what the person with autism can do himself or herself, to reduce the negative consequences of autism.

Introducing this theme carries a risk. In some cases, the young person harbours an illusion that he will succeed in bringing his autism completely under control. The facilitator needs to be vigilant about these too optimistic expectations and should keep the aims and content of the topic in the right perspective. One way to achieve this is to rely on the worksheets in the initial workbook and to point out:

1. that, regardless of interventions, autism is a disability and will always complicate certain situations

2. that there are two ways to reduce the negative consequences of autism: learning how to manage one's own difficulties and receiving support and help (see the worksheet '...but something can be done about it!')

In other words: be as independent as possible whenever possible and when this is not possible, ask others for support.

Another way of keeping things in perspective is to explain to the person that one cannot change the autism itself, but one can tackle the consequences of the autism, in (very) difficult and (very) troublesome situations. With adolescents and more gifted young adults, the facilitator can provide more details on the theme, 'you can do something yourself about your autism', and can explain this in more depth using a schematic representation of the social model of disability (see the suggestions given in the worksheets 'How do I deal with difficulties caused by my autism?'). With this model, the facilitator can highlight the rectangle below on their talents and compensations, thus making a visually apparent space for the worksheets as a whole:

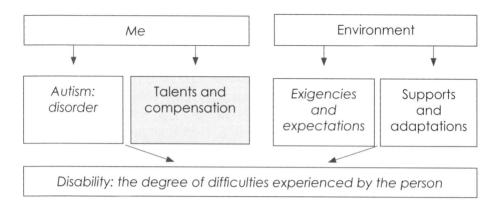

We want to warn against too great an optimism or having expectations that are too optimistic, both in the facilitator and in the wider environment of the youngsters with autism (such as their parents and teachers). Although the aim of the worksheets is to motivate the person with autism to confront their problems or to come up with ideas by themselves, the possibilities for these persons to control their autism are not limitless. Anyone who expects the person with autism to behave in a less autistic way (or be less difficult) after having completed these worksheets, is quite naive. Just as with the initial *I am Special* workbook, the purpose of these exercises is not to bring about a dramatic change in behaviour from the beginning. The main aim is and remains to inform the person with autism. In transferring this knowledge to real life, most adolescents are and will remain heavily dependent on the support of others. To that extent, the worksheets on managing blockages of thought and action are a bit paradoxical. The typical characteristic of a blockage is precisely to be blocked and therefore not to know how to effectively and efficiently manage a difficult situation. To apply strategies in a real situation, the majority of young people remain dependent on a repertoire, a scenario that will activate the strategies learned. To avoid the frustrations of the young person as well as those of the people around him/her (due to overly optimistic expectations with regard to the sessions 'How do I deal with difficulties caused by my autism?'), it is advisable to state clearly that the primary purpose of the sessions is to create an environment that is favourable to autism (see Chapter 2 on self-image in Part 1).

This adapted version of *I am Special* also particularly addresses adolescents and young adults who use their autism as an excuse for not having to do certain activities: 'There's no point asking me such a thing – there's no way I can do it, because I have autism.' The worksheets demonstrate that people with autism have very many ways of dealing with difficult situations. Adolescents who use their autism as an excuse for avoiding certain situations do not always do so for convenience. Sometimes they do not have the imagination necessary to see how they can deal with situations or they lack sufficient self-confidence.

 The worksheets on the CD ROM do not include illustrations or colours. If appropriate, in consultation with the person with autism, it is recommended they be added. For each of the main areas of impairment, for example, it is advisable to choose different colours. Different strategies for resolving difficult situations can be assigned different symbols. For example:

Talents

Aids

Asking for assistance

'Tricks'

Learning or improving skills.

For ease of use, the worksheets are, again, not numbered. In the manual, however, we have used page numbers for easy reference to the CD ROM documents.

Finally, the authors of this chapter (Marion Fuijkschot-Timmers and Bart Konings of *Pleincollege Antoon Schellens* in the Netherlands) have compiled the exercises under the name 'The world in fragments'. This title encompasses not only the actual worksheets but also their adapted version of the initial *I am Special* workbook. Depending on the range of vocabulary and preferences of the person with autism, the user/s can opt, if wished, and if appropriate in consultation with the person with autism or the group, for a more appealing title. The worksheets can be used both in an individual way and with a group.

5.2 Difficulties due to autism

Note: we have explicitly chosen to avoid the term 'problem'. This is a word with very negative connotations, especially for adolescents with autism. An expression such as 'difficult situation' is more neutral and indicates moreover that part of the difficulty resides not solely in the person with autism but also in the situation. This expression connects more closely to the social model of disability (see above). If the facilitator wishes to add to the information on difficulties already mentioned, he or she must be sure to use this wording. In accordance with the self-image of the person with autism, try to describe difficulties in terms of situations rather than in terms of personal characteristics. So do not say, 'I (or you) am unable to start a conversation properly,' but 'Starting a conversation is difficult for me (you).'

AIMS

- To recognise (identify or draw up an inventory) the difficulties associated with the main impairments in autism (social communication and interaction, imagination/flexibility) in oneself.

- To identify which are the three main ones, from these difficulties.

- If the facilitator wishes: test out the difficulties identified by the person with autism with those recognised by the people around him/her (this evaluation can help to establish a list of priorities).

METHOD AND ESSENTIAL ELEMENTS

If the person has already completed the characteristics of autism in the original *I am Special* workbook, this worksheet does not need to be repeated, unless the time elapsed is too long, in which case drawing up a new inventory is recommended.

Since it is not always easy for people with autism to have a more or less realistic view of their own potential and limitations, the facilitator can use, here, different sources of information. In order to give a more realistic assessment of difficulties, alongside the version for the person with autism, there are two supplementary versions for each worksheet, one for the parent(s) and one for another person. This can be a teacher or teaching assistant, a personal tutor, a therapist or another facilitator from a different group, etc.

Besides increasing the reliability of the information, letting several other people complete the exercise can also open up a conversation about the similarities and differences between the young person's self-image and how he is perceived by others. This can be presented visually by bringing together different people's information on one page. The aim is in no way to discuss with the young person who is right and who is wrong. It is preferable to avoid these kinds of discussions. The objective is simply to broaden the young person's viewpoint.

The fact that other people complete the lists undoubtedly raises questions on the part of the individual with autism. Explanations and clarifications are often necessary. For example, a discussion (group or individual) can be opened up to find out why parents ticked more, fewer or different options.

A minor point: it has happened that one boy with autism thought his parents had to fill in the page about themselves. He therefore asked about the worksheet 'What should I do when I'm faced with a blockage of thoughts or action?': 'Do my parents need to say how they react to a blockage of thoughts or action?' (In the meantime, the worksheet was adapted.) Some clarifications are therefore recommended, especially when one of the parents also presents with an autism spectrum disorder.

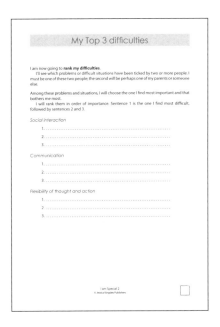

The above exercise reduces the lists of difficulties to a 'shortlist' which can be used again later. In view of the fact that choosing and prioritising are two tasks that can be very difficult for people with autism, a mathematical principle has been chosen for ranking the difficulties. In the previous worksheet, difficulties must be chosen by at least two people to make the top three. If this operation is too complicated, the young person can sort the difficulties as follows: first of all, those ticked by three people, then those ticked by two people, then those which only the young person has chosen, and finally, those ticked by only one other person.

To avoid a writing task that is too unwieldy, the original worksheets need to be photocopied and the difficulties cut into strips. These can thus be easily sorted into categories. These strips can be very useful, especially when choosing the top three: the different choices can be visualised and the young person has another opportunity to rearrange the strips. When the final choice has been made, the top three is complete. It is also possible to establish a top five.

5.3 How can I deal with difficulties caused by my autism?

This short text can serve as an introduction to all those who look over the previous worksheets, given that shortly before this, the person with autism has drawn up an inventory of their own difficulties.

5.4 How can I deal with a difficult situation?

This page gives a visual overview of difficult situations and problems. It serves as a kind of flowchart that gives a logical and chronological summary, a visual plan.

Furthermore, it is also possible to choose between dealing with the problem or not. Some people do not wish to deal with a problem and continue to live without seeking concrete solutions. This is a choice we need to respect. For the person who chooses to deal with difficult situations, there are four possibilities mentioned in the diagram, elaborated upon in the next two pages.

For a number of participants, especially younger ones and those with a lower level of intelligence, this worksheet can be too difficult (it contains a lot of information) and then it is better not to approach it. Moreover, the application to daily life is even more complicated. It is also advisable to mention to the participants that they can obtain help during certain stages, for example with 'What do you do if you are not sure of something or if you want to change something?' One must also take care not to inadvertently create the illusion that, through using the stages in this plan, the problem in question will be resolved. Even when the plan is followed, the problem may persist because the plan did not work well or was not sufficiently detailed.

5.5 Talents, assistance, 'tricks' and skills

This page gives an overview of the different options for dealing with difficult situations. Instead of simply asking the participant to read the worksheet, the facilitator can, if he or she wishes, encourage more active involvement by brainstorming different ways of dealing with a difficult situation, sorting and grouping them in a Socratic way.

5.6 Talents

AIMS

- To be aware of one's talents, to draw up an inventory of one's own talents, to relate one's talents to difficult situations by using the top three difficult situations and to develop practical and personalised advice.

Given that for people with autism, it is not always easy to have a more or less realistic view of their own potential and limitations, several sources of information can be used in this case (just as with the list of their difficulties). It is recommended, especially with adolescents who have quite a negative self-image, to have several people complete the worksheets on talents. For the young person who comes up without any or hardly any positive points, seeing a list of his talents can be a real turning point. For some, this list of talents is a revelation and can lead to conversations with others about their positive characteristics and thus contribute to the development of a positive self-image.

METHOD AND ESSENTIAL ELEMENTS

The method is the same as for the section on difficulties.

Again, the young person can gather information from different sources onto one page, where you can always see everyone's contribution. Compiling a simple list of all talents ticked (and the person who ticked them) or of the talents (also who ticked them) which the young person feels are important and which he recognises in himself is less complicated and clearer from a visual point of view. Abandoning the somewhat artificial division of the main categories of autism impairments is an even simpler way of reducing the number of pages. This reduction is especially advised for young people who quickly become lost with a large quantity of worksheets or for those who detest this kind of exercise.

Another disadvantage is that the young person may become confused and think that all the talents ticked on the page about social interaction are for use only and exclusively when dealing with difficult social situations (and those in the next section solely for difficulties in the area of communication). It is preferable to point out that talents in one domain can also be used to resolve difficult situations in another. For example, talents in communication can also be used in difficult social situations. The aim of sorting according to the main characteristics of autism is merely to show clearly that, despite their problems, people with autism also have talents and skills in these domains, and that they can use these to deal with difficult situations.

For young people who encounter problems during the numerous exercises and with sorting according to autism's main characteristics, it is preferable to start from concrete situations or examples. Indeed, due to their difficulties with episodic memory, people with autism experience greater difficulties with engaging in abstract reflections on themselves (in general terms) than with remembering concrete situations. Another option is to rely on the 'talent hunt' in the original *I am Special* workbook, and to continue filling this in, without grouping the elements into the three categories.

It is also advisable to give other people (for example parents) the pages preceding the list of talents, to complement these.

If he or she wishes, the young person can establish a 'Top 3' of their talents or bring together their main talents on one page. It is also recommended this is done when the list of talents is so long that it becomes unclear to the young person, and as a result, he or she experiences difficulty choosing from his talents when dealing with a specific situation.

Just as with ranking difficulties, a mathematical principle can be followed: first of all those talents mentioned by all the informers, then those ticked by two people, and so on.

'Dealing with difficult situations using talents: my personal advice' proposes a link between talents and difficult situations.

First of all, the top three difficult situations are repeated again on the worksheet. If autism's main areas of impairment were used during the inventory, it can be verified whether the problem is a difficulty linked to social communication, social interaction or flexibility of actions and thinking (imagination/rigidity). These concepts can be added if the distinction is clear and if they are related to the problem. Then, consider which talents can contribute towards alleviating each problem and which can help the situation. Thus talents are matched to problems and transformed into advice. This must be formulated as concretely as possible, in such a way that the young person will know when and how to act.

Depending on the young person's level, the whole process can be taken step by step, or the young person can complete the worksheets on their own first of all and then discuss them with the facilitator. In all cases, discussion is recommended before definitive advice takes shape and is noted down, to avoid the process ultimately leading to quite impractical advice. People with the capability to do so can complete the whole process on the computer. They themselves describe the problems they face, the talents that they can employ in these cases and even formulate some concrete advice. It is also essential to establish a contact person for this topic, to answer questions or provide clarifications. In every instance, it is essential that the advice provided by the young person is feasible and achievable and that they are also aware that the advice might help to ease complicated situations. In our experience, 'imposed' advice is generally not used.

VARIATIONS AND ADDITIONS

- Describe the concept of talent and look up the definition in a dictionary or on the internet.
- Name some people who have talent and draw up a list of one's own talents.
- Show photos of people who have a particular talent.
- Make collages of their own talents with diplomas, words, drawings, photos, medals, etc.
- Make a video recording of one of their talents, for example, a sport, hobby or music.
- Point out that a talent is not necessarily visible in someone's appearance, but can also stem from an ability to listen, relate well to others, ask for things, or to speak clearly.
- For adolescents who have or wish to have a more subtle image of themselves, ticking a list may seem too black-and-white and can therefore complicate the selection ('I know quite well how to do this, but it's not very well done.'). For them, it is easier to make a list that includes gradations, for example a scale of one to five (1: I am very poor in this area and 5: I am very good in this area).

5.7 Supports

AIMS

- To know the general meaning of the term 'support'.
- To know that supports are not specific to people with autism but can be used by everyone.
- To give details of examples described as supports.

- To understand that, for people with autism, certain supports may have advantages.

- To make a personal list of supports for their own use.

- To associate personal supports with difficult situations, if necessary for use in the top three difficult situations.

METHOD AND ESSENTIAL ELEMENTS

If necessary and if desired, the facilitator can repeat once more the worksheets on 'solutions and aids' in the initial version of *I am Special*. It is regularly the case that young people, especially those who received a late diagnosis, oppose the notion of 'supports'. It is recommended, and not only with them, to dissociate this notion from the concept of disability (negative for them). Everyone uses aids every day. First the facilitator can, in dissociating them from autism and from handicap, ask the participants to carry out a brainstorming activity to find supports used by everyone in general (diary, alarm, plans, reminders, etc.).

Then, it can be explained that for people with autism these supports can be very useful and that the only difference is that there are specific supports for them, which are not used by everyone.

The facilitator will review the list of supports and provide explanations of where they are needed. In a group, going around the table lets everyone see who has already used which supports and which, through experimenting, they have already abandoned. It is useful to provide illustrations or concrete examples and to advocate for usage or to let those who have already used the supports validate their usage. The facilitator must also provide sufficient time to add to the list of supports drawn up by the participants (regardless of any 'autistic' aspect). For adolescents interested in the field of computing, a specific session can be provided on using a computer, tablet or smart phone for different purposes (projects, diary, budget, spare time, communicating via e-mail, etc.). Then the young person can take note of which supports he thinks he could use for specific activities. It is essential to explain that the chosen support should actually be used to tackle the problem. To facilitate generalisation of learning, a concrete step by step plan can be drawn up on a separate page for the introduction and use of the support: who will buy it or make it, how it will be used, etc.

My personal advice worksheets

For some young people, always having to complete worksheets on their difficulties could pose problems. For them, it is more useful to use three different pages, one for each difficulty, and, below, the different categories: talents, support, skills and asking for help (see p.49). As a facilitator, be prepared for each category not to be filled in: this is not the point. For certain situations, there are no supports that can be used. For example: understanding the meaning of others' remarks.

5.8 Asking for help

Aims

These worksheets as designed are limited to an introduction to asking for help as a potential solution to difficult situations and problems. Depending on the young person and their previous experiences, other objectives (below) can be added.

- To impress upon the young person that asking for help and accepting it is a normal phenomenon. Everyone needs to ask for help now and then.
- To recognise a deadlock situation where asking for help is necessary.
- To know when it is necessary to ask for help.
- To learn to tell the difference between immediate and necessary help and that which possibly can be postponed.
- To know how to ask for help.
- To learn how to use an aid to ask for help.
- To draw up a social network giving an overview of people whom the young person can call upon for help.

(No worksheets have been drafted for these aims.)

Method and essential elements

The starting point is reading the 'Dealing with difficult situations using questions' worksheet with the participant. This page is essential because it gives good reasons for the situation and convinces the young person of the importance of asking others for help. It is advisable to invent (or ask the young person to name) a certain number of situations where it is hoped one would ask for help and where some practical advantages may become apparent. The practical examples are, in particular, asking the way, asking the time, asking about the start or finish of an event, asking for help to move an object, etc.

If the work is done in groups, the various participants can complete this and give other examples. These examples are perhaps going to be variations of the previous examples. This is not serious in itself, if other examples are cited. It is crucial that problems are recognised, as well as the positive consequences of a request for help. Some adolescents are hostile to this idea because they want to be as independent as possible and they associate asking for help with dependency. It is important to explain to them that asking for help increases one's (social) competence and therefore one's independence.

VARIATIONS AND ADDITIONS

People with autism function in different environments and situations. These environments present not only their own problems but they also require different communication styles. Asking for help at school is not done perhaps in the same way as at home or with other people. Since people with autism do not always have an overview of the different possibilities and limitations of these situations, it is advisable to draw a kind of social map. This is an overview of their social network, identifying people whom they may ask for help. In the middle of a page, the young person can, for example, draw themselves and draw around them, in boxes or circles, different situations (in class, at home, at youth groups, etc.) with beside these, the names of people who can help them and therefore whom they can actually ask for help.

To avoid needless frustration, it is also important to mention that a person is not always immediately available to help. The facilitator needs to explain the procedure to be followed should the need arise (look for someone else, write down the question, phone someone, put the problem aside, etc.).

Complementary role play around frequent situations is very useful and encourages the transfer of skills acquired in asking for help. In such role play, apart from the many repetitions, the rate of increasing difficulty is very important. For example: first practise in the usual place with people you trust; then ask for something within the same organisation with the usual facilitator helping the participant (the person whom the participant is asking for information is primed); in the next phase – still in a safe environment – the facilitator's help is no longer solicited and in the final phase, the young person practises asking questions outside this trusted environment.

If he or she wishes, the facilitator can use a video for feedback. The young people are recorded practising asking questions. These recordings are then viewed, discussed and evaluated according to aspects relating to asking for help (such as eye contact, use of language, intonation). Some people with autism find it very difficult to look at this sort of thing. However, our experience has shown us that this exercise if very helpful.

5.9 'Tricks'
AIMS

- To know that one can tackle a situation with a 'trick'.

- To know that a 'trick' is only a temporary solution and that, in the long run, may even further complicate a situation (if a person always avoids a problem, one might be forced into facing it, which would only increase one's stress).

- To establish a kind of repertoire of 'tricks' to survive in certain difficult situations.

The 'tricks' mentioned are always synonymous with either a '*deferment*' of the difficulty (counting 1 to 10 during a change, saying that for now you don't have the time), or an '*avoidance*' (fleeing the situation, letting another person make a decision).

METHOD AND ESSENTIAL ELEMENTS

There are two options for the 'Dealing with difficult situations using "tricks"' worksheet:

1. Read and discuss all the 'tricks'. Ask whether the young person has already been through such a situation, whether the advice mentioned would help and whether the young person would try it out, after which the facilitator can ask the young person to think of a concrete example of its application.

2. Proposing a list of 'tricks' is more difficult, but the person can, in this case, think of one situation where they would implement this advice.

To make things clearer, it is possible to illustrate a situation through role play. In our experience, the individual understands much better when he or she actually sees the problem and the implementation of the advice.

If necessary, other 'tricks' (no matter if they are 'autistic') can also be added.

Following on from this is the matching up of tricks to the difficult situations chosen by the person.

VARIATIONS AND ADDITIONS

Sometimes, some adolescents with autism invent 'tricks' which, even temporarily, are no solution, because they are socially unacceptable or intolerable, such as categorically refusing to carry out a task, pushing someone away or attacking them (verbally). Through (Socratic) questioning in the right direction, the facilitator can make the young person reflect on whether or not these options are adequate.

5.10 Skills

AIMS

The basic aim of these exercises is to know what skills are, to know and evaluate for oneself some important skills (especially communication skills) and match these to certain problem situations. The 'skills' worksheets in this section forms an excellent starting point for drawing up a plan with the young person for practising their social and communication skills.

METHOD AND ESSENTIAL ELEMENTS

Given that, in this area, young people with autism also face problems in evaluating their own difficulties and limitations, it is possible – just as for the exercises on difficulties and talents – to use different sources of information and, for example, to ask their parents and/or staff members to carry out an evaluation of the young person's level of competence.

Many of the skills cited here are very abstract and therefore either need to be made more concrete or explained by examples.

Most of the skills mentioned refer, again, to asking for help. These lines are not mandatory for adolescents who would struggle with this duplication (because of the repetition or because they would not know which part belongs to this chapter).

If the user wishes, the number of columns for rating competence can be reduced to two (I manage to use this very well/I still need to learn) or expanded to four (to avoid the participant always choosing the category in the middle).

Furthermore, with young people, it may be useful to indicate on the list of skills they still need to learn which ones the young person wants to learn first.

In 'My personal advice: skills' worksheet, the young person can indicate which skills he or she wants to use for their top three difficult situations. One colour could possibly indicate that the skill in question has yet to be acquired.

In the following worksheet, for each difficult situation, there is an immediate overview of what the person can do.

5.11 Solutions to problems

Note for the worksheet below: this page gives a visual and schematic summary of the two previous pages. The user needs to decide whether to use this page comprising the corresponding explanations first, then the previous pages with the numbered text, or *vice versa* (or only the summary). This page also partially overlaps with the worksheet on how to deal with difficult situations. The user can choose, if wished, one of the two versions.

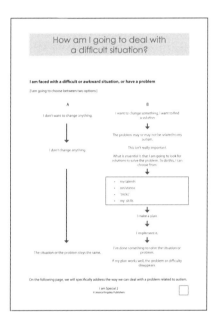

AIMS

- To increase the ability of the young person to resolve problems by having him or her understand the process of problem resolution.

- To establish a concrete plan in stages for tackling problems and difficult situations.

METHOD AND ESSENTIAL ELEMENTS

While the purpose of previous exercises was above all for the young person to learn different ways of dealing with difficult situations, these worksheets provide an overall plan in stages for addressing problems and difficult situations. The material on the previous pages can be used as concrete information for completing these exercises. Then, a particular and specific problem situation is chosen and, thanks to the exercises already completed, a very concrete plan is made for addressing the situation.

It is vital for everyone to have control over their life and its adherent problems. This control is also essential for people with autism, all the more so since it is lost more easily, due to difficulties with having a cohesive view of the world around them and of their inner world.

It is precisely because of this lack of a cohesive view (a result of weak central coherence, a characteristic of autism) that a systematic, step-by-step plan supports this control over situations and problems. The advantage of a step by step plan is that the problem is reduced to distinguishing a clear number of consecutive phases. Learning to work with a step by step plan is important because it can be applied to each problem that crops up, whatever its size and complexity.

The step-by-step plan presented here is composed of six parts or phases:

- two phases for identifying the problem (what is the problem and what would I like to change?)

- two phases for planning the change (how am I going to change and what am I going to do?)

- two phases for implementation and evaluation and/or amending the plan.

The plan is presented in different forms:

- a verbal description

- a visual plan

- pages with concrete questions to fill in.

In the identification of problems, a formula of five questions can be used:

- Where does the problem occur?

- When was it?

- Who was there?

- What happened, exactly?

- What do I want to change?

In the decision making towards finding a solution, we use the lists of advice, skills and 'tricks' previously established. Asking someone for help is also an option. The advantage of holding this session in a group is that much of the acceptable advice can be used by the majority of participants. The young people with autism can draw on the fruitful and positive experiences of other participants. Asking someone for help or telling a trusted person about a problem is advised fairly frequently.

It is recommended to divide the fourth step into small parts (making a plan: what am I going to do now?).

For example:

- What do I say?
- Who do I say it to?
- When do I say it?
- How do I say it?

The evaluation on the worksheet can of course be completed later. However, going through the exercise beforehand with the young person is recommended, so that he or she can visualise the outcome of the events.

The following questions play a role in the evaluation:

- Did the plan work?
- Are there any improvements to be made?
- Is the situation less difficult now, or less problematic?
- Did I do and say what I had planned?
- Did I forget something?
- Is the problem gone, or diminished?
- Am I pleased with the solution?

If the young person responds yes to these types of questions, the problem is resolved and nothing more needs to be changed. If the plan is not completely working, the young person and the facilitator can think of another way to approach it, and adapt the plan.

We wish to draw attention to the fact that the young person can fall into the trap of being naive and having too much optimism. Indeed, having finished the plan, the young person risks hoping for a complete and immediate success. To avoid frustration, it is advisable to mention to him/her beforehand that no plan works 100 per cent the first time and that adaptations will therefore be necessary.

VARIATIONS AND ADDITIONS

The layout and format of the pages can easily be adapted so that the young person can develop their own supports for 'solutions to problems'. The flowchart and the step-by-step plan can be presented in a numerical format.

IMPORTANT NOTE

Social difficulties constitute the greatest impairment in people with autism. Be aware that fruitful experiences will unfold more easily through using a step-by-step plan, when, in your choice of a concrete problem situation, you have not chosen a social difficulty straight away, but rather a practical problem. Often, with this kind of support, we tend to deal right away with serious and important problems (as a parent or facilitator, we derive many benefits from this). However, the risk of failure is fairly high and as a result, the young person may lose confidence in the support that we have presented for them (the step by step plan) and therefore refuse to continue using it. This is why it is recommended introducing the step-by-step plan for problems:

- which are quite practical in nature (and which do not pose too many social and/or communication demands)

- which are seen as a problem, especially by the young person (although parents and professionals may have totally different priorities)

- which are not too entrenched (problems which have existed for a long time are persistent and often complex)

- which can be solved in the short term.

Sometimes, a certain amount of direction or critical Socratic questioning in the choice of problem, without neglecting the wishes of the young person, is recommended. A compromise can eventually be found by subdividing a (very important and very difficult) given problem into parts, and beginning with one of these partial problems. Small steps ensure greater success than larger projects.

5.12 Blockage of thoughts and actions

Despite practising all sorts of skills, despite different kinds of support and assistance, adolescents with autism still regularly get out of their depth and block. Because of their autism and their autistic thinking style, they are easily overwhelmed by stimuli which they find difficult to understand and are, more often than other people, distressed, angry, confused or panicked. These reactions result in panic attacks, apathy, outbursts of anger or aggressiveness – depending on the person, his temperament and the situation experienced at the time. Since these reactions involve quite negative terms, it is preferable to choose more neutral expressions that start from the inner, real-life experiences of the person with autism, that is: *blockages of thoughts and actions (or 'getting stuck')*.

The previous worksheets on solving problems were used, above all, to deal with difficult situations in a structured way and therefore started more from a preventative and proactive point of view. Since, despite such preventative plans, young people with autism are at high risk of losing it in certain situations and therefore experiencing intense stress, some supplementary exercises have been developed to manage such 'blockages'.

AIMS

- To know what blockages of thoughts and actions are.

- To recognise blockages of thoughts and actions.

- To know when blockages of thoughts and actions occur and be able to link them to typical difficulties for people with autism (imprecision, unpredictability, sudden changes, misunderstandings arising from a literal understanding).

- To associate the notion of blockages of thought and action with the concept of stress.

- To be able to describe for oneself a situation in which a blockage develops.

- To be aware of these different reactions in such situations.

- To be able to assess one's own reactions during a blockage of thought and action in terms of the consequences for oneself and for others.

- To draw up a list of socially acceptable and inoffensive reactions to blockages of thoughts and actions.

- To draw up a personal plan for how to react during blockages of thoughts and actions in the future.

> ### Blockage of thoughts and action: a frequent problem in the world of autism
>
> **What is a blockage of thoughts or action?**
> This means that your thoughts and your actions are stuck.
>   You can no longer think about anything – **blockage of thoughts.**
>   You no longer know what to do, how to react – **blockage of action.**
>
> Other expressions have more or less the same meaning: to be in disarray, to be confused, to be paralysed by fear, to panic, not knowing what to do, experiencing a mental block, losing the plot.
>
> Are you familiar with blockages of thoughts and action?
>   Can you remember a time when you could no longer think or you no longer knew what to do?
>   Describe the situation below as well as how you reacted.
>
> Situation: ....
> ....
> ....
> ....
> ....
> ....
>
> My reaction: ....
> ....
> ....
> ....
> ....
>
> I am Special 2
> © Jessica Kingsley Publishers

METHOD AND ESSENTIAL ELEMENTS

Generally, explanation of the concept of 'blockage' is indeed possible, as well as the term 'blockage of thoughts and actions'. Problems often arise when the young person is required to give examples of these blockages. If this is the case, it is necessary to formulate the question differently. For example: 'Have you ever experienced a situation where you didn't know what to do or say?'; 'Have you ever been so confused or disoriented that you no longer knew what to say or do?' Young people can often give better responses to these questions than to questions about blockages. It is sometimes useful to recall a situation that is a diversion from the issue, for example, 'Have you ever been furious or very upset?'

Then, we explain why blockages of thoughts and actions are a frequent problem for people with autism and this notion is placed within the context of stress. These exercises contain a lot of text and for some young people, it is preferable to replace these with worksheets with less text, whether illustrated by graphics or not.

Various sources of information can again be utilised for completing the worksheets on the ways in which the young person usually reacts in stressful situations. The information from different sources can be gathered together on a summary worksheet. At this stage of the inventory, the goal is not, just yet, to include an assessment of the reactions listed (knowing whether a reaction is appropriate or not). Giving a judgement too soon prevents a certain number of responses from being expressed and generally results in the contribution of only socially desirable responses.

The 'Blockage of thoughts and action' worksheets introduce criteria from which the young person can, in the following pages, assess whether their reactions to stress are appropriate or not (appropriate here is synonymous with socially acceptable and inoffensive for the young person and those around him/her). The criteria are described in a very abstract way and, for some adolescents, they are therefore not concrete enough. Through a Socratic discussion, it is perhaps worth leaving young people to reflect on these criteria themselves.

Furthermore, due to the difficulties experienced by young people with autism in the area of theory of mind, it is very difficult for them to gauge the effects of their behaviour, in particular, how others experience it. There are different options for dealing with this during the assessment of reactions. People with autism also know the feeling of being teased or being hurt and some of them know very well how to explain it. In this case, the facilitator can start from their perspective in assessing behaviours, through questions such as: 'What would you think if someone behaved like this towards you?' The facilitator can then help the young person to understand that the other person experiences the same feeling if they behave similarly towards him. So do not ask the question 'How is the other person going to feel?' but 'How would you feel if such a thing happened to you?' or 'What is your reaction going to be, if someone behaves like that to you?'

For adolescents who find this exercise in reflection too difficult, it is possible to call upon external informants such as parents and assistants. In practical terms, this means that it is not the young person but others who complete the worksheets. It should preferably be people the young person has chosen himself. It is not impossible to call upon a peer, but we must be careful, in particular with regard to a too negative assessment on their part.

Usually, it is necessary to carry out a more nuanced assessment. Where appropriate, the worksheets should be adapted. There are situations where a certain behaviour is acceptable and situations where the environment does not support the same behaviour. Everything depends on the time, the place, the people present, etc. For example: playing music is not always a problem, but it is if it's the middle of the night and in a flat. On the basis of such observations, a diversified list can be made of acceptable reactions according to circumstances. Variations of reactions being acceptable or not is highly individualised and dependent on environmental tolerance. Sometimes this leads us to intervening with those closest to the young person, so that they will be more tolerant towards the young person with autism.

Again, some young people may find it tiresome to have to tick answers once again. One solution is to cut out all the reactions into strips and sort them into categories. If necessary, a new category can be created for the 'I don't know if this reaction is appropriate or not' strips. These strips will find their place thanks to a supplementary discussion.

Thanks to this list of appropriate reactions, the young person can create, for one or more situations, a personal manual.

To supplement what the young person himself can do in a blockage, he can also make a list stating his wishes with respect to his environment. The young person explains what he would want others to do during a blockage of his thoughts or actions (for example, talk to him), what helps when he faces an impasse (for example, leave him alone for a few minutes) and what he hates others saying or doing (for example, talking too much, touching him). In this way, we do not place a huge share of responsibility on the young person, when it comes to tackling the stress arising from autism. The environment also plays an important role in tackling autism.

With this page as a visual support, the young person can, thereafter, communicate their wishes to their parents, to a teacher and to other young people (carry over).

The CD ROM documents

 The CD ROM documents conclude the full version of 'The World in Fragments'.

Authors:

Marion Fuijkschot-Timmers, Bart Konings and Peter Vermeulen

CD ROM documents
Contents

I am Special

- I am unique
- My body
- The brain
- Being different: About people who are different
- Autism: A special disability

The big book about me

- Introduction
- My personal details
- My outside
- My inside
- My body
- My brain: A very special part of my body
- Being different
- Autism

That's me?!

- My hobbies
- The brain receives, processes and sends information

- True or false?
- Intelligence
- Learning disabilities
- The brain of someone with autism works differently
- Who am I?
- My future
- The tree: what I've learned about my intelligence

Version for siblings

- Autism
- Difficulties due to autism
- Other difficulties associated with autism
- People with autism are also different from one another, too
- True or false?
- Having a brother or sister with autism…

Various worksheets

- Our inside and our outside
- How the brain works
- My character 1: (for children and young people)
- My character 2: (for adolescents and adults)
- My strong points and my not-so-strong points (simplified version with illustrations)
- Identity card
- This is what others find special about me
- My favourite
- Frequently asked questions on autism

I am Special – game

- I am special – game board
- Communication cards
- Social interaction cards
- Imagination cards

Evaluation forms

- Referral form for the 'I am special' course
- Invitation to '*I am Special*'
- Evaluation of the 'I am special' course (children and young people)
- Evaluation of the 'I am special' course (adults)
- Evaluation of the 'I am special' course (parents and/or carers)
- Evaluation of the 'I am special' course (groups)

Examples of worksheets for adults

- Profile
- Your definition of a relationship
- Communication
- The brain receives, processes and sends information
- Explaining autism

The world in fragments

- Part 1: Difficulties due to autism
- Part 2: How do I deal with difficulties caused by my autism?
- Part 3: Solutions to problems
- Part 4: Blockages of thoughts and action

Literature

I am Special is one of the few psychoeducational manuals for people with autism spectrum disorders. For complementary information, other works are also available, some in other languages. Unlike *I am Special*, most of these publications are less interactive. Rather, they are books which explain autism. Publications marked with an asterisk (*) are available via the National Autistic Society (www.autism.org.uk).

Attwood, T. (1998) *Asperger's Syndrome*. London and Philadelphia: Jessica Kingsley Publishers.

Davies, J. (1994) (*) *Able Autistic Children – Children with Asperger's Syndrome: A Booklet for Brothers and Sisters*. Nottingham: The Early Years Diagnosis Centre.

Davies, J. (1994) (*) *Children with Autism – A Booklet for Brothers and Sisters*. Nottingham: The Early Years Diagnosis Centre.

De Clercq, H. (2003) *Mum, is that a human being or an animal? A book on autism*. Bristol: Lucky Duck Publishing.

Doherty, K., McNally, P. and Sherrard, E. (2000) (*) *I Have Autism...What's That?* Down Lisburn Trust.

Faherty, C. (2004) *Asperger's: What Does It Mean to Me?* Arlington: Future Horizons, Inc.

Fairfoot, E. (2004) (*) *My Special Brother Rory*. London: National Autistic Society.

Frender, S. and Schiffmiller, R. (2007) *Brotherly Feelings: Me, My Emotions, and My Brother with Asperger's Syndrome*. London and Philadelphia: Jessica Kingsley Publishers.

Gerland, G. (2000) (*) *Finding out About Asperger's Syndrome, High Functioning Autism and PDD*. London and Philadelphia: Jessica Kingsley Publishers.

Gorrod, L. (1997) (*) *My Brother is Different*. London: National Autistic Society.

Hénault, I. (2006) *Asperger's Syndrome and Sexuality: From Adolescence Through Adulthood*. London: Jessica Kingsley Publishers.

Hunter, S.T. (2006) (*) *My Sister is Different*. London: National Autistic Society.

Lawson, W., Murray, D., Neilson Walker, E. (2003) *Build Your Own Life: A Self-Help Guide for Individuals with Asperger's Syndrome*. London and Philadelphia: Jessica Kingsley Publishers.

National Autistic Society (2000) (*) *What is Asperger's Syndrome, and How Will It Affect Me? – A Guide for Young People*. London: National Autistic Society.

Newport, J. (2001) *Your Life is Not a Label*. Arlington: Future Horizons.

Peralta, S. (2002) *All About My Brother*. Shawnee Mission, Kansas: Autism Asperger Publishing Co.

Santomauro, J. (2009) *You Are Special Too: A Book for Brothers and Sisters of Children Diagnosed with Asperger's Syndrome*. London and Philadelphia: Jessica Kingsley Publishers.

Spilsbury, L. (2001) (*) *What Does It Mean to Have Autism?* London: Heinemann.

Vermeulen, P. (2010) (*) *Autisme et émotions* (translated by Wendy De Montis). Paris: De Boeck.

Endnotes

1. Centre for training, information and support in autism, Gent, Belgium.
2. See among others the review by Fiona Knott in the National Autistic Society's magazine (*Communication*, Spring 2001) and Professor Alec Webster's in *The Times Educational Supplement* (3rd November 2000).
3. Stemp, M. (2001) 'I Am Special, Introducing Children and Young People to their Autistic Spectrum Disorder.' *British Journal of Learning Disabilities 29*, 2, 77.
4. www.autismwestmidlands.org.uk/files/is_01-explaining%20asd%20to%20the%20 individual%20with%20asd.pdf, accessed 8 January 2013.
5. Chappell, A. *Disability and Society 16*, 2, 327–328.
6. Gerland, G. (1997) *Finding Out About Asperger's Syndrome, High-Functioning Autism and PDD.* London: Jessica Kingsley Publishers.
7. Gray, C. (1996) 'Pictures of Me.' *The Morning News,* pp. 1-14.
8. The ages given are approximate and should be understood to include the necessary margins: ten years therefore means 'circa' ten years. Just as we explicitly indicated in the first version, there are no strictly defined age criteria for the application of *I am Special*.
9. www.scotland.gov.uk/Resource/Doc/266126/0079626.pdf, accessed 14 January 2013.
10. Howlin, P. (2006) 'Reading about self-help books on autistic-spectrum disorders (autism, Asperger's Syndrome).' *The Psychiatrist 30*, 237–238.
11. Blijd-Hoogewijs, E.M.A. and Ketelaars, C.E.J. (2008) 'Behandeling ASS: psycho-educatie, gedragstherapieën, bejegening en psychofarmaca.' In E.H. Horwitz, C.E.J. Ketelaars and A.M.D.N. van Lammeren *Autisme Spectrum Stoornissen bij normaal begaafde volwassenen.* Assen: Van Gorcum.
12. Nederlandse Vereniging voor Psychiatrie (2009) *Richtlijn Diagnostiek en behandeling autismespectrumstoornissen bij kinderen en jeugdigen.* Utrecht: NVvP.
13. Zie onder meer (see amongst others): Bechdolf, A. e.a. (2010) 'Randomized comparison of group cognitive behaviour therapy and group psychoeducation in acute patients with schizophrenia: effects on subjective quality of life.' *Australian and New Zealand Journal of Psychiatry 44*, 2, 144–150. Colom, F. e.a. (2009) 'Psychoeducation for bipolar II disorder: An exploratory, 5-year outcome subanalysis.' *Journal of Affective Disorders 112*, 1–3, 30–35.
14. RCT: Randomized Control Trial. RCT studies are studies that test the efficacy of intervention. RCTs are considered to be the most rigorous method of determining the effects of an intervention (compared to no intervention or another intervention).
15. Rickhuss, S. (2006). Enabling Understanding of a diagnosis of Autism: Experiencing the Process. School of Education, Sheffield Hallam University.

16. Cann, A. (2007) Developing the understanding of self in secondary-aged children with autistic spectrum disorder. Good Autism Practice, 8(1), 49–63.

17. ibid.

18. Oslo Universitetssykehus (2011). *Erfaringer med metoden «Jeg er noe helt spesielt»: Individualsamtaler for å fremme selvforståelse hos barn og ungdom med Asperger's Syndrome.*

19. van der Meijden, S. and van der Stegen, B. (2009) 'Ik heb iets van autisme of zo...' Psychoeducatie voor slimme jongeren met ASS. *Kind en Adolescent Praktijk, 8*(4), 187–197.

20. M. Zimmerman (1998) 'Empowerment and Community Participation: a Review for the Next Millennium.' Paper presented at the 2nd European Congress of Community Psychology, Lisbon, 581–599.

21. In *The Times Educational Supplement* (3 November 2000).

22. Stemp, M. (2001), *ibid.*

23. Premack, D. and Woodruff, G. (1978) 'Does the Chimpanzee Have a Theory of Mind?' *Behavioural and Brain Sciences 4*, 515–526.

24. Frith, U. and Happé, F. (1999) 'Theory of Mind and Self-Consciousness: What is it like to be autistic?' *Mind and Language 14,* 1, 82–89. More recently, Happé has also suggested that reflecting on one's own thoughts relies on the same cognitive and neural functions used for attributing thoughts to others: Happé, F. (2003) 'Theory of Mind and the Self.' *Annals of the New York Academy of Sciences 1001,* (October), 134–144.

25. Williams, D. M. (2010) 'Theory of own mind in autism: Evidence for a specific deficit in self-awareness?' *Autism 14*, 474–494.

26. Capps, L., Sigman, M. and Yirmiya, N. (1995) 'Self-Competence and Emotional Understanding in High-Functioning Children with Autism.' *Development and Psychopathology 7,* 1, 137–149.

27. The discoveries by Mike Connor with a group of young people with autism spectrum disorders, at secondary school and with average intelligence, also indicate a low self perception of social competence, even lower than that of young people with emotional and behavioural problems in the control group. Connor, M. (2000) 'Asperger's Syndrome and the Self-Reports of Comprehensive School Students.' *Educational Psychology in Practice 16,* 3, 285–296.

28. We do not conclude that people with autism with a (severe) learning disability cannot have a negative self-image. However, it is not easy to prove through scientific research, given the limitation that such people know when they are being asked to express themselves spontaneously.

29. Lee, A. and Hobson, P.R. (1998) 'On Developing Self-Concepts: a Controlled Study of Children and Adolescents with Autism.' *Journal of Child Psychology and Psychiatry 39,* 8, 1132–1144.

30. See among others Baron-Cohen, S. (2000) 'Autism: Deficits in Folk Psychology Exist Alongside Superiority in Folk Physics.' In S. Baron-Cohen, H. Tager-Flusberg and D.J. Cohen (Eds) *Understanding Other Minds: Perspectives from Developmental Cognitive Neuroscience* (Second Edition). Oxford/New York: Oxford University Press.

31. ibid.

32. Green, J., Gilchrist, A., Burton, D. and Cox, A. (2000) 'Social and Psychiatric Functioning in Adolescents with Asperger's Syndrome Compared with Conduct Disorder.' *Journal of Autism and Developmental Disorders 30,* 4, 279–293.

33. Purkey, W. (1988) 'An Overview of Self-Concept Theory for Counselors. ERIC Clearinghouse on Counseling and Personnel Services.' Ann Arbor, Mich. (www.ericdigests.org/pre-9211/self.htm, accessed 15 January 2013)

34. Jordan, R.R. and Powell, S.D. (1995) *Understanding and Teaching Children with Autism*. New York: Wiley.

35. Damon, W. and Hart, D. (1982) 'The development of self understanding from infancy through adolescence.' *Child Development 53,* 4, 841–864.

36. ibid.

37. Millward, W., Powell, S., Messer, D. and Jordan, R. (2000) 'Recall for Self and Other in Autism: Children's Memory for Events Experienced by Themselves and their Peers.' *Journal of Autism and Developmental Disorders 30*, 1, 15–28.

38. Crane, L., and Goddard, L. (2008) 'Episodic and semantic autobiographical memory in adults with autism spectrum disorders.' *Journal of Autism and Developmental Disorders 38*, 498–506.

39. Lawson, W. (2000) *Life Behind Glass: a Personal Account of Autism Spectrum Disorder*. London: Jessica Kingsley Publishers.

40. Vermeulen, P. (2002) *Better sooner than later and better later than never: the recognition of autism in normal to gifted persons.* (In Flemish) Antwerp/Gent: EPO/ Vlaamse Dienst Autisme. The questions were not properly a part of the study but a preliminary study regarding the difficulties people with autism face in speaking about themselves.

41. *The Sentence Completion Test* (1989) Uitgeverij Berkhout B.V., Postbus 484, 6500 AL Nijmegen.

42. ibid.

43. Vermeulen, P. (2012) *Autism as Context Blindness*. Overland Park, KS: Autism Asperger Publishing Company.

44. Huskens, B.E.B.M. (1996) *Volwassen personen met autisme: factoren gerelateerd aan adaptief functioneren in de maatschappij*. Nijmegen: Nijmegen University Press.

45. ibid.

46. This is also the result of other studies carried out on self-concept among children with learning disabilities, for example: Cuskelly, M. and de Jong, I. (1996) 'Self-Concept in Children with Down Syndrome.' *Down Syndrome Research and Practice 4*, 2, 59–64.

47. Vermeulen, P. (2012) ibid.

48. Vermeulen P. (2012) ibid.

49. One may use autobiographies of people with autism to refute the hypothesis of a deficit in self-awareness. In their accounts, they sometimes show an extremely detailed knowledge of themselves, not only of facts but of feelings and thoughts too. Strangely, they are capable of this retrospectively, for the past, but not for the present. Uta Frith and Francesca Happé (1999) mention an experiment they did with three adults with Asperger's Syndrome. They showed that introspection regarding present sensations was very limited in even able persons with an autism spectrum disorder. The form the introspections took was also very visual and concrete, and the report of their inner experiences did not differ from their objective descriptions of the situation. Frith, U. & Happé , F. (1999) Theory of mind and self-consciousness: What is it like to be autistic? *Mind and Language 14*, 1–22.

50. Bandura, A. (1993) 'Perceived Self-Efficiency in Cognitive Development and Functioning.' *Educational Psychologist 28*, 117–148.

51. ibid.

52. James, W. (1890. *The Principles of Psychology*. New York: Henry Holt.

53. Toichi, M. *et al.* (2002) 'A Lack of Self-Consciousness in Autism.' *American Journal of Psychiatry 159*, 1422–1424.

54. See also 'sense of self', above.

55. A tip mentioned by Klin and Volkmar (2000). Klin, A. and Volkmar, F.R. (2000) *Treatment and Intervention Guidelines for Individuals with Asperger's Syndrome.* In A. Klin, F.R. Volkmar and S.S. Sparrow (eds.) *Asperger's Syndrome.* New York/London: The Guilford Press.

56. Van Doorn, E.C. and Verheij, F. (2002) 'Psycho-educatie in kaart gebracht op het grensviak van onderwijs en jeugdzorg.' *Tijdschrift voor Orthopedagogiek 41*, 550–558.

57. Renou, M. (1989) 'La psychoéducation: une perspective historique.' *Revue Canadienne de Psychoéducation 18*, 2, 63–68.

58. Ivey, A.E. (1974) 'The Clinician as a Teacher of Interpersonal Skills: Let's give away what we've got.' *The Clinical Psychologist 27*, 3, 6–9. – Ivey, A.E. (1977) 'Cultural Expertise: If the Counsellor is to Become a Teacher, Toward What Should That Teaching Be Directed?' *Canadian Journal of Counselling and Psychotherapy 12*, 1, 23–29.

59. The very first article on the application of psychoeducation in psychiatry dates back to 1980: Anderson, C. M., Hogarty, G. and Reiss, D. J. (1980) 'Family Treatment of Adult Schizophrenic Patients: a Psychoeducational Approach.' *Schizophrenia Bulletin 6*, 490–505.

60. Bisbee, C. C. (2000) 'Psychiatric Patient Education.' *Psychiatric Times 17*, 4.

61. Vermeulen, P. (1985) *Het onderwijskundige model van psychosociale hulpverlening (The educational model of psychosocial support).* Leuven: KU Leuven, Fac. Psych. et Ped. Wetenschappen. (ongepubliceerde licentiaatsverhandeling [unpublished masters thesis]). In the early 1970s, personalities such as Guerney were already describing therapists as psychoeducators: Guerney, B.G., Stollak, G.E. and Guerney, L. (1971) 'The Practicing Psychologist as an Educator: an Alternative to the Medical Practitioner Model.' *Professional Psychology 2*, 3, 276–282.

62. ibid.

63. For example, at the Center for Psychiatric Rehabilitation at the University of Chicago, where Robert Liberman and his colleagues outlined psychoeducational resources and developed a set of nine modules for people with schizophrenia, which included managing medication, managing symptoms, conversation skills and developing a network of friends.

64. Goldman, C.R. (1988) 'Towards a Definition of Psychoeducation.' *Hospital Community Psychiatry 39*, 6, 666–668.

65. ibid.

66. Van Doorn and Verheij (2002) distinguished between three levels of psychoeducation: informative, supportive and therapeutic. The informative level focuses on the transfer of information and knowledge, the supportive level is focused on the process of acceptance, and the therapeutic level on identifying solutions at an *impasse.*

67. Henselmans, H. (1999) 'Eerst weten, dan handelen, dan leiden.' (First know, then act, then lead.) *Ypsilon Nieuws 83,*10.

68. ibid.

69. See for example Dannon, P.N., Inacu, I. and Grunhaus, L. (2002) 'Psychoeducation in Panic Disorder Patients: Effect of a Self-information Booklet in a Randomised, Masked-Rater Study.' *Depression and Anxiety 16*, 2, 71–76.

70. Swaim, K.F. and Morgan, S.B. (2001) 'Children's Attitudes and Behavioral Intentions Toward a Peer with Autistic Behaviors: does a brief educational intervention have an effect?' *Journal of Autism and Developmental Disorders 31*, 2, 195–205.

71. Vermeulen, P. (2012). *Autism as context blindness.* ibid..

72. Vermeulen, P. (1985). ibid.

73. Vermeulen, P. (1998), *Brein bedriegt: als autisme niet op autisme lijkt. ['The Deceiving Brain']* Antwerpen/Gent: EPO/Vlaamse Dienst Autisme (in the chapter on the approach for more able people with autism, see pp.88–89).

74. Socrates drinking hemlock is magnificently depicted in the famous work 'The death of Socrates' (1787), by the Neoclassical painter Jacques-Louis David.

75. Reich, B. (1998) 'Confusion About the Socratic Method: Socratic Paradoxes and Contemporary Invocations of Socrates.' *Philosophy of Education Society Yearbook.* Urbana: Philosophy of Education Society.

76. For more information: Nelson, L. (2007) *Socratic Method and Critical Philosophy: Selected Essays.* Translated by T. K. Brown. Montana, USA: Kessinger Publishing.

77. Socrates makes reference to the importance of self-examination in the quest for wisdom (the adage 'know thyself' is associated with Socrates). In the same vein, Kant speaks of the importance of examining our own reason (*Critique of Pure Reason* and *Critique of Practical Reason*).

78. www.princetonreview.com/law/socratic-method.aspx, accessed 10 January 2013.

79. Reference is being made to something 'non-democratic', at least in the negative sense of the word. There is also the notion of authority, which, unlike power, is an attribute given by someone else. For example, the authority accorded to someone in a certain domain.

80. Baron-Cohen, S. (2009) 'Autism: the empathizing-systemizing (E-S) theory.' *Annals of the New York Academy of Sciences 1156*, 68–80.

81. It is for this reason that *Autisme Centraal* organises numerous workshops on the Socratic method. More information is available at www.autisme.be, accessed 16 January 2013.

82. For more information about the development and understanding of concepts in autism spectrum disorders, see Chapter 6 (Context in Knowledge) in "*Autism as context blindness*" (Vermeulen 2012).

83. Naturally, in addition to the tests mentioned in the book, there are many other usable lists and tests. The data bank of tests at the *Educational Testing Service* (www.ets.org) mentions 43 instruments for charting self-image. Unfortunately, there are very few with questions suitable for use with the target group for *I am special*.

84. Damon, W. and Hart, D. (1988) *Self-understanding in Childhood and Adolescence.* Cambridge: Cambridge University Press. This is the interview used by Lee and Hobson (1988) for their study of self-concept in children and adolescents with autism.

85. For more information, see among others Marsh, H., Craven, R. and Debus, R. (1991) 'Self-Concepts of Young Children 5 to 8 Years of Age. Measurement and Multidimensional Structure.' *Journal of Educational Psychology 83*, 377–392 and Marsh, H.W. and O'Neill, R. (1994) 'Self Description Questionnaire III (SDQ III): The Construct Validity of Multidimensional Self-Concept Ratings by Late Adolescents.' *Journal of Educational Measurement 21*, 153–174.

86. Harter, S. (1985) *Manual of the Self-Perception Profile for Children.* University of Denver: Denver Co.

87. Harter, S. (1988) *Self-Perception Profile for Adolescents.* USA: University of Denver.

88. Messer, B. and Harter, S. (1986) *Self-Perception Profile for Adults.* USA: University of Denver.

89. Renick, M.J. and Harter, S. (1988) *Self-Perception Profile for Learning Disabled Students.* USA: University of Denver.

90. Harter, S. and Pike, R. (1984) 'The Pictorial Scale of Perceived Competence and Social Acceptance for Young Children.' *Child Development 55*, 1969–1982.

91. For more information please see http//www.autisme.be, accessed 15 January 2013.

92. Sinclair, J. (1993) 'Don't mourn for us.' *Our Voice 1*, 3.

93. Holliday Willey, L. (1999) *Pretending to be Normal: Living with Asperger's Syndrome.* London: Jessica Kingsley Publishers.
94. Gerland, G. (2003) *A Real Person: life on the outside.* London: Souvenir Press Ltd.
95. Grandin, T. (1996) *Emergence: Labeled Autistic.* New York: Warner Books.
96. Williams, D. (1998) *Nobody Nowhere: The Remarkable Autobiography of an Autistic Girl.* London: Jessica Kingsley Publishers.
97. Jackson, L. (2002) *Freaks, Geeks and Asperger's Syndrome: A User Guide to Adolescence.* London: Jessica Kingsley Publishers.
98. Haddon, M. (2004) *The Curious Incident of the Dog in the Night-time.* London: Vintage.
99. Vermeulen, P. (2001) *Autistic Thinking: This is the Title.* London: Jessica Kingsley Publishers.
100. Peralta, S. (2007) *All About My Brother.* Autism Asperger Publishing Co.
101. Frender, S. and Schiffmiller, R. *Brotherly Feelings: Me, My Emotions, and My Brother with Asperger's Syndrome.* London: Jessica Kingsley Publishers.
102. Gorrod, L. (1997) *My Brother is Different.* National Autistic Society.
103. McKee, D. (2007) *Elmer.* London: Andersen Press.
104. Dowd, S. (2010) The London Eye Mystery. Oxford: David Fickling Books.
105. Available from the National Autistic Society (UK): www.autism.org.uk
106. Davies, J. (1998) University of Nottingham: Child Developmental Research Unit. Available from the National Autistic Society (UK): Davies, J. (1998) The Early Years Diagnostic Centre.
107. Hunter, S. H. (2006) National Autistic Society.
108. Fairfoot, E. (2004) National Autistic Society.
109. (2009) London: Jessica Kingsley Publishers.
110. Swaim, K.F. and Morgan, S.B. (2001) 'Children's Attitudes and Behavioral Intentions Toward a Peer with Autistic Behaviors: Does a Brief Educational Intervention Have an Effect?' *Journal of Autism and Developmental Disorders 31*, 2, 195–205.
111. For more information, see: Vermeulen, P. (2012) ibid.

Index